# Sunday by Sunday

A S B   Y E A R   2

# Sunday by Sunday
### A S B   Y E A R   2

## Joy Tetley

**>> The Bible Reading Fellowship**
O P E N I N G   T H E   B I B L E

Text copyright © 1995 Joy Tetley
Illustrations copyright © 1995 BRF and Fred Apps

The author asserts the moral right to be
identified as the author of this work.

Published by
**The Bible Reading Fellowship**
Peter's Way, Sandy Lane West
Oxford OX4 5HG
ISBN 0 7459 3200 2
**Albatross Books Pty Ltd**
PO Box 320, Sutherland
NSW 2232, Australia
ISBN 0 7324 1210 2

First edition 1995
10 9 8 7 6 5 4 3 2 1 0

**Acknowledgments**                                                        ✢
Biblical passages are reproduced with permission from

The Revised Standard Version of the Bible (RSV), copyright
1946, 1952, © 1971, 1973 by The Division of Christian
Education of the National Council of the Churches of Christ
in the USA

The New English Bible (NEB), © 1961, 1970 Oxford and
Cambridge University Presses

The Jerusalem Bible (JB), © 1966 by Darton, Longman & Todd
Ltd and Doubleday and Company Inc.

Today's English Version (TEV), © American Bible Society 1966,
1971, 1976. British usage edition Good News Bible published 1976
by The Bible Societies and Collins.

The lectionary and the Collects are from The Alternative
Service Book 1980 copyright © The Central Board of Finance
of the Church of England 1980. Used by permission.

A catalogue record for this book is
available from the British Library

Printed and bound in Slovenia

# Contents

# Introduction

Worship is at the heart of our relationship with God. It expresses our response 'at all times and in all places' to God's outgoing and sacrificial love. It is a focus for meeting with the living God; for being encouraged, challenged, broken open and transformed. It is an invitation to hold the whole of life in the blessing of God. It is an opportunity to realize our communion with angels and archangels and all the company of heaven—as well as with the richly varied expressions of humankind amongst whom we find ourselves. Yet, all too often, it can seem more like 'duty' than 'joy'. It is my prayer that the material contained in this book may be used in however modest a way to trigger thoughts and reflections that will inform the enterprise of worship.

The comments on the readings first appeared as a weekly column in the *Church Times*. My brief was to offer a short reflection on the readings for the coming Sunday, as set out in the *Alternative Service Book*, noting particularly the connecting themes between the lections. As my column began in October 1993, my reflections were based on the lessons set for Year 2 in the ASB lectionary. To these reflections have been added the relevant Bible passages (in the versions selected for the ASB), the Collect for the day, a quotation from the set Psalm and prayers that take up the day's theme in a fresh way.

As this book has sprung from meditations on the readings for a particular calendar year, 1993–94, there are potential gaps. A moveable Easter leads to disparities from year to year in the number of Sundays after Christmas, Epiphany and Pentecost. Where there is no reflection for a particular Sunday in these seasons, the reader might find it helpful to use material from another Sunday with a similar theme.

As we enter more deeply into worship, may the searching God take hold of us for good.

*Joy Tetley*

# Ninth Sunday before Christmas

## Collect

Almighty God,
you have created the heavens and the earth
and made man in your own image.
Teach us to discern your hand in all your works,
and to serve you with reverence and thanksgiving;
through Jesus Christ our Lord,
who with you and the Holy Spirit reigns supreme over all things
now and for ever.

### *Psalms 104.1-10; 29*

## Old Testament *Genesis 2.4-9, 15-end NEB*

This is the story of the making of heaven and earth when they were created.

When the Lord God made earth and heaven, there was neither shrub nor plant growing wild upon the earth, because the Lord God had sent no rain on the earth; nor was there any man to till the ground. A flood used to rise out of the earth and water all the surface of the ground. Then the Lord God formed a man from the dust of the ground and breathed into his nostrils the breath of life. Thus the man became a living creature. Then the Lord God planted a garden in Eden away to the east, and there he put the man whom he had formed. The Lord God made trees spring from the ground, all trees pleasant to look at and good for food; and in the middle of the garden he set the tree of life and the tree of the knowledge of good and evil.

The Lord God took the man and put him in the garden of Eden to till it and care for it. He told the man, 'You may eat from every tree in the garden, but not from the tree of the knowledge of good and evil; for on the day that you eat from it, you will certainly die.' Then the Lord God said, 'It is not good for the man to be alone. I will provide a partner for him.' So God formed out of the ground all the wild animals and all the birds of heaven. He brought them to the man to see what he would call them, and whatever the man called each living creature, that was its name. Thus the man gave names to all cattle, to the birds of heaven, and to every wild animal; but for the man himself no partner had yet been found. And so the Lord God put the man into a trance, and while he slept, he took one of his ribs and closed the flesh over the place. The Lord God then built up the rib, which he had taken out of the man, into a woman. He brought her to the man, and the man said:

'Now this, at last—
bone from my bones,
flesh from my flesh!—
this shall be called woman,
for from man was this taken.'

That is why a man leaves his father and mother and is united to his wife,
and the two become one flesh. Now they were both naked, the man and his
wife, but they had no feeling of shame towards one another.

## New Testament *Revelation 4 NEB*

I looked, and there before my eyes was a door opened in heaven; and the
voice that I had first heard speaking to me like a trumpet said, 'Come up here,
and I will show you what must happen hereafter.' At once I was caught up by
the Spirit. There in heaven stood a throne, and on the throne sat one whose
appearance was like the gleam of jasper and cornelian; and round the throne
was a rainbow, bright as an emerald. In a circle about this throne were
twenty-four other thrones, and on them sat twenty-four elders, robed in white
and wearing crowns of gold. From the throne went out flashes of lightning
and peals of thunder. Burning before the throne were seven flaming torches,
the seven spirits of God, and in front of it stretched what seemed a sea of
glass, like a sheet of ice.

In the centre, round the throne itself, were four living creatures, covered
with eyes, in front and behind. The first creature was like a lion, the second
like an ox, the third had a human face, the fourth was like an eagle in flight.
The four living creatures, each of them with six wings, had eyes all over,
inside and out; and by day and by night without a pause they sang:

'Holy, holy, holy is God the sovereign Lord of all, who was, and is, and is
to come!'

As often as the living creatures give glory and honour and thanks to the
One who sits on the throne, who lives for ever and ever, the twenty-four
elders fall down before the One who sits on the throne and worship him who
lives for ever and ever; and as they lay their crowns before the throne they
cry:

'Thou art worthy, O Lord our God, to receive glory and honour and power,
because thou didst create all things; by thy will they were created, and have
their being!'

## Gospel *John 3.1-8 NEB*

There was one of the Pharisees named Nicodemus, a member of the Jewish
Council, who came to Jesus by night. 'Rabbi,' he said, 'we know that you are a
teacher sent by God; no one could perform these signs of yours unless God
were with him.' Jesus answered, 'In truth, in very truth I tell you, unless a
man has been born over again he cannot see the kingdom of God.' 'But how is

it possible,' said Nicodemus, 'for a man to be born when he is old? Can he enter his mother's womb a second time and be born?' Jesus answered, 'In truth I tell you, no one can enter the kingdom of God without being born from water and spirit. Flesh can give birth only to flesh; it is spirit that gives birth to spirit. You ought not to be astonished, then, when I tell you that you must be born over again. The wind blows where it wills; you hear the sound of it, but you do not know where it comes from, or where it is going. So with everyone who is born from spirit.'

# A creative artist with a world canvas and a personal touch

*Ascribe to the Lord the honour due to his name,*
*O worship the Lord in the beauty of his holiness. (Ps 29.2)*

Out of their differing contexts, the readings for this Sunday present us with some striking perspectives on the Creator God. The 'Lord God' of Genesis 2 is a creative artist, prepared to be decidedly down-to-earth. In 'the making of heaven and earth', he has an eye to aesthetic pleasure as well as usefulness. So the trees are good to look at as well as good for food. God brings forth a garden, full of life and variety. When it comes to producing humankind, the Lord God is very much a 'hands on' operative, working with dust and shaping human flesh. He is also willing to experiment, looking at his creative work as it emerges and determining how it might be further improved. And in this process, he works collaboratively with the human being into whom he has breathed the divine breath of life. Responsibility for creation becomes a shared enterprise (as in the naming of the animals), though not an equal partnership (the making of woman is *God's* stroke of genius). The Lord God realizes the man's need for personal relationship, for 'mutual society and comfort'. Only one of the same substance can effectively address that need. When man meets woman, there is thus profound recognition and—at this stage, at least—an equal openness to one another that leads to fulfilment and celebration.

The vision of God in Revelation 4 is seen through a somewhat different lens. The medium is that of Jewish/Christian apocalyptic, a language given to vivid and cryptic imagery about ultimate reality, a language born of suffering, persecution and threat. When so much on earth seems to argue against it, how can belief in a sovereign God of creation be sustained? Only by looking through the door of heaven. Only by wholehearted self-abandonment to the risky foolishness of worship. In that context, faith may break through to a measure of understanding, albeit inarticulate.

When Nicodemus journeys through the darkness to the Light of the world, understanding still does not come easily. That is not surprising. This experienced religious teacher is being challenged by the God of radical new beginnings to go through the trauma of a new birth, to start all over again, to learn a fresh way of seeing. Old perceptions of the power of God have to be reinterpreted. The God who will not be trapped by human definition gives birth to children animated by the freedom of divine life (see John 1.12f). As the Fourth Gospel proclaims so eloquently, the power and the glory of this God are to be seen most clearly in the creative travail of the cross. There is God's kingdom paradoxically realized.

In these readings, then, we encounter a God greater than all things, yet intimately involved with all things; a God given to beautiful artistry and to sharing the vitality of his own life; a God who works to bring out the best and labours to bring forth new life; a God whose sovereign mystery can only be fruitfully explored in the risk of personal relationship. Does not the world, in many and various ways, cry out for such a God?

*God of heaven and earth,*
*artist and artisan,*
*free us to see things afresh,*
*that we may be fully alive*
*and truly for your glory.*

# Eighth Sunday before Christmas

## Collect

Heavenly Father,
whose blessed Son was revealed
that he might destroy the works of the devil
and make us the sons of God
and heirs of eternal life:
grant that we, having this hope,
may purify ourselves even as he is pure;
that when he shall appear in power and great glory
we may be made like him in his eternal and glorious kingdom;
where he is alive and reigns with you and the Holy Spirit,
one God, now and for ever.

## *Psalms 130; 10.13-end*

## Old Testament *Genesis 3.1-15 NEB*

The serpent was more crafty than any wild creature that the Lord God had
made. He said to the woman, 'Is it true that God has forbidden you to eat
from any tree in the garden?' The woman answered the serpent, 'We may eat
the fruit of any tree in the garden, except for the tree in the middle of the
garden; God has forbidden us either to eat or to touch the fruit of that; if we
do, we shall die.' The serpent said, 'Of course you will not die. God knows
that as soon as you eat it, your eyes will be opened and you will be like God
knowing both good and evil.' When the woman saw that the fruit of the tree
was good to eat, and that it was pleasing to the eye and tempting to
contemplate, she took some and ate it. She also gave her husband some and
he ate it. Then the eyes of both of them were opened and they discovered that
they were naked; so they stitched fig-leaves together and made themselves
loincloths.

The man and his wife heard the sound of the Lord God walking in the
garden at the time of the evening breeze and hid from the Lord God among
the trees of the garden. But the Lord God called to the man and said to him,
'Where are you?' He replied, 'I heard the sound as you were walking in the
garden, and I was afraid because I was naked, and I hid myself.' God
answered, 'Who told you that you were naked? Have you eaten from the tree
which I forbade you?' The man said, 'The woman you gave me for a
companion, she gave me fruit from the tree and I ate it.' Then the Lord God

said to the woman, 'What is this that you have done?' The woman said, 'The serpent tricked me, and I ate.' Then the Lord God said to the serpent:
'Because you have done this you are accursed
more than all cattle and all wild creatures.
On your belly you shall crawl, and dust you shall eat
all the days of your life.
I will put enmity between you and the woman,
between your brood and hers.
They shall strike at your head,
and you shall strike at their heel.'

## New Testament *Romans 7.7-13 TEV*

Shall we say that the Law itself is sinful? Of course not! But it was the Law that made me know what sin is. If the Law had not said, 'Do not desire what belongs to someone else,' I would not have known such a desire. But by means of that commandment sin found its chance to stir up all kinds of selfish desires in me. Apart from law, sin is a dead thing. I myself was once alive apart from law; but when the commandment came, sin sprang to life, and I died. And the commandment which was meant to bring life, in my case brought death. Sin found its chance, and by means of the commandment it deceived me and killed me.

So then, the Law itself is holy, and the commandment is holy, right, and good. But does this mean that what is good caused my death? By no means! It was sin that did it; by using what is good, sin brought death to me, in order that its true nature as sin might be revealed. And so, by means of the commandment sin is shown to be even more terribly sinful.

## Gospel *John 3.13-21 RSV*

Jesus said, 'No one has ascended into heaven but he who descended from heaven, the Son of Man. And as Moses lifted up the serpent in the wilderness, so must the Son of Man be lifted up, that whoever believes in him may have eternal life.'

For God so loved the world that he gave his only Son, that whoever believes in him should not perish but have eternal life. For God sent the Son into the world, not to condemn the world, but that the world might be saved through him. He who believes in him is not condemned; he who does not believe is condemned already, because he has not believed in the name of the only Son of God. And this is the judgement, that the light has come into the world, and men loved darkness rather than light, because their deeds were evil. For everyone who does evil hates the light, and does not come to the light, lest his deeds should be exposed. But he who does what is true comes to the light, that it may be clearly seen that his deeds have been wrought in God.

# Questionable behaviour?

*Surely you see the trouble and sorrow,*
*you look on and will take it into your own hands. (Ps 10.15)*

It is patently obvious that all is not well with the world. Such a state of affairs is clearly not new, as this Sunday's readings testify. These passages, born out of very different ages and cultures, still speak eloquently to our contemporary context because they address the heart of the human condition. In their several ways, they illuminate how things are and how things might be. In so doing, they give us much to ponder about the character and involvement of God.

With a vivid and memorable story, the writer of Genesis 3 presents us with a telling analysis and some tantalizing questions. Humanity (of both genders) is shown to be prone to behaviour which leads to disharmony, tension and conflict. The eating of forbidden fruit (attractive to both mind and senses) shatters innocence and throws up barriers. Instead of trustful openness and happy coexistence, there come shame, fear, and enmity, a failure to accept responsibility and the compulsion to hide. All that, we can recognize. Yet we may also find objections rising within us. What is wrong with a thirst for knowledge, especially in relation to an open-eyed awareness of good and evil? If, in some sense, humanity shares the divine life (enlivened by God's breath, made in God's image), what is wrong with the desire to be like God? And was not the serpent (a creature of God) fundamentally right? The man and the woman did not die. They lived on to struggle with issues of good and evil, no longer blissfully ignorant but with a more knowing capacity to work with and against the God with whom they are so intimately related. These objections surely need to be taken seriously and pursued prayerfully. And God, it seems, relishes questioning dialogue. The first recorded comment in the Bible from God to humanity comes in the form of a devastating question: 'Where are you?' 'What is the truth of your condition?' With that question we are still confronted and challenged into response. The evidence of the rest of scripture is that God's *modus operandi* involves the throwing out of a great many questions and the provoking of a good many in return. In such exchanges is understanding stretched and relationship deepened.

The apostle Paul certainly bears witness to that, from his conversion experience onward. In Romans, he is grappling with some enormous, well nigh intractable questions, not least the relationship between divine sovereignty and human free will. In Sunday's passage, Paul struggles with the apparently perverse character of God's law in acting as an incentive for sin. Yet the law is good, because it exposes sin for what it is. So does God's light, as the Fourth Evangelist so powerfully reminds us. But this is no cause for despair. The light emanates from One whose motive force is love. So the descendants of Adam and Eve may be confident that exposure can be the painful prelude to salvation, for those who will. In the time of Moses, God used the image of a deadly serpent to bring healing. So, in Jesus, God brings life out of death. The cost to God is enormous. Having asked us where we are, he takes to himself the crucifying consequences. Such a God we can trust, not only with our questions but with our lives.

*God of dialogue,*
*challenge us to question our ways*
*in the light of your truth,*
*the beauty of your holiness,*
*and our down-to-earth Saviour, Jesus.*

# Seventh Sunday before Christmas

## Collect

Almighty God,
whose chosen servant Abraham
faithfully obeyed your call
and rejoiced in your promise
that, in him, all the families of the earth should be blessed:
give us a faith like his,
that, in us, your promises may be fulfilled;
through Jesus Christ our Lord.

## Psalms 1; 105.1-11

## Old Testament *Genesis 22.1-18 NEB*

The time came when God put Abraham to the test. 'Abraham', he called, and Abraham replied, 'Here I am.' God said, 'Take your son Isaac, your only son, whom you love, and go to the land of Moriah. There you shall offer him as a sacrifice on one of the hills which I will show you.' So Abraham rose early in the morning and saddled his ass, and he took with him two of his men and his son Isaac; and he split the firewood for the sacrifice, and set out for the place of which God had spoken. On the third day Abraham looked up and saw the place in the distance. He said to his men, 'Stay here with the ass while I and the boy go over there; and when we have worshipped we will come back to you.' So Abraham took the wood for the sacrifice and laid it on his son Isaac's shoulder; he himself carried the fire and the knife, and the two of them went on together. Isaac said to Abraham, 'Father', and he answered, 'What is it, my son?' Isaac said, 'Here are the fire and the wood, but where is the young beast for the sacrifice?' Abraham answered, 'God will provide himself with a young beast for a sacrifice, my son.' And the two of them went on together and came to the place of which God had spoken. There Abraham built an altar and arranged the wood. He bound his son Isaac and laid him on the altar on top of the wood. Then he stretched out his hand and took the knife to kill his son; but the angel of the Lord called to him from heaven, 'Abraham, Abraham.' He answered, 'Here I am.' The angel of the Lord said, 'Do not raise your hand against the boy; do not touch him. Now I know that you are a God-fearing man. You have not withheld from me your son, your only son.' Abraham looked up, and there he saw a ram caught by its horns in a thicket. So he went and took the ram and offered it as a sacrifice instead of his son. Abraham named that place Jehovah-jireh; and to this day the saying is, 'In the mountain of the Lord it was provided.' Then the angel of the Lord called from heaven a second time to Abraham, 'This is the word of the Lord: By my own self I swear: inasmuch as you have done this and have not withheld your son, your only son, I will bless you abundantly and greatly multiply your descendants until they are as numerous as the stars in the sky and the grains of sand on the sea-shore. Your descendants shall possess the cities of their enemies. All nations on earth shall pray to be blessed as your descendants are blessed, and this because you have obeyed me.'

## New Testament *James 2.14-24 (25, 26) NEB*

My brothers, what use is it for a man to say he has faith when he does nothing to show it? Can that faith save him? Suppose a brother or sister is in rags with not enough food for the day, and one of you says, 'Good luck to you, keep yourselves warm, and have plenty to eat', but does nothing to supply their bodily needs, what is the good of that? So with faith; if it does not lead to action, it is in itself a lifeless thing.

But someone may object: 'Here is one who claims to have faith and another who points to his deeds.' To which I reply: 'Prove to me that this faith you speak of is real though not accompanied by deeds, and by my deeds I will prove to you my faith.' You have faith enough to believe that there is one God. Excellent! The devils have faith like that, and it makes them tremble. But can you not see, you quibbler, that faith divorced from deeds is barren? Was it not by his action, in offering his son Isaac upon the altar, that our father Abraham was justified? Surely you can see that faith was at work in his actions, and that by these actions the integrity of his faith was fully proved. Here was fulfilment of the words of Scripture: 'Abraham put his faith in God, and that faith was counted to him as righteousness'; and elsewhere he is called 'God's friend'. You see then that a man is justified by deeds and not by faith in itself. (The same is true of the prostitute Rahab also. Was not she justified by her action in welcoming the messengers into her house and sending them away by a different route? As the body is dead when there is no breath left in it, so faith divorced from deeds is lifeless as a corpse.)

## Gospel *Luke 20.9-17 JB*

Jesus went on to tell the people this parable: 'A man planted a vineyard and leased it to tenants, and went abroad for a long while. When the time came, he sent a servant to the tenants to get his share of the produce of the vineyard from them. But the tenants thrashed him, and sent him away empty-handed. But he persevered and sent a second servant; they thrashed him too and treated him shamefully and sent him away empty-handed. He still persevered and sent a third; they wounded this one also, and threw him out. Then the owner of the vineyard said, "What am I to do? I will send them my dear son.

Perhaps they will respect him." But when the tenants saw him they put their heads together. "This is the heir," they said, "let us kill him so that the inheritance will be ours." So they threw him out of the vineyard and killed him.

'Now what will the owner of the vineyard do to them? He will come and make an end of those tenants and give the vineyard to others.' Hearing this they said, 'God forbid!' But he looked hard at them and said, 'Then what does this text in the scriptures mean:

It was the stone rejected by the builders
that became the keystone?'

## Faith in action: searching for truth

*Seek the Lord and his strength,*
*O seek his face continually. (Ps 105.4)*

As the saying goes, 'Actions speak louder than words'. This Sunday's readings are eloquent with activity; but what is being said? That question is particularly apposite in relation to the story told in Genesis 22. On one level, it is horrifying in what it is implying about God. Though the beloved child of promise was not slaughtered, he was put through a terrifying ordeal. How could God countenance such a thing? That it was set up as a test of the father's faith could well intensify rather than mitigate the modern reader's sense of outrage. In the narrative, the child is silent, apart from one poignant question. He is victim, with no rights and no choice. Only Abraham had choice. It is interesting that later Judaism developed the tradition that Isaac gave willing consent and encouragement to his sacrificial fate, thereby accumulating merit that could be pleaded in Israel's favour. We need to remember, of course, that the biblical narrative emerged out of a different culture from ours and that, at the climax of the story, God is revealed as *not* requiring child sacrifice (unlike other cults of the time). It is also true that the primary theme of the narrative is costly obedience which releases an assurance of God's faithfulness. Yet the essential theological question remains. What kind of God would use such methodology and could this kind of God really be 'good news' for a hurting world?

Perhaps the New Testament passages can help us in our struggle. While presenting Abraham's willingness to sacrifice Isaac as a powerful example of faith issuing in action, the Epistle of James nonetheless also points to active faith as behaviour which meets the needs of those who cannot help themselves. God, it seems, has a profound care for those who have nothing and are powerless. The Gospel reading takes us even further in our theological search. Here we encounter the parabolic form which was evidently a favourite teaching method of Jesus. Parables are not just engaging stories (though they can be received at that level). They are meant to encourage their hearers to tease out truth, to wrestle for themselves with the riddle of meaning. Characteristically and fittingly, Jesus caps the parable with a question. What follows on immediately from the passage set for the Gospel shows that both parable and question have hit home to their intended target, the 'scribes and chief priests'. They had not been left short of clues to work on, the main one being the familiarity of the vineyard as a symbol for Israel (cf Psalm 80.8ff; Isaiah 5.1-7). For us, the challenge is still there. How do *we* receive the messengers of God, not least God's 'dear son'? Here is a God who perseveres in inviting positive response, who takes many cruel rebuffs and who risks to our mercy the self-expression of his heart. This God does not demand sacrifice from others; he lays himself open to it. And his Son is killed. Yet even as we wonder at the extent of his loving humility, the parable's ending raises another subject for searching: that of judgment. The riddle of God remains.

*God of promise,*
*help us to welcome your messengers,*
*wrestle with your truth,*
*and lay ourselves open to others*
*in your service.*

# Sixth Sunday before Christmas

## Collect

Lord God our redeemer,
who heard the cry of your people
and sent your servant Moses to lead them out of slavery:
free us from the tyranny of sin and death
and, by the leading of your Spirit,
bring us to our promised land;
through Jesus Christ our Lord.

### *Psalms 135.1-6; 77.11-end*

## Old Testament *Exodus 6.2-8 NEB*

God spoke to Moses and said, 'I am the Lord. I appeared to Abraham, Isaac, and Jacob as God Almighty. But I did not let myself be known to them by my name JEHOVAH. Moreover, I made a covenant with them to give them Canaan, the land where they settled for a time as foreigners. And now I have heard the groaning of the Israelites, enslaved by the Egyptians, and I have called my covenant to mind. Say therefore to the Israelites, "I am the Lord. I will release you from your labours in Egypt. I will rescue you from slavery there. I will redeem you with arm outstretched and with mighty acts of judgement. I will adopt you as my people, and I will become your God. You shall know that I, the Lord, am your God, the God who releases you from your labours in Egypt. I will lead you to the land which I swore with uplifted hand to give to Abraham, to Isaac and to Jacob. I will give it you for your possession. I am the Lord."'

## New Testament *Hebrews 11.17-31 RSV*

By faith Abraham, when he was tested, offered up Isaac, and he who had received the promises was ready to offer up his only son, of whom it was said, 'Through Isaac shall your descendants be named.' He considered that God was able to raise men even from the dead; hence, figuratively speaking, he did receive him back. By faith Isaac invoked future blessings on Jacob and Esau. By faith Jacob, when dying, blessed each of the sons of Joseph, bowing in worship over the head of his staff. By faith Joseph, at the end of his life, made mention of the exodus of the Israelites and gave directions concerning his burial.

By faith Moses, when he was born, was hid for three months by his parents, because they saw that the child was beautiful; and they were not afraid of the king's edict. By faith Moses, when he was grown up, refused to be called the son of Pharaoh's daughter, choosing rather to share ill-treatment with the people of God than to enjoy the fleeting pleasures of sin. He considered abuse suffered for the Christ greater wealth than the treasures of Egypt, for he looked to the reward. By faith he left Egypt, not being afraid of the anger of the king; for he endured as seeing him who is invisible. By faith he kept the Passover and sprinkled the blood, so that the Destroyer of the first-born might not touch them.

By faith the people crossed the Red Sea as if on dry land; but the Egyptians, when they attempted to do the same, were drowned. By faith the walls of Jericho fell down after they had been encircled for seven days. By faith Rahab the harlot did not perish with those who were disobedient, because she had given friendly welcome to the spies.

## Gospel *Mark 13.5-13 NEB*

Jesus said to his disciples, 'Take care that no one misleads you. Many will come claiming my name, and saying, "I am he", and many will be misled by them.

'When you hear the noise of battle near at hand and the news of battles far away, do not be alarmed. Such things are bound to happen; but the end is still to come. For nation will make war upon nation, kingdom upon kingdom; there will be earthquakes in many places; there will be famines. With these things the birth- pangs of the new age begin.

'As for you, be on your guard. You will be handed over to the courts. You will be flogged in synagogues. You will be summoned to appear before governors and kings on my account to testify in their presence. But before the end the Gospel must be proclaimed to all nations. So when you are arrested and taken away, do not worry beforehand about what you will say, but when the time comes say whatever is given you to say; for it is not you who will be speaking, but the Holy Spirit. Brother will betray brother to death, and the father his child; children will turn against their parents and send them to their death. All will hate you for your allegiance to me; but the man who holds out to the end will be saved.'

# Hope and endurance in times of tribulation

*You led your people like sheep,*
*by the hand of Moses and Aaron. (Ps 77.20)*

The bright thread that runs through this Sunday's readings is that God is able to save out of adversity. The darker strand is that God's people are by no means exempt from hardship and suffering. Indeed, they can expect their commitment to increase the probability of pain rather than render it less likely. It is not an attractive prospect. Yet, paradoxically, neither is it a recipe for despair. The testimony of these readings is that the surpassing worth and faithfulness of God mean that tribulation is shot through with hope.

For the enslaved Israelites in Egypt, hope must have been in short supply. And as the Exodus saga unfolds, it is clear that they found it hard to hold on to the positive message of God's deliverance as proclaimed by Moses. The evidence of their experience seemed to give the lie to it. Moses himself found it difficult enough. Nonetheless, against enormous odds, liberation is achieved. The promised divine act of rescue takes place. As it turns out, this exodus event, this gaining of freedom, becomes the prelude to a long and stringently testing journey of faith. The promised land is not easily reached. The elation of redemption gives way to the dryness and danger of the wilderness. The call to blessed escape becomes an exhortation to dogged endurance and radical trust.

So it must have seemed to those beneficiaries of the new covenant addressed by the writer of Hebrews. Here were Christians, apparently well into their pilgrimage, under grave pressure to give up and go back to the familiar security of their former way of life. In his sermon (for such is Hebrews) the author holds before them both profound encouragement and fearful challenge, each born of his pastoral passion and his sense of the enormity of God's new act of redemption in Jesus. In this great section on faith he parades in front of his endangered community some of the great heroes and heroines of the old covenant (including the outsider Rahab). The faith of these people, he claims, was characterized by a trusting relationship with an unseen God, unshaken by the force of circumstances. Their faith displayed 'the assurance of things hoped for, the evidence of things not seen' (11.1). What a salutary example for a new covenant people with the inestimable advantage of 'seeing Jesus' (2.9; 12.2), the self-expression of the living God (1.1-4). In this light, endurance is infinitely worthwhile.

It seems likely that the recipients of Mark's Gospel were also facing testing times. On the face of it, Sunday's extract gives little comfort.

Disaster, deprivation, appalling suffering, conflict, hatred, rejection, betrayal: not the most desirable of experiences. And they are still very much with us. Where is the good news? Where is the faithfulness of God? Even a bleak passage like this gives us some clues. One is the empowering involvement of the Holy Spirit in times of trial. Another is the effective creativity of God, somehow bringing new life to birth out of the extremities of pain. Were we to read on in Mark, we would also discover that God is to be found, crying out, in the middle of the darkness. There is the essence of our hope.

*God of deliverance,*
*uphold those you set free,*
*encourage us on our journey,*
*and help us face our time of trial*
*with you as our strength and shield.*

# Fifth Sunday before Christmas

## Collect

Almighty God,
who spoke to the prophets
that they might make your will and purpose known:
inspire the guardians of your truth,
that through the faithful witness of the few
the children of earth may be made one with the saints in glory;
by the power of Jesus Christ our Lord,
who alone redeemed mankind
and reigns with you and the Holy Spirit,
one God, now and for ever.

Stir up, O Lord,
the wills of your faithful people;
that richly bearing the fruit of good works,
they may by you be richly rewarded;
through Jesus Christ our Lord.

## *Psalms 80.1-7; 80.8-end*

## Old Testament *Isaiah 10.20-23 RSV*

On the day of the Lord the remnant of Israel and the survivors of the house of Jacob will no more lean upon him that smote them, but will lean upon the Lord, the Holy One of Israel, in truth. A remnant will return, the remnant of Jacob, to the mighty God. For though your people Israel be as the sand of the sea, only a remnant of them will return. Destruction is decreed, overflowing with righteousness. For the Lord, the Lord of hosts, will make a full end, as decreed, in the midst of all the earth.

## New Testament *Romans 9.19-28 JB*

You will ask, 'How can God ever blame anyone, since no one can oppose his will?' But what right have you, a human being, to cross-examine God? The pot has no right to say to the potter: 'Why did you make me this shape?' Surely a potter can do what he likes with the clay? It is surely for him to decide whether he will use a particular lump of clay to make a special pot or an ordinary one?

Or else imagine that although God is ready to show his anger and display his power, yet he patiently puts up with the people who make him angry, however much they deserve to be destroyed. He puts up with them for the sake of those other people, to whom he wants to be merciful, to whom he wants to reveal the richness of his glory, people he had prepared for this glory long ago. Well, we are those people; whether we are Jews or pagans we are the ones he has called.

This is exactly what God says in Hosea: 'I shall say to a people that was not mine, "You are my people", and to a nation I never loved, "I love you". Instead of being told, "You are no people of mine", they will now be called the sons of the living God.' Referring to Israel Isaiah had this to say: 'Though Israel should have as many descendants as there are grains of sand on the seashore, only a remnant will be saved, for without hesitation or delay the Lord will execute his sentence on the earth.'

## Gospel *Mark 13.14-23 NEB*

Jesus said, 'But when you see "the abomination of desolation" usurping a place which is not his (let the reader understand), then those who are in Judaea must take to the hills. If a man is on the roof, he must not come down into the house to fetch anything out; if in the field, he must not turn back for his coat. Alas for women with child in those days, and for those who have children at the breast! Pray that it may not come in winter. For those days will bring distress such as never has been until now since the beginning of the world which God created—and will never be again. If the Lord had not cut short that time of troubles, no living thing could survive. However, for the sake of his own, whom he has chosen, he has cut short the time.

'Then, if anyone says to you, "Look, here is the Messiah", or "Look, there he is", do not believe it. Imposters will come claiming to be messiahs or prophets, and they will produce signs and wonders to mislead God's chosen, if such a thing were possible. But you be on your guard; I have forewarned you of it all.'

# Holding fast to the covenant God

*Turn to us again, O Lord of hosts,*
*look down from heaven and see. (Ps 80.14)*

We must beware of taking this Sunday's readings in isolation. To do so might well push us into a 'gloom and doom' mentality, with a less than wholesome view of God. Nonetheless, these passages give us much cause for thought and incentive for response. A sense of crisis is dominant. In the prophecy of Isaiah, the air is heavy with judgment. The people of God have turned elsewhere for their succour and support. They will bear the consequences of removing themselves from God's protection. Divine righteousness will have its day. Yet all is not lost. Some will turn again to God, recognizing at last that in God is their only true strength and security. And the covenant God will not turn them away. Divine promises are kept. Though there be only a remnant, it is honoured. This is not, however, a God to be trifled with. This is the holy and righteous God, the God of power and might.

For Paul, devout Jew that he was, this God was very much to be acknowledged and reckoned with. The new covenant to which Paul was committed might differ from the the old in its expression, but the covenant God remained the same. What, then, of the chosen people who, according to Paul's conviction, had rejected God's Messiah? Were they to be rejected by God? Where did that leave God's covenant faithfulness? In chapters 9 to 11 of Romans, Paul almost tears himself apart in trying to argue a theological way through his dilemma, a dilemma with deeply personal dimensions. He was sure that Jesus was the Christ. He was equally sure that the good news of Jesus the Christ was for Gentiles as well as Jews. But so many of his Jewish kindred were in active opposition to what he saw as the gracious purposes of God. He himself, on not a few occasions, had felt the painful force of their negativity. In labouring away at the issue, Paul explores a number of areas. From Sunday's extract we can observe his emphasis on the 'long-term planning' of God. Using the Jewish scriptures (to him, as to the early Church generally, the 'living utterances of God') he stresses that God's intention had always been to call outsiders into covenant relationship. In Isaiah 10 he also finds an indicator that not all Israel was bound to be saved by God, only that remnant which turned to God in responsive faith. In the end, in this passage and in the climactic paragraph towards the end of chapter 11, Paul takes refuge in the mysterious sovereignty of God. That course, especially if resorted to too rapidly, has its dangers. We need to recall that elsewhere in scripture there are many 'pots' who object to the potter—and not a few obtain blessing for their temerity. Honest questioning of God on matters of passionate concern can, indeed, be true worship.

What the original 'reader' of Sunday's Gospel might have understood by it is a matter of debate. It seems that a traditional 'day of the Lord' scenario is being associated with a specific situation known to the Gospel's recipients. For us the warning still holds. In time of crisis, our security lies in faithfulness to the faithful God. The power and might of this God are not always to be identified with spectacular shows of strength. As St Mark so powerfully discerned, there is a deeper truth.

*Sovereign God,*
*in times of crisis, strengthen our faith,*
*in times of falling away, draw us back,*
*and when we seem to be on our own,*
*remind us of all who follow you in Jesus.*

# Advent Sunday

## Collect

Almighty God,
give us grace to cast away the works of darkness
and to put on the armour of light,
now in the time of this mortal life,
in which your Son Jesus Christ came to us in great humility:
so that on the last day,
when he shall come again in his glorious majesty to judge the
living and the dead,
we may rise to the life immortal;
through him who is alive and reigns with you and the Holy Spirit,
one God, now and for ever.

*Psalms 50.1-6; 82*

## Old Testament *Isaiah 51.4-11 NEB*

Pay heed to me, my people,
and hear me, O my nation;
for my law shall shine forth
and I will flash the light of my judgement over the nations.
My victory is near, my deliverance has gone forth
and my arm shall rule the nations;
for me coasts and islands shall wait
and they shall look to me for protection.
Lift your eyes to the heavens,
look at the earth beneath:
the heavens grow murky as smoke;
the earth wears into tatters like a garment,
and those who live on it die like maggots;
but my deliverance is everlasting
and my saving power shall never wane.
Listen to me, my people who know what is right,
you who lay my law to heart:
do not fear the taunts of men,
let no reproaches dismay you;
for the grub will devour them like a garment
and the moth as if they were wool,
but my saving power shall last for ever
and my deliverance to all generations.

Awake, awake, put on your strength, O arm of the Lord,
awake as you did long ago, in days gone by.
Was it not you
who hacked the Rahab in pieces and ran the dragon through?
Was it not you
who dried up the sea, the waters of the great abyss,
and made the ocean depths a path for the ransomed?
So the Lord's people shall come back, set free,
and enter Zion with shouts of triumph,
crowned with everlasting joy;
joy and gladness shall overtake them as they come,
and sorrow and sighing shall flee away.

## New Testament *Romans 13.8-end NEB*

Leave no claim outstanding against you, except that of mutual love. He who loves his neighbour has satisfied every claim of the law. For the commandments, 'Thou shalt not commit adultery, thou shalt not kill, thou shalt not steal, thou shalt not covet', and any other commandment there may be, are all summed up in the one rule, 'Love your neighbour as yourself.' Love cannot wrong a neighbour; therefore the whole law is summed up in love.

In all this, remember how critical the moment is. It is time for you to wake out of sleep, for deliverance is nearer to us now than it was when first we believed. It is far on in the night; day is near. Let us therefore throw off the deeds of darkness and put on armour as soldiers of the light. Let us behave with decency as befits the day: no revelling or drunkenness, no debauchery or vice, no quarrels or jealousies! Let Christ Jesus himself be the armour that you wear; give no more thought to satisfying the bodily appetites.

## Gospel *Matthew 25.31-end NEB*

Jesus said to his disciples, 'When the Son of Man comes in his glory and all the angels with him, he will sit in state on his throne, with all the nations gathered before him. He will separate men into two groups, as a shepherd separates the sheep from the goats, and he will place the sheep on his right hand and the goats on his left. Then the king will say to those on his right hand, "You have my Father's blessing; come, enter and possess the kingdom that has been ready for you since the world was made. For when I was hungry, you gave me food; when I was thirsty, you gave me drink; when I was a stranger you took me into your home, when naked you clothed me; when I was ill you came to my help, when in prison you visited me." Then the righteous will reply, "Lord, when was it that we saw you hungry and fed you, or thirsty and gave you drink, a stranger and took you home, or naked and clothed you? When did we see you ill or in prison, and come to visit you?" And the king will answer, "I tell you this: anything you did for one of my brothers here, however humble, you did for me." Then he will say to those on his left hand, "The curse is upon you; go from my sight to the eternal fire that is ready for the devil and his angels. For when I was hungry you gave me nothing to eat, when thirsty nothing to drink; when I was a stranger you gave me no home, when naked you did not clothe me; when I was ill and in prison you did not come to my help." And they too will reply, "Lord, when was it that we saw you hungry or thirsty or a stranger or naked or ill or in prison, and did nothing for you?" And he will answer, "I tell you this: anything you did not do for one of these, however humble, you did not do for me." And they will go away to eternal punishment, but the righteous will enter eternal life.'

# Liberation through disturbance; hope through faith in action

*Arise, O God, and judge the earth,*
*for you shall take all nations as your possession. (Ps 82.8)*

The ASB theme for this Sunday is 'The Advent Hope'. Where is this hope to be found and what is its substance? The set readings point us in a heartening direction as, in a disillusioned world, we look for real hope. They also face us with radical challenge.

The Isaiah passage radiates confidence in a God of deliverance. The God who in the act of creation slew the monster of chaos (Rahab), who at the exodus held back the mighty death-dealing waters, this God of surpassing strength was about to act again—this time to liberate his people from their Babylonian exile. With great rejoicing God was going to bring them home to a new life, where misery would be banished for ever. If the exiles found this hard to believe, they must pay heed not to the depressing circumstances of their physical context but to the greater reality of a creative and redeeming God. The believer has always to remember that immediate appearances can be deceptive. Stubborn faith in God against all the odds can, indeed, open windows into heaven—and pave the way for God's saving acts. Yet, despite the prophet's spiritual elation and confident faith, and though the exile was ended, those who returned did not experience heaven on earth. The new creation glimpsed in this magnificent prophetic poem was to find its fullest realization in a more wonderful act of liberation: one in which God was to come to his people and set them free, strong arms outstretched upon a cross.

God's love demonstrated in Jesus, though rejected and destroyed, is paradoxically more powerful than all the evil in the world. Out of this love, joy and hope are born. Out of this love, unexpected victories are won. With this love, lives are transformed. And, as Paul insists again and again, not least in today's Epistle, this love—outpouring of the uninhibited generosity of God—is to be willingly shared. Whatever the circumstances, the critical moment is now. Now is the time to wake out of complacency. Now is the time to cast off dirty old clothes, all behaviour that undermines genuine love, that obstructs the bringing out of God's best. Now is the time to acknowledge, in all humility, that we can only begin to do such a thing if we place ourselves within the strong and recreative love of Christ Jesus.

It is in that spirit that we should hear the parable which forms the Gospel reading. It is both deeply disturbing and profoundly hopeful (rather like the God to whom it points us). When it comes to the ultimate moment of crisis, the acid test will not be our theological orthodoxy, nor even our fine words about love. It will be whether we have expressed God's love in action; whether we have met crying human need. That is the challenge. The hope is this: that the God who disturbs us identifies with the weak and the powerless. The implications of that are awesome. Such a God is the world's true hope.

*Disturbing God,*
*you identify with the weak and powerless,*
*and surprise us as we seek to do your will.*
*Help us to find true hope*
*in the now of our action*
*rather than in the distant future of our longing.*

# *Advent 2*

## Collect

Blessed Lord,
who caused all holy Scriptures to be written for our learning:
help us so to hear them,
to read, mark, learn, and inwardly digest them
that, through patience, and the comfort of your holy word,
we may embrace and for ever hold fast the hope of everlasting life,
which you have given us in our Saviour Jesus Christ.

### Psalms *19.7-end; 119.129-136*

## Old Testament *Isaiah 64.1-7 JB*

Oh, that you would tear the heavens open and come down
—at your Presence the mountains would melt,
as fire sets brushwood alight,
as fire causes water to boil—
to make known your name to your enemies,
and make the nations tremble at your Presence,
working unexpected miracles
such as no one has ever heard of before.
No ear has heard,
no eye has seen
any god but you act like this
for those who trust him.
You guide those who act with integrity
and keep your ways in mind.
You were angry when we were sinners;
we had long been rebels against you.
We were all like men unclean,
all that integrity of ours like filthy clothing.
We have all withered like leaves
and our sins blew us away like the wind.
No one invoked your name
or roused himself to catch hold of you.
For you hid your face from us
and gave us up to the power of our sins.
And yet, Lord, you are our Father.

# New Testament *Romans 15.4-13 NEB*

All the ancient scriptures were written for our own instruction, in order than through the encouragement they give us we may maintain our hope with fortitude. And may God, the source of all fortitude and all encouragement, grant that you may agree with one another after the manner of Christ Jesus, so that with one mind and one voice you may praise the God and Father of our Lord Jesus Christ.

In a word, accept one another as Christ accepted us, to the glory of God. I mean that Christ became a servant of the Jewish people to maintain the truth of God by making good his promises to the patriarchs, and at the same time to give the Gentiles cause to glorify God for his mercy. As Scripture says, 'Therefore I will praise thee among the Gentiles and sign hymns to thy name'; and again, 'Gentiles, make merry together with his own people'; and yet again, 'All Gentiles, praise the Lord; let all peoples praise him.' Once again, Isaiah says, 'There shall be the Scion of Jesse, the one raised up to govern the Gentiles; on him the Gentiles shall set their hope.' And may the God of hope fill you with all joy and peace by your faith in him, until, by the power of the Holy Spirit, you overflow with hope.

## Gospel *Luke 4.14-21 NEB*

Jesus, armed with the power of the Spirit, returned to Galilee; and reports about him spread through the whole country-side. He taught in their synagogues and all men sang his praises.

So he came to Nazareth, where he had been brought up, and went to synagogue on the Sabbath day as he regularly did. He stood up to read the lesson and was handed the scroll of the prophet Isaiah. He opened the scroll and found the passage which says,

'The spirit of the Lord is upon me because he has anointed me; he has sent me to announce good news to the poor, to proclaim release for prisoners and recovery of sight for the blind; to let the broken victims go free, to proclaim the year of the Lord's favour.'

He rolled up the scroll, gave it back to the attendant, and sat down; and all eyes in the synagogue were fixed on him.

He began to speak: 'Today,' he said, 'in your very hearing this text has come true.'

# Stubborn faith in a God of communication

*The unfolding of your words gives light,*
*it gives understanding to the simple. (Ps 119.130)*

Why doesn't God do something? That heart-cry has battered the doors of heaven countless times throughout human history. In our contemporary context, it has certainly not lost its force. In the midst of disaster and cruelty, why does God seem to be (in R.S. Thomas' phrase) 'this great absence'? Why does God hide his face and his power? The opening verses of Isaiah 64 express in vivid summary the yearning common to many times and many places: that God would show himself and make the world feel the effect of divine might. This psalm-like passage probably originated with those left in Palestine after the Babylonian conquest and the removal of large numbers into exile. It reflects a time of desolate questioning, a time of penitent acknowledgement of the failings of God's people. Out of such honesty and longing come assertions of faith. The God who brought Israel into being, their 'Father', the God of Exodus who caused Sinai to quake, this God will surely act for those who patiently wait on his mercy. Naked trust holds on, the raw material of hope.

The Jewish scriptures are permeated by stubborn faith in a God who cares enough to get involved, a God who is faithful to his people and his promises. When circumstances serve to deny this, vigorous appeal can be made, explanation demanded. Though God might be perceived as holy terror, he is also known as inviting relationship, relationship designed to bring out the best for all the world. So, as Paul asserts in Romans 15, these 'ancient scriptures' are shot through with encouragement, even for those of non-Jewish background. They put us in touch with the God who is prime source of encouragement, fortitude (stickability) and full-blown hope. They point us to the divine purpose that the whole earth should live to praise God's name—and thereby find true joy and peace. Above all, in setting before us a God committed to communication, a God who evokes prayer and longing for salvation, these scriptures point us to Jesus. It is in Jesus that God decisively shows himself. It is in Jesus that God comes to meet our longing. It is in Jesus that God acts with power for the sake of the world. But God's kind of power turns out to be very different from that of human definition. So it is that in Jesus, God is despised and rejected.

To fulfil the prophet's promise of good news and freedom for the world's disadvantaged victims, God expresses himself in an unauthorized figure on the edge of things. There were times when all spoke well of him, even those among whom he had been brought up. It did not last. The immediate sequel to the Gospel reading has the people of Nazareth trying to throw Jesus over a cliff. He had dared to challenge their ingrained prejudice. When God's Word becomes flesh, he says some unpalatable things.

In Jesus, God has done something. It is when we look at what humankind does to him that we begin to discern just how deep is God's determination to love us into redemption. It is at the cross that we realize the indestructibility of hope.

*God of the margins,*
*show yourself to those who long for you;*
*help us to find you in the unlikely and unpalatable*
*as well as in the encouraging comfort of your word.*

# Advent 3

## Collect

Almighty God,
who sent your servant John the Baptist
to prepare your people for the coming of your Son:
inspire the ministers and stewards of your truth
to turn our disobedient hearts to the law of love;
that when he comes again in glory,
we may stand with confidence before him as our judge;
who is alive and reigns with you and the Holy Spirit,
one God, now and for ever.

### *Psalms 126; Benedictus*

## Old Testament *Malachi 3.1-5 NEB*

Look, I am sending my messenger who will clear a path before me.
Suddenly the Lord whom you seek will come to his temple; the messenger
of the covenant in whom you delight is here, here already, says the Lord
of Hosts. Who can endure the day of his coming? Who can stand firm
when he appears? He is like a refiner's fire, like fuller's soap; he will take
his seat, refining and purifying; he will purify the Levites and cleanse
them like gold and silver, and so they shall be fit to bring offerings to the
Lord. Thus the offerings of Judah and Jerusalem shall be pleasing to
the Lord as they were in days of old, in years long past. I will appear
before you in court, prompt to testify against sorcerers, adulterers, and
perjurers, against those who wrong the hired labourer, the widow, and the
orphan, who thrust the alien aside and have no fear of me, says the Lord of
Hosts.

## New Testament *Philippians 4.4-9 RSV*

Rejoice in the Lord always; again I will say, Rejoice. Let all men know your
forbearance. The Lord is at hand. Have no anxiety about anything, but in
everything by prayer and supplication with thanksgiving let your requests be
made known to God. And the peace of God, which passes all understanding,
will keep your hearts and minds in Christ Jesus.

Finally, brethren, whatever is true, whatever is honourable, whatever is
just, whatever is pure, whatever is lovely, whatever is gracious, if there is any
excellence, if there is anything worthy of praise, think about these things.
What you have learned and received and heard and seen in me, do; and the
God of peace will be with you.

# Gospel *Matthew 11.2-15 NEB*

John, who was in prison, heard what Christ was doing, and sent his own disciples to him with this message: 'Are you the one who is to come, or are we to expect some other?' Jesus answered, 'Go and tell John what you hear and see: the blind recover their sight, the lame walk, the lepers are made clean, the deaf hear, the dead are raised to life, the poor are hearing the good news—and happy is the man who does not find me a stumbling-block.'

When the messengers were on their way back, Jesus began to speak to the people about John; 'What was the spectacle that drew you to the wilderness? A reed-bed swept by the wind? No? Then what did you go out to see? A man dressed in silks and satins? Surely you must look in palaces for that. But why did you go out? To see a prophet? Yes indeed, and far more than a prophet. He is the man of whom Scripture says,

"Here is my herald, whom I send on ahead of you,
and he will prepare your way before you."

'I tell you this: never has there appeared on earth a mother's son greater than John the Baptist, and yet the least in the kingdom of Heaven is greater than he.

'Ever since the coming of John the Baptist the kingdom of Heaven has been subjected to violence and violent men are seizing it. For all the prophets and the Law foretold things to come until John appeared, and John is the destined Elijah, if you will but accept it. If you have ears, then hear.'

# Signpost or scarecrow?

*You, my child, shall be called the prophet of the Most High,*
*for you will go before the Lord to prepare his way.*
*(Benedictus 7)*

The coming of God may be 'a consummation devoutly to be wished' but
we should beware of assuming that his advent will conform to our
expectations. The people addressed by the prophecy of Malachi looked for
God to return in glory to his restored temple, even as Ezekiel had promised
(Ezekiel 43.2-5). In no uncertain terms, they were warned that they might
get more than they bargained for. The Lord would come suddenly, bringing
purifying crisis as well as 'delight'. That which was amiss in worship and
in personal and social relationships would be exposed and eradicated in a
refining process that would be far from comfortable. Who, indeed, would
be able to endure the day of God's coming? The day of the Lord would not
make God's people feel good, nor confirm them in a sense of complacent
superiority. It would put them to rights. That they needed it is underlined
by the prediction that God's action would take them by surprise
(compare 1 Thessalonians 5.2). Had they heeded the messenger sent on
ahead, they might have been better prepared.

The coming of God in Jesus brings both surprise and crisis—but
reactions are mixed. Divine glory, it seems, is not to be identified with the
obvious or the coercive. Its radiance and effectiveness are of a different
order to that of human imagining. John the Baptist, messenger of God *par
excellence*, has much to ponder as he languishes in Herod's prison. In the
wilderness of Judea he had preached powerfully about the one who would
come in refining judgment and with a baptism of fire. That one he had
recognized and acknowledged as Jesus (Matthew 3.1-17). Yet Jesus, it
seems, is not living up to John's expectations. The day of the Lord has not
come with decisive power. The herald is left to suffer in the dungeon of an
immoral king who is weak yet ruthless. No salvation. No vindication. Has
his discernment been wrong? As presented in Matthew's Gospel, the
response of Jesus is characteristically tantalizing. Though not benefitting
from it himself, John is to consider the liberating ministry of Jesus and trust
that the messianic age has dawned. Whatever else Jesus has brought, he
had certainly provoked a major crisis of faith in this giant of a spiritual
leader. To the crowds (but not to John) Jesus opens up the Baptist's
significance. He is the herald (Malachi 3.1), the Elijah figure signalling the
Messiah's coming (Malachi 4.5f). But privileged vocation does not mean
privileged status in God's kingdom. It is wholehearted response to Jesus
that opens doors into heaven. And however much power-hungry humanity
might desire it, the blessings of God cannot be seized by force.

It is the peace of God that Jesus offers, a peace which, as Paul recognized, defies human explanation or description. This peace is born out of trusting relationship with the God revealed in Jesus, the God who is near, even in the darkest of situations, the God who cares about our anxieties and our needs. It is interesting to recall that the encouraging conviction expressed in Philippians comes from one who was also in prison because of his courageous ministry for God.

*God who comes to us,*
*shake us out of our complacency.*
*Turn our hearts and our minds,*
*that we may respond to you in Jesus,*
*and so know your peace.*

# *Advent 4*

## Collect

Heavenly Father,
who chose the Virgin Mary, full of grace,
to be the mother of our Lord and Saviour:
fill us with your grace,
that in all things we may accept your holy will
and with her rejoice in your salvation;
through Jesus Christ our Lord.

### *Psalms 45.10-end; Magnificat*

## Old Testament *Zechariah 2.10-end NEB*

Shout aloud and rejoice, daughter of Zion; I am coming, I will make my
dwelling among you, says the Lord. Many nations shall come over to the
Lord on that day and become his people, and he will make his dwelling with
you. Then you shall know that the Lord of Hosts has sent me to you. The
Lord will once again claim Judah as his own possession in the holy land, and
make Jerusalem the city of his choice.

Silence, all mankind, in the presence of the Lord! For he has bestirred
himself out of his holy dwelling-place.

## New Testament *Revelation 21.1-7 RSV*

I saw a new heaven and a new earth; for the first heaven and the first earth
had passed away, and the sea was no more. And I saw the holy city, new
Jerusalem, coming down out of heaven from God, prepared as a bride
adorned for her husband; and I heard a great voice from the throne saying,
'Behold, the dwelling of God is with men. He will dwell with them, and they
shall be his people, and God himself will be with them; he will wipe away
every tear from their eyes, and death shall be no more, neither shall there be
mourning nor crying nor pain any more, for the former things have passed
away.'

And he who sat upon the throne said, 'Behold, I make all things new.' Also
he said, 'Write this, for these words are trustworthy and true.' And he said to
me, 'It is done! I am the Alpha and the Omega, the beginning and the end. To
the thirsty I will give water from the fountain of the water of life without
payment. He who conquers shall have this heritage, and I will be his God and
he shall be my son.'

## Gospel *Matthew 1.18-23 RSV*

Now the birth of Jesus Christ took place in this way. When his mother Mary had been betrothed to Joseph, before they came together she was found to be with child of the Holy Spirit; and her husband Joseph, being a just man and unwilling to put her to shame, resolved to divorce her quietly. But as he considered this, behold, an angel of the Lord appeared to him in a dream, saying, 'Joseph, son of David, do not fear to take Mary your wife, for that which is conceived in her is of the Holy Spirit; she will bear a son, and you shall call his name Jesus, for he will save his people from their sins.' All this took place to fulfil what the Lord had spoken by the prophet:

'Behold, a virgin shall conceive and bear a son,
and his name shall be called Emmanuel'
(which means, God with us).

# Giving flesh to the longing of ages

*The Almighty has done great things for me, and holy is his name. (Magnificat 3)*

In their different settings, all Sunday's readings celebrate the promise of God to come and dwell with his people. After the Babylonian exile, Zechariah looks confidently to the time when God will claim back Jerusalem as his home. When he does so, the special covenant relationship with his people will be not only renewed but extended. The 'holy land' will become the focal meeting-place between God and the 'many nations' who will be drawn to his Presence. And the proper response of everyone to the coming of this holy God must be the silence of awe and worship.

In the terms that Zechariah understood it, that vision was clearly not realized. The restored temple did not see God coming into his own and attracting universal reverence. In its turn, that temple was desecrated by those who certainly had no respect for the God to whom it was dedicated. Was it that Zechariah's vision still awaited its time? Or was it to be seen in a different light? Some began to look to a heavenly Jerusalem where everything would be as the glorious God intended. The Christian writer of Revelation takes up this theme. At a time of severe trial and crisis, he perceives the ultimate triumph of God—and of the steadfast believer. Sometimes the coded imagery he uses to express this can seem harsh to the point of savagery. In Sunday's extract, however, the nature of the triumphant God is unambiguously apparent. The God of the new Jerusalem, who comes to dwell with humankind, is one who has both power and tenderness: power to put an end to pain and death, and tenderness to wipe away the many tears shed by his long-suffering children (cf Isaiah 25.7-9). This God cares. This God can bring about new beginnings. This God offers a personal relationship that will freely satisfy the deepest desire. And this covenant God is utterly faithful.

It is as we look at the Gospel reading that substance is given to vision and hope. God's final coming is not his only visitation. Giving flesh to the longing of ages, God has already come to dwell with his people. But how unexpected is the nature of his coming; how risky, how unspectacular: a vulnerable baby, born out of dubious circumstances. In this strange and hidden way God appears among us. Little wonder that even upright, caring Joseph needs convincing. Such a God is hard for us to take; it is easier to argue him out of existence or smother him with sentimentality. The challenge of unadulterated divine love is radical in the extreme. We are free to reject it; and we are free to open ourselves to its transforming (if disturbing) power. The God who in love goes to such lengths should indeed reduce us to adoring silence.

*God of the new Jerusalem,*
*help us to blend the silence of awe and worship*
*with the rejoicing of those whose tears are wiped away.*
*May we, like Joseph, be so convinced of your will,*
*that, like Mary, we may be open*
*to your transforming power.*

# *Christmas Day*

## Collect

All praise to you,
Almighty God and heavenly king,
who sent your Son into the world
to take our nature upon him
and to be born of a pure virgin.
Grant that, as we are born again in him,
so he may continually dwell in us
and reign on earth as he reigns in heaven
with you and the Holy Spirit,
now and forever.

Eternal God,
who made this most holy night
to shine with the brightness of your one true light:
bring us, who have known the revelation
of that light on earth,
to see the radiance of your heavenly glory;
through Jesus Christ our Lord.

### *Psalms 85; 96; 98*

### Old Testament *Isaiah 9.2, 6-7 RSV*

The people who walked in darkness
have seen a great light;
those who dwelt in a land of deep darkness,
on them has light shined.
For to us a child is born, to us a son is given;
and the government will be upon his shoulder,
and his name will be called
'Wonderful Counsellor, Mighty God,
Everlasting Father, Prince of Peace.'
Of the increase of his government and of peace
there will be no end,
upon the throne of David, and over his kingdom,
to establish it, and to uphold it with justice and with righteousness
from this time forth and for evermore.
The zeal of the Lord of hosts will do this.

# New Testament *Hebrews 1.1-5 (6-12) JB*

At various times in the past and in various different ways, God spoke to our ancestors through the prophets; but in our own time, the last days, he has spoken to us through his Son, the Son that he has appointed to inherit everything and through whom he made everything there is. He is the radiant light of God's glory and the perfect copy of his nature, sustaining the universe by his powerful command; and now that he has destroyed the defilement of sin, he has gone to take his place in heaven at the right hand of divine Majesty. So he is now as far above the angels as the title which he has inherited is higher than their own name. God has never said to any angel: 'You are my Son, today I have become your father'; or: 'I will be a father to him and he a son to me.'

(Again, when he brings the First-born into the world, he says: 'Let all the angels of God worship him.' About the angels, he says: 'He makes his angels winds and his servants flames of fire', but to his Son he says: 'God, your throne shall last for ever and ever', and: 'his royal sceptre is the sceptre of virtue; virtue you love as much as you hate wickedness. This is why God, your God, has anointed you with the oil of gladness, above your rivals.' And again: 'It is you, Lord, who laid earth's foundations in the beginning, the heavens are the work of your hands; all will vanish, though you remain, all wear out like a garment, you will roll them up like a cloak, and like a garment they will be changed. But yourself, you never change and your years are unending.')

## Gospel *John 1.1-14 RSV*

In the beginning was the Word, and the Word was with God, and the Word was God. He was in the beginning with God; all things were made through him, and without him was not anything made that was made. In him was life, and the life was the light of men. The light shines in the darkness, and the darkness has not overcome it.

There was a man sent from God, whose name was John. He came for testimony, to bear witness to the light, that all might believe through him. He was not the light, but came to bear witness to the light.

The true light that enlightens every man was coming into the world. He was in the world, and the world was made through him, yet the world knew him not. He came to his own home, and his own people received him not. But to all who received him, who believed in his name, he gave power to become children of God; who were born, not of blood nor of the will of the flesh nor of the will of man, but of God.

And the Word became flesh and dwelt among us, full of grace and truth; we have beheld his glory, glory as of the only Son from the Father.

# 'Heaven on earth': God's self-expression in Jesus

*Truly his salvation is near to those that fear him,*
*and his glory shall dwell in our land. (Ps 85.9)*

The message of Christmas is that, as the hymn puts it, 'the great God of heaven is come down to earth'. The coming of this God among us brings both profound hope and radical challenge. The world badly needs both.

Yearning for the intervention of God, for the advent of true and lasting peace is nothing new. We find it throughout the scriptures. In the prophecy of Isaiah we read of the idealistic expectations surrounding the birth of a king (Hezekiah?), expectations which become staple ingredients in the profile of the longed-for Davidic Messiah. God's messianic king will bring light, clear authority, wise counsel, divine power, unfailing fatherly care and real peace. The government of this figure and the peace his rule engenders will be characterized by justice and righteousness. And this highly desirable state of affairs will be brought about by a God who is passionately concerned for the welfare of his people.

The author of Hebrews is in no doubt that it is in Jesus that God has acted decisively to give expression to his concern. The people of God were given even more than they hoped for: not just a messianic king but God's eternal Son. In the resounding opening section of this epistle (which is really a sermon), the preacher sets out his agenda—the conviction on which his entire writing is based.

The one in whom God speaks comprehensively and authoritatively is indeed no less than God's Son, the one in whom we see the exact likeness of God. When we look to Jesus, we encounter God's creativity, God's sustaining power and God's sovereign righteousness and majesty. We also meet God's awesome humility, God's willingness to go to any lengths to bring cleansing from the deadly pollution of sin. This is not a God who keeps himself to himself, maintaining a holy distance. This is a God who gets involved, who comes into the middle of human experience to put things right. As his sermon unfolds, the preacher of Hebrews powerfully reminds us that the cost to God is enormous. And so are the blessings which his ministry in Jesus releases. To say the least, this God is worthy of commitment.

John the Evangelist would wholeheartedly agree. That is why he wrote his Gospel (see John 20.31). In the Prologue to his work (1.1-18), he offers us a rich meditation on the meaning of the incarnation, God becoming flesh in Jesus. Even after many readings, it would be difficult to exhaust the significance of this Prologue. There are many themes here that are taken up in the body of the Gospel: creation/new creation, light/darkness, witness, acceptance/rejection, the offer of new life. Above all, there is the claim that Jesus is God's supreme act of communication, God's Word, who was with God from the beginning and God's agent in creation (cf Genesis 1.1ff). More wonderful even than that, God's Word becomes flesh. The self-expression of God becomes a human being, so that human beings should not only see God's glory but also have the opportunity to share God's very life. What more can God say? And all we have to say in response (the 'word' God longs for from us) is 'Yes'. Here is both invitation and challenge.

As St Paul puts it (2 Corinthians 9.15), 'Thanks be to God for his indescribable gift.'

> *God of heaven,*
> *you came to earth to claim your own,*
> *and your own received you not.*
> *Claim us and hold us, we pray,*
> *in our flesh and to all eternity.*

## A suggested worship activity for Christmas Day

### (This is based on a custom from continental Europe.)

1. On Christmas Day, place on or in a display near the Christmas tree: an apple, to represent humankind's sin and disobedience (see Genesis 2.15-17; 3.1-24); a candle, to represent the light of Christ coming to the world's darkness (see John 1.1-14); a small piece of bread, to represent Jesus the Bread of Life, and the offering to God in thanksgiving of our own lives (see John 6.48-51). The setting of the dressed Christmas tree reminds us not only of the joy of Christ's birth but also of the hard wood of Christ's cross, which underlies the glory of Easter.

2. On Christmas Day, and perhaps on each of the days of Christmas, the candle should be lit whilst a prayer is said (the prayer above could be used).

3. If more than one person is present, members of the group can share out the little actions involved. (Take great care with the candle, especially if it is on the tree! Do not leave the candle alight and unattended.)

4. After Christmas, save a couple of branches from the tree to use during Lent, Holy Week and Easter (see page 87).

# *Sunday after Christmas Day*

## Collect

Almighty Father,
whose Son Jesus Christ was presented in the Temple
and acclaimed the glory of Israel and the light of the nations:
grant that in him we may be presented to you
and in the world may reflect his glory;
through Jesus Christ our Lord.

### *Psalms 2; 116.11-18*

## Old Testament *1 Samuel 1.20-end NEB*

Elkanah had intercourse with his wife Hannah, and the Lord remembered her. She conceived, and in due time bore a son, whom she named Samuel, 'because', she said, 'I asked the Lord for him.'

Elkanah, with his whole household, went up to make the annual sacrifice to the Lord and to redeem his vow. Hannah did not go with them, but said to her husband, 'When the child is weaned I will come up with him to enter the presence of the Lord, and he shall stay there always.' Her husband Elkanah said to her, 'Do what you think best; stay at home until you have weaned him. Only, may the Lord indeed see your vow fulfilled.' So the woman stayed and nursed her son until she had weaned him; and when she had weaned him, she took him up with her. She took also a bull three years old, an ephah of meal, and a flagon of wine, and she brought him, child as he was, into the house of the Lord at Shiloh. They slaughtered the bull, and brought the boy to Eli. Hannah said to him, 'Sir, as sure as you live, I am the woman who stood near you here praying to the Lord. It was this boy that I prayed for and the Lord has given me what I asked. What I asked I have received; and now I lend him to the Lord; for his whole life he is lent to the Lord.' And they prostrated themselves there before the Lord.

## New Testament *Romans 12.1-8 NEB*

My brothers, I implore you by God's mercy to offer your very selves to him: a living sacrifice, dedicated and fit for his acceptance, the worship offered by mind and heart. Adapt yourselves no longer to the pattern of this present world, but let your minds be remade and your whole nature thus transformed. Then you will be able to discern the will of God, and to know what is good, acceptable, and perfect.

In virtue of the gift that God in his grace has given me I say to everyone among you: do not be conceited or think too highly of yourself; but think your way to a sober estimate based on the measure of faith that God has dealt to each of you. For just as in a single human body there are many limbs and organs, all with different functions, so all of us, united with Christ, form one body, serving individually as limbs and organs to one another.

The gifts we possess differ as they are allotted to us by God's grace, and must be exercised accordingly: the gift of inspired utterance, for example, in proportion to a man's faith; or the gift of administration, in administration. A teacher should employ his gift in teaching, and one who has the gift of stirring speech should use it to stir his hearers. If you give to charity, give with all your heart; if you are a leader, exert yourself to lead; if you are helping others in distress, do it cheerfully.

## Gospel *Luke 2.22-40 JB*

When the day came for them to be purified as laid down by the Law of Moses, the parents of Jesus took him up to Jerusalem to present him to the Lord—observing what stands written in the Law of the Lord: Every first-born male must be consecrated to the Lord—and also to offer in sacrifice, in accordance with what is said in the Law of the Lord, a pair of turtledoves or two young pigeons. Now in Jerusalem there was a man named Simeon. He was an upright and devout man; he looked forward to Israel's comforting and the Holy Spirit rested on him. It had been revealed to him by the Holy Spirit that he would not see death until he had set eyes on the Christ of the Lord. Prompted by the Spirit he came to the Temple; and when the parents brought in the child Jesus to do for him what the Law required, he took him into his arms and blessed God; and he said:

'Now, Master, you can let your servant go in peace,
just as you promised;
because my eyes have seen the salvation
which you have prepared for all the nations to see,
a light to enlighten the pagans
and the glory of your people Israel.'

As the child's father and mother stood there wondering at the things that were being said about him, Simeon blessed them and said to Mary his mother, 'You see this child: he is destined for the fall and for the rising of many in Israel, destined to be a sign that is rejected—and a sword will pierce your own soul too—so that the secret thoughts of many may be laid bare.'

There was a prophetess also, Anna the daughter of Phanuel, of the tribe of Asher. She was well on in years. Her days of girlhood over, she had been married for seven years before becoming a widow. She was now eighty-four years old and never left the Temple, serving God night and day with fasting and prayer. She came by just at that moment and began to praise God; and she spoke of the child to all who looked forward to the deliverance of Jerusalem.

When they had done everything the Law of the Lord required, they went back to Galilee, to their own town of Nazareth. Meanwhile the child grew to maturity, and he was filled with wisdom; and God's favour was with him.

## *Given by God, given to God*

*I will pay my vows to the Lord*
*in the presence of all his people (Ps 116.11)*

The gifts of God are both precious and challenging. They bring much joy and fulfilment. They also call out for response, and that response can be searching in its demands.

Hannah's child was asked for from the Lord in circumstances of deep personal distress (1 Samuel 1.1-18). In all its desperate honesty, her prayer bore fruit. A son was born. Yet only too soon, the longed-for gift had to be given back. A promise had been made. When we look at this story in human terms (and why shouldn't we?) we recognize pain as well as joy. As Hannah at last brought herself to leave her child in 'the house of the Lord', a sword must have pierced her heart. Obedience can be very costly. For the small boy, too, the experience must have been bewildering. And much was to be subsequently laid upon his shoulders. From an early age he was entrusted with the truth of God. Communicating that truth to Israel and its leaders was not always a comfortable vocation. Samuel, given by God and to God, knew the wounding of God as well as the blessing.

So it was, in far greater degree, for Mary's child, the truth of God made flesh. Luke's narrative of the Presentation carries powerful echoes of the Samuel infancy story, but the Evangelist leaves us in no doubt that a greater than Samuel is here. This is the one prayerfully awaited by the faithful: the one who would bring salvation to both Israel and the nations. This is 'the Christ of the Lord'. He is recognized by sheer spiritual discernment. Simeon and Anna had no external evidence to go on, nor can they have lived to see any corroboration of their inner conviction. They knew because of their disciplined openness to God and their refusal to give up hope. And Simeon knew that this gift of a child would not be universally welcomed. He would bring too much to light. He would be more than many could bear. Expressing the honesty of God's love, he would be grievously hurt. And so would his mother. Hannah and Mary are what a later age might call soul-sisters. As Mary's Magnificat reinterprets Hannah's song, so Hannah's obedience and maternal suffering point to Mary's more searing experience.

hat comes to its climax at the cross, but from conception onwards it was ever absent. Mary had to learn that this child of God's saving love was not ers to possess; and, for all her pondering, she found him hard to nderstand. In both respects we have to share her experience.

To be effectively appreciated, the gift of God in Christ demands of us no ess than complete transformation. If we say 'yes' to that and seek onstantly to offer the whole of our being to the giving God, we shall know he piercing of God's sword. But we shall know also the release of God's fe in our lives; the setting free of gifts which, as they are used, will build p the kind of community God intended. Paul's words to the Romans need o be heeded afresh in each generation.

*Generous God,*
*given life by you,*
*may we be wholly given over to you;*
*loved by you,*
*may we be wholly given over to love of you,*
*gifted by you,*
*may we ever use those gifts in your service.*

# Christmas 2

## Collect

> Eternal God,
> who by the shining of a star
> led the wise men to the worship of your Son:
> guide by his light the nations of the earth,
> that the whole world may behold your glory;
> through Jesus Christ our Lord.

## *Psalms Nunc Dimittis; 27.1-8*

## Old Testament *Isaiah 60.1-6 NEB*

> Arise, Jerusalem,
> rise clothed in light; your light has come
> and the glory of the Lord shines over you.
> For, though darkness covers the earth
> and dark night the nations,
> the Lord shall shine upon you
> and over you shall his glory appear;
> and the nations shall march towards your light
> and their kings to your sunrise.
> Lift up your eyes and look all around:
> they flock together, all of them, and come to you;
> your sons also shall come from afar,
> your daughters walking beside them leading the way.
> Then shall you see, and shine with joy,
> then your heart shall thrill with pride:
> the riches of the sea shall be lavished upon you
> and you shall possess the wealth of nations.
> Camels in droves shall cover the land,
> dromedaries of Midian and Ephah,
> all coming from Sheba
> laden with golden spice and frankincense,
> heralds of the Lord's praise.

## New Testament *Revelation 21.22-22.5 NEB*

> I saw no temple in the city; for its temple was the sovereign Lord God and the Lamb. And the city had no need of sun or moon to shine upon it; for the glory of God gave it light, and its lamp was the Lamb. By its light shall the nations walk, and the kings of the earth shall bring into it all their splendour. The

gates of the city shall never be shut by day—and there will be no night. The wealth and splendour of the nations shall be brought into it; but nothing unclean shall enter, nor anyone whose ways are false and foul, but only whose who are inscribed in the Lamb's roll of the living.

Then the angel showed me the river of the water of life, sparkling like crystal, flowing from the throne of God and of the Lamb down the middle of the city's street. On either side of the river stood a tree of life, which yields twelve crops of fruit, one for each moth of the year; the leaves of the trees serve for the healing of the nations. Every accursed thing shall disappear. The throne of God and of the Lamb will be there, and his servants shall worship him; they shall see him face to face, and bear his name on their foreheads. There shall be no more night, nor will they need the light of lamp or sun, for the Lord God will give them light; and they shall reign for evermore.

## Gospel *Matthew 2.1-12, 19-23 RSV*

When Jesus was born in Bethlehem of Judaea in the days of Herod the king, behold, wise men from the East came to Jerusalem, saying, 'Where is he who has been born king of the Jews? For we have seen his star in the East, and have come to worship him.' When Herod the king heard this, he was troubled, and all Jerusalem with him; and assembling all the chief priests and scribes of the people, he enquired of them where the Christ was to be born. They told him, 'In Bethlehem of Judaea; for so it is written by the prophet: "And you, O Bethlehem, in the land of Judah, are by no means least among the rulers of Judah; for from you shall come a ruler who will govern my people Israel." '

Then Herod summoned the wise men secretly and ascertained from them what time the star appeared; and he sent them to Bethlehem, saying, 'Go and search diligently for the child, and when you have found him bring me word, that I too may come and worship him.' When they had heard the king they went their way; and lo, the star which they had seen in the East went before them, till it came to rest over the place where the child was. When they saw the star, they rejoiced exceedingly with great joy; and going into the house they saw the child with Mary his mother, and they fell down and worshipped him. Then, opening their treasures, they offered him gifts, gold and frankincense and myrrh. And being warned in a dream not to return to Herod, they departed to their own country by another way.

But when Herod died, behold, an angel of the Lord appeared in a dream to Joseph in Egypt, saying, 'Rise, take the child and his mother, and go to the land of Israel, for those who sought the child's life are dead.' And he rose and took the child and his mother, and went to the land of Israel. But when he heard that Archelaus reigned over Judaea in place of his father Herod, he was afraid to go there, and being warned in a dream he withdrew to the district of Galilee. And he went and dwelt in a city called Nazareth, that what was spoken by the prophets might be fulfilled, 'He shall be called a Nazarene.'

# True subjection to divine sovereignty

*The Lord is my light and my salvation,*
*whom then shall I fear?*
*The Lord is the stronghold of my life,*
*of whom then shall I be afraid? (Ps 27.1)*

In one way or another, all the readings set for Sunday are concerned with the nature and expression of sovereign power. The prophecy of Isaiah 60 holds out the radiant promise of a renewed Jerusalem. After the traumatic battering of the Babylonian conquest, the city will again become the focus of God's presence. It will fulfil its vocation to reflect the glory of God, so that nations, with their rulers, will be drawn to its light. They will bring handsome tribute, signifying their submission and making Jerusalem overflow with wealth. No wonder the personified city will thrill with pride and joy. The poetry of this passage is compelling in its beauty. It vibrates with excitement and hope. Yet it also carries the potential of movement to a darker side of glory. All too easily, the glorification of Jerusalem could replace the glorification of God. Exercising power and control over others is an attractive prospect. Abuse of such power is so much the more insidious when justified in the name of God. To whom, in reality, are 'the nations' becoming subject? That question, and its implications, could be transposed to many contexts, personal and ecclesiastical, as well as global.

The new Jerusalem of Revelation is certainly the domain of God but, here again, there is a question. The passage ends by proclaiming the eternal reign of the servants of God. What is the substance of their sovereignty? Presumably, its character is determined by their attitude of worship and their face-to-face vision of God. In the light of such an emphasis, their rule should be an agency of divine governance. At the consummation of all things anticipated in Revelation, God's servants will no doubt be perfect in their obedience and behaviour. Until then, it would be as well for those servants (especially when in positions of leadership and influence) to be constantly aware of the pitfalls of power. But how is God's power expressed? In the Revelation passage, divine sovereignty involves a range of qualities. It dispels darkness. It excites worship and allegiance from the peoples of earth and their leaders. It brings security and freedom of access (open gates), it offers healing and purity. It is the sovereignty of one who has made himself known in a figure tellingly described by the image of a lamb—a lamb who was slain.

The Gospel reading makes it clear that the acknowledgement of God's superior authority by earthly rulers is very much a future hope. Herod is fearful, scheming and savage in his reaction to the threat of competition from a messianic king. The ruthless Archelaus has to be avoided when the holy family return from Egypt. God, however, does not respond in kind to power-hungry defensiveness. It is those who discern the signs and have the will to search who see the star of God's presence and rejoice. For Matthew, that star is yet another indicator of the fulfilment of God's promises (compare Numbers 24.17). It is perceived by those who are neither leaders of the people of God nor even Gentile kings. They are magi, practitioners of esoteric wisdom, mysterious in their identity. Their perception, perseverance and devotion put rulers to shame. They also lead to a God prepared to dwell with us in humble obscurity. With such a God lies true power, power that can save the world.

*Magnetic God,*
*you attract nations to your light,*
*and your servants to your worship.*
*Draw us, like the magi,*
*to perceive you, to persevere in finding you,*
*and to be continually devoted to you.*

# Epiphany of Our Lord

## Collect

Eternal God,
who by the shining of a star
led the wise men to the worship of your Son:
guide by his light the nations of the earth,
that the whole world may behold your glory;
through Jesus Christ our Lord.

## *Psalms 72.1-8; 72.10-end*

## Old Testament *Isaiah 49.1-6 NEB*

Listen to me, you coasts and islands,
pay heed, you peoples far away:
from birth the Lord called me,
he named me from my mother's womb.
He made my tongue his sharp sword
and concealed me under cover of his hand;
he made me a polished arrow
and hid me out of sight in his quiver.
He said to me, 'You are my servant,
Israel through whom I shall win glory;
so I rose to honour in the Lord's sight
and my God became my strength.
Once I said, 'I have laboured in vain;
I have spent my strength for nothing, to no purpose';
yet in truth my cause is with the Lord
and my reward is in God's hands.
And now the Lord who formed me in the womb to be his servant,
to bring Jacob back to him
that Israel should be gathered to him,
now the Lord calls me again:
it is too slight a task for you, as my servant,
to restore the tribes of Jacob,
to bring back the descendants of Israel:
I will make you a light to the nations,
to be my salvation to earth's farthest bounds.

# New Testament *Ephesians 3.1-12 TEV*

For this reason I, Paul, the prisoner of Christ Jesus for the sake of you Gentiles, pray to God. Surely you have heard that God in his grace has given me this work to do for your good. God revealed his secret plan and made it know to me. (I have written briefly about this, and if you will read what I have written, you can learn about my understanding of the secret of Christ.) In past times mankind was not told this secret, but God has revealed it now by the Spirit to his holy apostles and prophets. The secret is that by means of the gospel the Gentiles have a part with the Jews in God's blessings; they are members of the same body and share in the promise that God made through Christ Jesus.

I was made a servant of the gospel by God's special gift, which he gave me through the working of this power. I am less than the least of all God's people; yet God gave me this privilege of taking to the Gentiles the Good News about the infinite riches of Christ, and of making all people see how God's secret plan is to be put into effect. God, who is the Creator of all things, kept his secret hidden through all the past ages, in order that at the present time, by means of the church, the angelic rulers and powers in the heavenly world might learn of his wisdom in all its different forms. God did this according to his eternal purpose, which he achieved through Christ Jesus our Lord. In union with Christ and through our faith in him we have the boldness to go into God's presence with all confidence.

# Gospel *Matthew 2.1-12 RSV*

When Jesus was born in Bethlehem of Judaea in the days of Herod the king, behold, wise men from the East came to Jerusalem, saying, 'Where is he who has been born king of the Jews? For we have seen his star in the East, and have come to worship him.' When Herod the king heard this, he was troubled, and all Jerusalem with him; and assembling all the chief priests and scribes of the people, he inquired of them where the Christ was to be born. They told him, 'In Bethlehem of Judaea; for so it is written by the prophet:
"And you, O Bethlehem, in the land of Judah,
are by no means least among the rulers of Judah;
for from you shall come a ruler
who will govern my people Israel."'

Then Herod summoned the wise men secretly and ascertained from them what time the star appeared; and he sent them to Bethlehem, saying, 'Go and search diligently for the child, and when you have found him bring me word, that I too may come and worship him.' When they had heard the king they went their way; and lo, the star which they had seen in the East went before them, till it came to rest over the place where the child was. When they saw the star, they rejoiced exceedingly with great joy; and going into the house they saw the child with Mary his mother, and they fell down and worshipped

him. Then, opening their treasures, they offered him gifts, gold and
frankinsence and myrrh. And being warned in a dream not to return to
Herod, they departed to their own country by another way.

## *Light to the nations,*
## *treasure for the world*

*Let all peoples use his name in blessing,*
*and all nations call him blessed. (Ps 72.19)*

It is difficult to see the point of the passage from Ephesians without relating
it to what has gone before. Paul has been specifically addressing his Gentile
audience, showing how, through the death and resurrection of Jesus, God
has acted to bring them together with the Jews to newness of life. It is Jesus
who has brought them hope; it is Jesus who has accepted them into God's
household in a new way. This is why Paul prays for them. He emphasizes
how the Gentiles are to share the blessings and promises formerly thought
to belong solely to the Jews. With God there are no outsiders.

Paul writes, a little modestly, of his own part in taking the good news of
Jesus Christ to the Gentiles. He reminds them that as a result of his
endeavours, he is now a prisoner. And yet, in view of the way God has
revealed himself to the world, by opening up 'the infinite riches of Christ',
Paul and all those united with Christ are able to approach God in confident
boldness. The time has come for this 'secret' to be blazed abroad.

The passage from Isaiah 49 is one of those known as the Servant Songs.
Like Paul, the Servant figure is called to go far beyond what might seem to
have been his vocation. He addresses the people farthest away. Whilst
previously it had been thought that the Servant's task was to convict the
people of Israel of the errors of their ways and to bring them back to God,
now the prophet is given the sense of a much wider vocation. Restoration
of Israel is indeed part of the task, but beyond this the Servant is to be
God's 'salvation to earth's farthest bounds'. The Servant is called to be 'a
light to the nations'.

Unlike Luke (Luke 2.28-32), Matthew does not link the revelation of
God's coming in Jesus directly with the 'light to the nations'. But the
narrative of the coming of the 'wise men' and all that surrounded that
coming suggests that Matthew saw the wider significance of their coming
to Bethlehem to worship the new king. Whatever the precise significance of
the star and the involvement of the highly political King Herod, there is a
sense of mysterious revelation that catches something of what has gone
before in Isaiah and elsewhere, and builds on it. The coming of Jesus is an
opening up to the whole world of God's purposes. Those purposes are not

going to be thwarted by a jealous politician. Nor are they going to be monopolized by the magi. Like the Servant, the child of Bethlehem is for all people, to earth's farthest coast. In an obscure little town, God opens up his treasure for the world. The magi respond by opening up their treasures in worship. So must we.

*God of illumination,*
*you call us beyond our imagining*
*to tasks beyond our powers.*
*Empower our service and enlighten our worship*
*that we may know and proclaim the light of the world.*

# Epiphany 1

## Collect

Almighty God,
who anointed Jesus at his baptism with the Holy Spirit
and revealed him as your beloved Son:
inspire us, your children,
who are born of water and the Spirit,
to surrender our lives to your service,
that we may rejoice to be called the sons of God;
through Jesus Christ our Lord.

## Psalms 36.5-10; 89.19-30

## Old Testament *Isaiah 42.1-7 NEB*

Here is my servant, whom I uphold,
my chosen one in whom I delight,
I have bestowed my spirit upon him,
and he will make justice shine on the nations.
He will not call out or lift his voice high,
or make himself heard in the open street.
He will not break a bruised reed,
or snuff out a smouldering wick;
he will make justice shine on every race,
never faltering, never breaking down,
he will plant justice on earth,
while coasts and islands wait for his teaching.
Thus speaks the Lord who is God,
he who created the skies and stretched them out,
who fashioned the earth and all that grows in it,
who gave breath to its people,
the breath of life to all who walk upon it:
I, the Lord, have called you with righteous purpose
and taken you by the hand;
I have formed you, and appointed you
to be a light to all peoples,
a beacon for the nations,
to open eyes that are blind,
to bring captives out of prison,
out of the dungeons where they lie in darkness.

# New Testament *Ephesians 2.1-10 JB*

You were dead, through the crimes and the sins in which you used to live when you were following the ways of this world, obeying the ruler who governs the air, the spirit who is at work in the rebellious. We all were among them too in the past, living sensual lives, ruled entirely by our own physical desires and our own ideas; so that by nature we were as much under God's anger as the rest of the world. But God loved us with so much love that he was generous with his mercy: when we were dead through our sins, he brought us to life with Christ—it is through grace that you have been saved—and raised us up with him and gave us a place with him in heaven, in Christ Jesus.

This was to show for all ages to come, through his goodness towards us in Christ Jesus, how infinitely rich he is in grace. Because it is by grace that you have been saved, through faith; not by anything of your own, but by a gift from God; not by anything that you have done, so that nobody can claim the credit. We are God's work of art, created in Christ Jesus to live the good life as from the beginning he had meant us to live it.

# Gospel *John 1.29-34 JB*

Seeing Jesus coming towards him, John said, 'Look, there is the lamb of God that takes away the sin of the world. This is the one I spoke of when I said: "A man is coming after me who ranks before me because he existed before me." I did not know him myself, and yet it was to reveal him to Israel that I came baptizing with water.' John also declared, 'I saw the Spirit coming down on him from heaven like a dove and resting on him. I did not know him myself, but he who sent me to baptize with water had said to me, "The man on whom you see the Spirit come down and rest is the one who is going to baptize with the Holy Spirit." Yes, I have seen and I am the witness that he is the Chosen One of God.'

# Strength and gentleness—the vocation of God's servants

*I have found my servant David,*
*and anointed him with my holy oil. (Ps 89.21)*

Despite much scholarly probing, the servant figure of Deutero-Isaiah continues to resist firm identification. Yet this anonymous character has been profoundly influential, not least for many struggling to articulate the significance of Jesus of Nazareth, including New Testament writers (see e.g. Mark 1.11; Matthew 12.17-21; Luke 22.37; John 12.38). Certainly there are powerful connections between the vocation of the servant and the ministry of the one who came not to be served but to serve. In Sunday's passage from Isaiah 42 we are introduced (as by God himself) to one who is specially chosen and empowered by God to undertake a staggering mission: to bring justice and revealing light to the nations and to set people free from their prisons. This servant, anointed with God's Spirit, will persevere in the task given to him, daunting though it might be. Held by the hand of God, his proclamation of God's message will be free of stridency and infused with discerning gentleness. Strong though he is, he will not break the bruised reed.

It does not take a great leap of the imagination to detect the effective realization of the servant's calling in the person of Jesus. At his baptism, the divine Spirit descends on Jesus and, as the Fourth Evangelist insists, remains upon him. Emerging from obscurity (not even the Baptist knew him) he is marked out by God. The time has come to go public, to begin unveiling God's glory to the world. But, as Isaiah's servant was also to discover (cf Isaiah 53), the mission of God is not universally welcomed, nor even recognized. The strong minister becomes himself the bruised reed. The truth of God, deeply disturbing in character, provokes a harshly negative reaction. The light shines in the darkness. Yet the darkness is not total. There are those with eyes to see who bear witness to the light, of whom the Baptist is a prime example. Nor is the darkness ultimately triumphant. Despite the insidious forces of destruction, God will have his way in dealing decisively with sin and evil. His way is strange. His Chosen One is given over to the less than tender mercies of the world. Here is the Lamb of God—mysterious sacrificial offering, expressing the extremity of love. Though truth and goodness might be led to the slaughter, they will break out with power from the very place of death. That is the message which 'the nations' so desperately need to hear and receive.

John's Gospel as a whole is a testimony to the truth of God as shown forth in Jesus—a Jesus who is not just God's chosen servant/Lamb but the embodiment of God's eternal love. In Jesus, God is directly involved. That means that the act of grace celebrated in the Letter to the Ephesians is indeed fully and finally effective, though for its effects to be enjoyed a responsive commitment is needed. God's lavish love is not dictatorial. Though sin grieves him sorely, he will not force us to turn away from its futile attractions. The fruits of repentance are far more delightful. New life in Christ is heavenly in its truest sense. But it is not without costly responsibility. Living 'the good life' will surely involve, in one way or another, sharing the painful vocation of Jesus the servant.

*God of vocation,*
*you call us, as you called your servant,*
*to bring justice and light to your world*
*and to set people free;*
*Empower our commitment to new life in Christ,*
*and strengthen us as we share his suffering.*

# Epiphany 2

## Collect

Almighty God,
by whose grace alone we are accepted
    and called to your service:
strengthen us by your Holy Spirit
and make us worthy of our calling;
through Jesus Christ our Lord.

## Psalms 100; 145.1-12

## Old Testament *1 Samuel 3.1-10 RSV*

Now the boy Samuel was ministering to the Lord under Eli. And the word of
the Lord was rare in those days; there was no frequent vision.

At that time Eli, whose eyesight had begun to grow dim, so that he could
not see, was lying down in his own place; the lamp of God had not yet gone
out, and Samuel was lying down within the temple of the Lord, where the ark
of God was. Then the Lord called, 'Samuel! Samuel!' and he said, 'Here I am!'
and ran to Eli, and said, 'Here I am, for you called me.' But he said, 'I did not
call; lie down again.' So he went and lay down. And the Lord called again,
'Samuel!' And Samuel arose and went to Eli, and said, 'Here I am, for you
called me.' But he said, 'I did not call you, my son; lie down again.' Now
Samuel did not yet know the Lord, and the word of the Lord had not yet been
revealed to him. And the Lord called Samuel again the third time. And he
arose and went to Eli, and said 'Here I am, for you called me.' Then Eli
perceived that the Lord was calling the boy. Therefore Eli said to Samuel, 'Go,
lie down; and if he calls you, you shall say, "Speak, Lord, for your servant
hears." ' So Samuel went and lay down in his place.

And the Lord came and stood forth, calling as at other times, 'Samuel!
Samuel!' And Samuel said, 'Speak, for your servant hears.'

## New Testament *Galatians 1.11-end NEB*

I must make it clear to you, my friends, that the gospel you heard me preach
is no human invention. I did not take it over from any man; no man taught it
me; I received it through a revelation of Jesus Christ.

You have heard what my manner of life was when I was still a practising
Jew: how savagely I persecuted the church of God, and tried to destroy it; and
how in the practice of our national religion I was outstripping many of my
Jewish contemporaries in my boundless devotion to the traditions of my
ancestors. But then in his good pleasure God, who had set me apart from

birth and called me through his grace, chose to reveal his Son to me and through me, in order that I might proclaim him among the Gentiles. When that happened, without consulting any human being, without going up to Jerusalem to see those who were apostles before me, I sent off at once to Arabia, and afterwards returned to Damascus.

Three years later I did go up to Jerusalem to get to know Cephas. I stayed with him for a fortnight, without seeing any other of the apostles, except James the Lord's brother. What I write is plain truth; before God I am not lying.

Next I went to the region of Syria and Cilicia, and remained unknown by sight to Christ's congregations in Judaea. They only heard it said, 'Our former persecutor is preaching the good news of the faith which once he tried to destroy'; and they praised God for me.

## Gospel *John 1.35-end NEB*

John was standing with two of his disciples when Jesus passed by. John looked towards him and said, 'There is the Lamb of God.' The two disciples heard him say this, and followed Jesus. When he turned and saw them following him, he asked, 'What are you looking for?' They said, 'Rabbi' (which means a teacher), 'where are you staying?' 'Come and see', he replied. So they went and saw where he was staying, and spent the rest of the day with him. It was then about four in the afternoon.

One of the two who followed Jesus after hearing what John said was Andrew, Simon Peter's brother. The first thing he did was to find his brother Simon. He said to him, 'We have found the Messiah' (which is the Hebrew for 'Christ'). He brought Simon to Jesus, who looked at him and said, 'You are Simon son of John. You shall be called Cephas' (that is, Peter, the Rock).

The next day Jesus decided to leave for Galilee. He met Philip, who, like Andrew and Peter, came from Bethsaida, and said to him, 'Follow me.' Philip went to find Nathanael, and told him, 'We have met the man spoken of by Moses in the Law, and by the prophets: it is Jesus son of Joseph, from Nazareth.' 'Nazareth!' Nathanael exclaimed; 'can anything good come from Nazareth?' Philip said, 'Come and see.' When Jesus saw Nathanael coming, he said, 'Here is an Israelite worthy of the name; there is nothing false in him.' Nathanael asked him, 'How do you come to know me?' Jesus replied, 'I saw you under the fig-tree before Philip spoke to you.' 'Rabbi,' said Nathanael, 'you are the son of God; you are the king of Israel.' Jesus answered, 'Is this the ground of your faith, that I told you I saw you under the fig-tree? You shall see greater things than that.' Then he added, 'In truth, in very truth I tell you all, you shall see heaven wide open, and God's angels ascending and descending upon the Son of Man.'

# Challenge and courage— the vocation to discipleship

*They speak of the glory of your kingdom,*
*and tell of your great might,*
*that all mankind may know your mighty acts*
*and the splendour of your kingdom. (Ps 145.11-12)*

People are called to discipleship in many and various ways. Sunday's readings present us with an instructive selection. In the case of both Samuel and Paul, God takes direct action. Samuel's situation should have provided the ideal context for a developing relationship with God, issuing in committed service. As God's gift of a child to devout parents, Samuel had been dedicated to God in his infancy, brought to live in a holy place and entrusted to the care of a priest of God. But promise was not fulfilled. Eli's failing eyesight is a parable of the loss of spiritual vision among the people of God and their leaders. Samuel had not been nurtured in an awareness of the reality of God. When eventually, Eli comes to himself, he does, at least, facilitate communication between the boy and God. Not all has been lost. But it is God who intervenes to take the situation in hand. As so often, his choice of helper is surprising. An unaware child is singled out to bring a fearful message to the leadership (1 Samuel 3.13-18). It was not the last time Samuel's calling as God's prophet was to bring challenge and stress.

So it was also for Paul, though he was hardly an innocent child when God turned his life around. By his own admission, he had been savagely persecuting the church of God. Precisely why remains a matter for conjecture, but there is little doubt that passionate zeal for his ancestral faith was a driving force in his extreme behaviour. He is not alone in that. Over the centuries, so much savagery has been perpetrated in the name of God. Behind it lies an intensity of feeling and energy that needs redeeming and channelling for good. In Paul's case, God was able to work that work with (to say the least) far-reaching results. Fierce defender of God Paul remains, but his encounter with the risen Christ transforms ferocity into force of love, campaign of terror into courageous mission to the outsider. God uses dramatic gesture to break through to one who undoubtedly possessed a keen sense of high drama. The distorted vision of a believer is emphatically corrected by one who is the true light. For this particular chosen one of God, human agency was not enough.

It was of great significance, however, according to the Fourth Gospel, in the coming together of the first disciples of Jesus. Beginning with the Baptist, personal testimony excites a compelling curiosity which becomes exploration. Questioning begins to turn into relationship—and an awareness of the presence of mystery. Very quickly Jesus is perceived as Messiah, Son of God and king of Israel. Yet these standard categories of expectation seem not to exhaust his significance. There is far more to this puzzling man than meets the eye. A journey has begun which will take the disciples into a strange land. It will be both the breaking and the making of them.

The vocation to discipleship, however experienced, rarely leads to unalloyed comfort. Following the living God is not a leisure activity. But there is no greater destiny, no deeper fulfilment. That claim needs testing. As the Johannine Jesus puts it, 'Come and see'.

*God of invitation,*
*open our eyes to your presence*
*our ears to your call,*
*our minds to your truth,*
*and our lives in your service.*

# Epiphany 3

## Collect

Almighty God,
whose Son revealed in signs and miracles
the wonder of your saving love:
renew your people with your heavenly grace,
and in all our weakness
sustain us by your mighty power;
through Jesus Christ our Lord.

### Psalms 46; 107.1-9

## Old Testament *Deuteronomy 8.1-6 NEB*

Moses said to Israel, 'You must carefully observe everything that I command
you this day so that you may live and increase and may enter and occupy the
land which the Lord promised to your forefathers upon oath. You must
remember all that road by which the Lord your God has led you these forty
years in the wilderness to humble you, to test you and to discover whether or
no it was in your heart to keep his commandments. He humbled you and
made you hungry; then he fed you on manna which neither you nor your
fathers had known before, to teach you that man cannot live on bread alone
but lives by every word that comes from the mouth of the Lord. The clothes
on your backs did not wear out nor did your feet swell all these forty years.
Take this lesson to heart: that the Lord your God was disciplining you as a
father disciplines his son; and keep the commandments of the Lord your God,
conforming to his ways and fearing him.'

## New Testament *Philippians 4.10-20 JB*

It is a great joy to me, in the Lord, that at last you have shown some concern
for me again; though of course you were concerned before, and only lacked
an opportunity. I am not talking about shortage of money: I have learnt to
manage on whatever I have, I know how to be poor and I know how to be
rich too. I have been through my initiation and now I am ready for anything
anywhere: full stomach or empty stomach, poverty or plenty. There is
nothing I cannot master with the help of the One who gives me strength. All
the same, it was good of you to share with me in my hardships. In the early
days of the Good News, as you people of Philippi well know, when I left
Macedonia, no other church helped me with gifts of money. You were the
only ones; and twice since my stay in Thessalonica you have sent me what I
needed. It is not your gift that I value; what is valuable to me is the interest

that is mounting up in your account. Now for the time being I have everything that I need and more: I am fully provided now that I have received from Epaphroditus the offering that you sent, a sweet fragrance— the sacrifice that God accepts and finds pleasing. In return my God will fulfil all your needs, in Christ Jesus, as lavishly as only God can. Glory to God, our Father, for ever and ever. Amen.

## Gospel *John 6.1-14 NEB*

Jesus withdrew to the farther shore of the Sea of Galilee (or Tiberias), and a large crowd of people followed who had seen the signs he performed in healing the sick. Then Jesus went up the hill-side and sat down with his disciples. It was near the time of Passover, the great Jewish festival. Raising his eyes and seeing a large crowd coming towards him, Jesus said to Philip, 'Where are we to buy bread to feed these people?' This he said to test him; Jesus himself knew what he meant to do. Philip replied, 'Twenty pounds would not buy enough bread for every one of them to have a little.' One of his disciples, Andrew, the brother of Simon Peter, said to him, 'There is a boy here who has five barley loaves and two fishes; but what is that among so many?' Jesus said, 'Make the people sit down.' There was plenty of grass there, so the men sat down, about five thousand of them. Then Jesus took the loaves, gave thanks, and distributed them to the people as they sat there. He did the same with the fishes, and they had as much as they wanted. When everyone had had enough, he said to his disciples, 'Collect the pieces left over, so that nothing may be lost.' This they did, and filled twelve baskets with the pieces left uneaten of the five barley loaves.

When the people saw the sign Jesus had performed, the word went round, 'Surely this must be the prophet that was to come into the world.'

# The lavish provision of a dependable God

*Let them thank the Lord for his goodness,*
*and for the wonders that he does for the children of men;*
*for he satisfies the thirsty,*
*and fills the hungry with good things. (Ps 107.8-9)*

The God of glory is not easy to comprehend. Nor are the signs that point to him. Yet the emphatic assertion of all three of Sunday's readings is that this God makes generous provision for the needs of his people. In this respect, his glory is very down-to-earth. It is seen, as the Collect puts it, in 'the wonder of [his] saving love'.

For the Israelites addressed by Deuteronomy, God's saving love must have been decidedly double-edged. They had to travel a long way round to get to the promised land and the going was hard. Faith and obedience were, indeed, tested to the limit—and failure met with a severe response. Where, then, the God of mercy and salvation? It is a question of more than antiquarian interest. The writer of Deuteronomy offers as a means of interpretation the formative discipline a good father administers to his child (cf. Proverbs 3.11-12; Hebrews 12.5-6). Its astringency is matched by a day-to-day care which is attentive to the basic necessities of life: food, clothing, physical well-being. Even in the most trying of circumstances, daily dependence on God is honoured (cf Matthew 6:25-34).

John's account of the feeding of the five thousand has very much in mind God's supplying of manna to his people in the wilderness. The discourse that follows the feeding narrative explores the connections and contrasts, underlining that Jesus is greater than Moses. He is also far more significant than the promised prophet like Moses (Deuteronomy 18:15) with whom he was identified by the beneficiaries of the sign (John 6.14). This dispenser of life-giving bread is himself the bread of life (John 6.48). That truth is difficult to swallow (John 6.52-59) but for those who receive it, it brings not just daily survival but eternal life. For here is the Word made flesh, through whom (if we will) we can experience God's mysterious glory (John 1.14-18).

Paul had certainly had some close encounters with the glory of God. He was also intimately acquainted with hardship and suffering, much of it inflicted by fellow-believers as well as non-Christian opponents. Through the challenges of nastiness, pain and frustration, he had come to rely trustfully on the resources of God. Strong in the strength which God supplied, he was the master rather than the victim of circumstances. In fact, his dependence on God was so direct that he almost falls into the trap of undervaluing the generosity of his sisters and brothers in Christ. He doesn't really need their gift, he tells the Philippians, but he appreciates the thought behind it and what it says about their spiritual condition. That response perhaps leaves a little to be desired. However, Paul does correctively acknowledge that he has benefitted from their ministry in the past and that their present gift is useful to him. It is in this passage, too, that he enunciates one of the glories of faith. Sacrificial generosity is met with an overflowing response from a lavish God. That is a lesson worth learning.

*God of glory,*
*help us to accept our dependence on you,*
*through the generosity of others*
*and in all you provide for us*
*in Jesus, our true and living bread.*

# Ninth Sunday before Easter

## Collect

Eternal God,
whose Son Jesus Christ is for all mankind
the way, the truth, and the life:
grant us to walk in his way,
and to rejoice in his truth,
and to share his risen life;
who is alive and reigns with you and the Holy Spirit,
one God, now and for ever.

### Psalms 103.1-13; 34.11-18

## Old Testament *Proverbs 3.1-8 RSV*

My son, do not forget my teaching,
but let your heart keep my commandments;
for length of days and years of life
and abundant welfare will they give you.
Let not loyalty and faithfulness forsake you;
bind them about your neck,
write them on the tablet of your heart.
So you will find favour and good repute
in the sight of God and man.
Trust in the Lord with all your heart,
and do not rely on your own insight.
In all your ways acknowledge him,
and he will make straight your paths.
Be not wise in your own eyes;
fear the Lord, and turn away from evil.
It will be healing to your flesh
and refreshment to your bones.

## New Testament *1 Corinthians 2.1-10 NEB*

Brothers, when I came to you, I declared the attested truth of God without
display of fine words or wisdom. I resolved that while I was with you I
would think of nothing but Jesus Christ—Christ nailed to the cross. I came
before you weak, nervous, and shaking with fear. The word I spoke, the
gospel I proclaimed, did not sway you with subtle arguments; it carried

conviction by spiritual power, so that your faith might be built not upon human wisdom but upon the power of God.

And yet I do speak words of wisdom to those who are ripe for it, not a wisdom belonging to this passing age, nor to any of its governing powers, which are declining to their end; I speak God's hidden wisdom, his secret purpose framed from the very beginning to bring us to our full glory. The powers that rule the world have never known it; if they had, they would not have crucified the Lord of glory. But, in the words of Scripture, 'Things beyond our seeing, things beyond our hearing, things beyond our imagining, all prepared by God for those who love him', these it is that God has revealed to us through the Spirit. For the Spirit explores everything, even the depths of God's own nature.

## Gospel *Luke 8.4b-15 RSV*

Jesus said in a parable, 'A sower went out to sow his seed; and as he sowed, some fell along the path, and was trodden under foot, and the birds of the air devoured it. And some fell on the rock; and as it grew up, it withered away, because it had no moisture. And some fell among thorns; and the thorns grew with it and choked it. And some fell into good soil and grew, and yielded a hundredfold.' As he said this, he called out, 'He who has ears to hear, let him hear.'

And when his disciples asked him what this parable meant, he said, 'To you it has been given to know the secrets of the kingdom of God; but for others they are in parables, so that seeing they may not see, and hearing they may not understand. Now the parable is this: The seed is the word of God. The ones along the path are those who have heard; then the devil comes and takes away the word from their hearts, that they may not believe and be saved. And the ones on the rock are those who, when they hear the word, receive it with joy; but these have no root, they believe for a while and in time of temptation fall away. And as for what fell among the thorns, they are those who hear, but as they go on their way they are choked by the cares and riches and pleasures of life, and their fruit does not mature. And as for that in the good soil, they are those who, hearing the word, hold it fast in an honest and good heart, and bring forth fruit with patience.'

# The beginning and spring of wisdom

*Come, my children, listen to me,*
*and I will teach you the fear of the Lord. (Ps 34.11)*

Where is wisdom to be found? That question is just as crucial now as when it was posed in the book of Job. Perhaps even more so, for the explosion of human knowledge carries with it many and great dangers.

Those who produced the passages set for Sunday are in no doubt that the way through to wisdom lies in serious attention to God. For them, God is the supreme teacher, committed to bringing insight and understanding. So the one addressed in Proverbs is told that a respectful relationship with God will make him far more wise than relying on his own native wit and intelligence. Moreover, in opening himself to divine wisdom, he will find a fulfilment that affects his whole person and not just his cerebral activity. That is not to say that he should abdicate mental responsibility. It is rather that a person's best powers of heart and mind should be dedicated and referred to the One who is wisdom's essence. Such advice might still be fruitfully heeded by those who would be wise (whether male or female).

God's wisdom has a tendency to surprise and challenge, to defy rational analysis and the expectations of the world. Who would have believed that the focal expression of God's truth could be shown forth in the crucifixion of a low-born troublemaker? Sheer foolishness. But, as Paul profoundly discovered, the figure on the cross takes us into the heart of God. When we have the courage to accept that, the Spirit of God can open up perspectives we could not even have imagined. We shall begin to know even as also we are known. The world sorely needs such 'hidden wisdom' but not all are 'ripe for it'. Proclamation of God's truth will not always attract a positive response. In human terms, speaking of 'the foolishness of God' can be a costly business (cf 1 Corinthians 1.18-30). It even rendered the zealous Paul 'weak, nervous and shaking with fear', difficult though that is to envisage. Yet (as on the cross) out of human weakness comes the power of God.

When we look to Jesus we see the teaching of God incarnate. The post-communion sentence (Matthew 7.28-29) points to its compelling authority. The Gospel reading gives us a flavour of its character. Jesus starts from people's everyday experience. He sees the messages of God in the ongoing life of the world. Here it is the mundane and familiar activity of sowing seed. But his vivid story-telling does not spell out meaning. That emerges for those who have ears to hear and the will to struggle with God for insight. In this case, unusually, we have a detailed interpretation given to those disciples who asked for an explanation. Responses to the seed of

God's word are not vastly dissimilar today. In relation to the fertile soil, it is worth noting a feature unique to Luke. For those in this category, fruit is brought forth 'with patience'. Perseverance yields a rich harvest.

And persevering attention to the only wise God is the beginning and spring of wisdom.

*God only wise,*
*encourage us to accept the seeming foolishness*
*that is both yours and ours.*
*Open up our best powers of heart and mind,*
*that all who search after wisdom*
*may find it in you.*

# Eighth Sunday before Easter

## Collect

Almighty and everliving God,
whose Son Jesus Christ healed the sick
and restored them to wholeness of life:
look with compassion on the anguish of the world,
and by your healing power
make whole both men and nations;
through our Lord and Saviour Jesus Christ,
who is alive and reigns with you and the Holy Spirit,
one God, now and for ever.

### Psalms 147.1-11; 131

## Old Testament *2 Kings 5.1-14 NEB*

Naaman, commander of the king of Aram's army, was a great man highly
esteemed by his master, because by his means the Lord had given victory to
Aram; but he was a leper. On one of their raids the Aramaeans brought back
as a captive from the land of Israel a little girl, who became a servant to
Naaman's wife. She said to her mistress, 'If only my master could meet the
prophet who lives in Samaria, he would get rid of the disease for him.'
Naaman went in and reported to his master word for word what the girl from
the land of Israel had said. 'Very well, you may go,' said the king of Aram,
'and I will send a letter to the king of Israel.' So Naaman went, taking with
him ten talents of silver, six thousand shekels of gold, and ten changes of
clothing. He delivered the letter to the king of Israel, which read thus: 'This
letter is to inform you that I am sending to you my servant Naaman, and I
beg you to rid him of his disease.' When the king of Israel read the letter, he
rent his clothes and said, 'Am I a god to kill and to make alive, that this fellow
sends to me to cure a man of his disease? Surely you must see that he is
picking a quarrel with me.' When Elisha, the man of God, heard how the king
of Israel had rent his clothes, he sent to him saying, 'Why did you rend your
clothes? Let the man come to me, and he will know that there is a prophet in
Israel.' So Naaman came with his horses and chariots and stood at the
entrance to Elisha's house. Elisha sent out a messenger to say to him, 'If you
will go and wash seven times in the Jordan, your flesh will be restored and
you will be clean.' Naaman was furious and went away, saying, 'I thought he
would at least have come out and stood, and invoked the Lord his God by

name, waved his hand over the place and so rid me of the disease. Are not Abana and Pharpar, rivers of Damascus, better than all the waters of Israel? Can I not wash in them and be clean?' So he turned and went off in a rage. But his servants came up to him and said, 'If the prophet had bidden you to do something difficult, would you not do it? How much more then, if he tells you to wash and be clean?' So he went down and dipped himself in the Jordan seven times as the man of God had told him, and his flesh was restored as a little child's, and he was clean.

## New Testament *2 Corinthians 12.1-10 JB*

Must I go on boasting, though there is nothing to be gained by it? But I will move on to the visions and revelations I have had from the Lord. I know a man in Christ who, fourteen years ago, was caught up—whether still in the body or out of the body, I do not know; God knows—right into the third heaven. I do know, however, that this same person—whether in the body or out of the body, I do not know; God knows—was caught up into paradise and heard things which must not and cannot be put into human language. I will boast about a man like that, but not about anything of my own except my weaknesses. If I should decide to boast, I should not be made to look foolish, because I should only be speaking the truth; but I am better than he can actually see and hear me to be.

In view of the extraordinary nature of these revelations, to stop me from getting too proud I was given a thorn in the flesh, an angel of Satan to beat me and stop me from getting too proud! About this thing, I have pleaded with the Lord three times for it to leave me, but he has said, 'My grace is enough for you: my power is at its best in weakness.' So I shall be very happy to make my weaknesses my special boast so that the power of Christ may stay over me, and that is why I am quite content with my weaknesses, and with insults, hardship, persecutions, and the agonies I go through for Christ's sake. For it is when I am weak that I am strong.

## Gospel *Mark 7.24-end NEB*

Jesus left that place and went away into the territory of Tyre. He found a house to stay in, and he would have liked to remain unrecognized, but this was impossible. Almost at once a woman whose young daughter was possessed by an unclean spirit heard of him, came in, and fell at his feet. (She was a Gentile, a Phoenician of Syria by nationality.) She begged him to drive the spirit out of her daughter. He said to her, 'Let the child be satisfied first; it is not fair to take the children's bread and throw it to the dogs.' 'Sir,' she answered, 'even the dogs under the table eat the children's scraps.' He said to her, 'For saying that, you may go home content; the unclean spirit has gone out of your daughter.' And when she returned home, she found the child lying in bed; the spirit had left her.

On his return journey from Tyrian territory he went by way of Sidon to the Sea of Galilee through the territory of the Ten Towns. They brought to him a man who was deaf and had an impediment in his speech, with the request that he would lay his hand on him. He took the man aside, away from the crowd, put his fingers into his ears, spat, and touched his tongue. Then, looking up to heaven, he sighed, and said to him, 'Ephphatha', which means 'Be opened.' With that his ears were opened, and at the same time the impediment was removed and he spoke plainly. Jesus forbade them to tell anyone; but the more he forbade them, the more they published it. Their astonishment knew no bounds: 'All that he does, he does well,' they said; 'he even makes the deaf hear and the dumb speak.'

## *Healing for outsiders first?*

*O Israel trust in the Lord,*
*from this time forward and for ever. (Ps 131.4)*

The scriptures in general and Sunday's readings in particular bear consistent witness to God's propensity to minister saving health. They also make it clear that such ministry is God's prerogative And God moves in mysterious ways. Frequently they are hard to understand. Often they surprise. Always, they emanate from a God who will not be manipulated by human expectations nor confined by human attempts to systematize (and therefore control) divine activity. God the healer, it seems, does not work to set formulae.

'There were many lepers in Israel in the time of the prophet Elisha and none of them was cleansed except Naaman the Syrian' (Luke 4.27). That reminder of God's selectivity and bias to the outsider enraged the people of Nazareth. Who was Naaman to deserve such favouritism? He was, after all, an enemy leader—and one whose humility left something to be desired. To add insult to injury, Naaman's healing was prompted by the generosity of a captive Israelite slave-child—who presumably remained a captive. What strange behaviour for the God of Israel.

Another native of Syria comes to the foreground in Sunday's Gospel narrative. Here is a woman of spirit and initiative. Determined to find help for her daughter, she is prepared to abandon her dignity and risk her reputation by breaking in on this famed Jewish healer (trying to have a private retreat). She throws herself at his feet. As Mark is at pains to point out, this woman is a Gentile. It is no accident that he has placed her encounter with Jesus immediately after a section dealing with the true nature of cleanness and defilement. Unlike the rule-bound Pharisees and the uncomprehending disciples, this Gentile woman goes to the heart of the matter. Her care for her daughter overcomes all else. What are ritual taboos and racial/religious differences in the face of crying human need? The dialogue between the woman and Jesus is a fascinating one, open to much speculation. Why was the response of Jesus apparently so harsh? Was he annoyed by her interruption? Was he asserting the primacy of God's chosen people? Was he testing the woman's faith? Did he have something to learn from her? Or, being aware of her character, was he giving her back her dignity; lifting her to her feet metaphorically if not actually by an exchange designed to give expression to her courage, tenacity and wit? Perhaps it was something of all of these. Certainly, the woman is in no way shamed, and she gets what she wants. Nor can it be without significance that the subsequent healing of a deaf man also takes place in Gentile territory. Outsiders are important in God's sight, whether they be outsiders through race or physical circumstance. And they are dealt with individually.

Paul was an insider, a Jew who had met with Christ and become a Christian. He had been through a great deal for Christ (see 2 Corinthians 11) and had been blessed with profound spiritual experiences. Yet he did not receive the healing he begged for. Rather, he was given God's grace to live with and through his affliction. By this means, the power of God was shown forth. Therein lies a pointer to bedrock truth. Whatever our physical circumstance, we have freely and constantly available to us the saving power of the God of cross and Resurrection. That power can bring out of appalling suffering the life and joy of heaven.

*God of wholeness,*
*fill us with thankfulness for your healing*
*and prayerfulness for all who need it,*
*whoever they may be,*
*and whatever their condition.*

# Seventh Sunday before Easter

## Collect

Merciful Lord,
grant to your faithful people pardon and peace:
that we may be cleansed from all our sins
and serve you with a quiet mind;
through Jesus Christ our Lord.

### Psalms 32; 119.65-72

## Old Testament *Numbers 15.32-36 NEB*

During the time that the Israelites were in the wilderness, a man was found
gathering sticks on the sabbath day. Those who had caught him in the act
brought him to Moses and Aaron and all the community, and they kept him
in custody, because it was not clearly known what was to be done with him.
The Lord said to Moses, 'The man must be put to death; he must be stoned by
all the community outside the camp.' So they took him outside the camp and
all stoned him to death, as the Lord had commanded Moses.

## New Testament *Colossians 1.18-23 NEB*

Christ is the head of the body, the church. He is its origin, the first to return
from the dead, to be in all things alone supreme. For in him the complete
being of God, by God's own choice, came to dwell. Through him God chose
to reconcile the whole universe to himself, making peace through the
shedding of his blood upon the cross—to reconcile all things, whether on
earth or in heaven, through him alone.

Formerly you were yourselves estranged from God; you were his enemies
in heart and mind, and your deeds were evil. But now by Christ's death in his
body of flesh and blood God has reconciled you to himself, so that he may
present you before himself as dedicated men, without blemish and innocent
in his sight. Only you must continue in your faith, firm on your foundations,
never to be dislodged from the hope offered in the gospel which you heard.
This is the gospel which has been proclaimed in the whole creation under
heaven; and I, Paul, have become its minister.

# Gospel *John 8.2-11 NEB*

At daybreak Jesus appeared in the temple, and all the people gathered round him. He had taken his seat and was engaged in teaching them when the doctors of the law and the Pharisees brought in a woman caught committing adultery. Making her stand out in the middle they said to him, 'Master, this woman was caught in the very act of adultery. In the Law Moses has laid down that such women are to be stoned. What do you say about it?' They put the question as a test, hoping to frame a charge against him. Jesus bent down and wrote with his finger on the ground. When they continued to press their question he sat up straight and said, 'That one of you who is faultless shall throw the first stone.' Then once again he bent down and wrote on the ground. When they heard what he said, one by one they went away, the eldest first; and Jesus was left alone, with the woman still standing there. Jesus again sat up and said to the woman, 'Where are they? Has no one condemned you?' She answered, 'No one, sir.' Jesus said, 'Nor do I condemn you. You may go; do not sin again.'

# The life-changing love that faces the destructiveness of sin

*Lord you have done good to your servant,
in accordance with your word. (Ps 119.65)*

One important lesson the scriptures can teach us is to take sin seriously. The word 'sin' is not popular these days, though the reality behind it continues to take its tragic toll. Sin involves a failure to live out God's healthy purposes for creation. It therefore brings suffering and heartache in its wake, pain that is all too frequently felt most keenly by the innocent.

How do Sunday's readings speak to this state of affairs? The Old Testament passage seems brutally stark in its message. By divine guidance and command the offender is stoned to death. He has flagrantly transgressed the sabbath law (see e.g. Exodus 31.14-15; 35.2-3), despising God's rest and failing to trust in God's provision. His is an example of that 'high-handed' sin which is treated of in the immediately preceding verses of Numbers 15. For such a deliberate defiance of God's law there could be no ritual atonement. For those who look to and proclaim a God of forgiveness, this raises fundamental theological questions. Granted that sin is serious, is killing the sinner the most fitting remedy? Surely there is more to God than grim justice? Such was the perception of many other contributors to the Jewish scriptures, and their insight should be viewed alongside this passage. Hosea, for example, encapsulates the issue, with all its painful tension, in the oracle of 11.1-9, culminating in the words 'I am God and not man, the Holy One in your midst, and I will not come to destroy' (v. 9).

When God comes in Christ, that assertion is realized, even in 'flesh and blood' (Colossians 1.22). The true character of divine holiness is expressed in a human being, one who makes it clear that the holy God's way is not to keep himself to himself. Nor is it to extinguish life as a punishment for failure. The truth, as portrayed in Colossians 1, is even harder to comprehend. In Christ, God opens up his own life in a passionate mission to bring forgiveness, reconciliation and peace to a creation gone awry. Genuine forgiveness is always costly. On a cosmic scale it must be sacrificial beyond imagining. The sin of the world is indeed a crucifying burden to bear and to forgive. In a real, yet deeply mysterious sense, God came in Christ not to destroy but to be destroyed. Penitent response to that death can be life-changing. It releases the potential for new beginnings. It offers access to the life of God. And it gives the motivation and resources to live more faithfully in the way God intended. To call this 'good news' is an understatement.

At some stage on his path to the cross, Jesus is forced by his opponents into a encounter with a woman taken in adultery (where was the man, one wonders?). Though the provenance and location of this narrative are matters for debate, it is entirely consistent with the Jesus we meet in all strands of the Gospel tradition. The behaviour of the woman's respectable accusers is distinctly unsavoury. Their concern is not so much for morality as to trap a troublesome upstart teacher. The woman is being used. In response, and by reference to the law that witnesses should throw the first stones, Jesus faces these religious leaders with the truth about themselves. To the woman he offers not condemnation but forgiveness. As, supremely, on the cross, an act of grace precedes the call for repentance. Divine love does not wait for the fulfilment of conditions. It is the experience of love and forgiveness that most effectively changes hearts and lives.

*God, friend of sinners,*
*help us to copy you*
*in the graciousness of acceptance*
*and the costliness of forgiveness.*

# Ash Wednesday

## Collect

Almighty and everlasting God,
you hate nothing that you have made
and forgive the sins of all those who are penitent.
Create and make in us new and contrite hearts,
that, lamenting our sins
and acknowledging our wretchedness,
we may receive from you, the God of all mercy,
perfect forgiveness and peace;
through Jesus Christ our Lord.

## *Psalms 6; 51.1-17; 90.1-12*

## Old Testament *Isaiah 58.1-8 TEV*

The Lord says, 'Shout as loud as you can! Tell my people Israel about their
sins! They worship me every day, claiming that they are eager to know my
ways and obey my laws. They say they want me to give them just laws and
that they take pleasure in worshipping me.'

The people ask, 'Why should we fast if the Lord never notices? Why
should we go without food if he pays no attention?'

The Lord says to them, 'The truth is that at the same time as you fast, you
pursue your own interests and oppress your workers. Your fasting makes
you violent, and you quarrel and fight. Do you think this kind of fasting will
make me listen to your prayers? When you fast, you make yourselves suffer;
you bow your heads low like a blade of grass, and spread out sackcloth and
ashes to lie on. Is that what you call fasting? Do you think I will be pleased
with that?

'The kind of fasting I want is this: Remove the chains of oppression and
the yoke of injustice, and let the oppressed go free. Share your food with
the hungry and open your homes to the homeless poor. Give clothes to
those who have nothing to wear, and do not refuse to help your own
relatives.

'Then my favour will shine on you like the morning sun, and your
wounds will be quickly healed. I will always be with you to save you; my
presence will protect you on every side.'

### New Testament *1 Corinthians 9.24-end NEB*

You know (do you not?) that at the sports all the runners run the race, though only one wins the prize. Like them, run to win! But every athlete goes into strict training. They do it to win a fading wreath; we, a wreath that never fades. For my part, I run with a clear goal before me; I am like a boxer who does not beat the air; I bruise my own body and make it know its master, for fear that after preaching to others I should find myself rejected.

### Gospel *Matthew 6.16-21 NEB*

Jesus said, 'When you fast, do not look gloomy like the hypocrites: they make their faces unsightly so that other people may see that they are fasting. I tell you this: they have their reward already. But when you fast, anoint your head and wash your face, so that men may not see that you are fasting, but only your Father who is in the secret place; and your Father who sees what is secret will give you your reward.

'Do not store up for yourselves treasure on earth, where it grows rusty and moth-eaten, and thieves break in to steal it. Store up treasure in heaven, where there is no moth and no rust to spoil it, no thieves to break in and steal. For where your treasure is, there will your heart be also.'

# *The surprising—and liberating— nature of true worship*

*Create in me a clean heart, O God, and renew a right spirit within me. (Ps 51.10)*

The writings of the prophets contain a good deal of criticism of ways of worship. Their most severe criticism, however, is reserved for the wrong attitudes that people adopt towards worship. It is clear from both Isaiah and the Gospel reading that, for the people of Israel, fasting had become something of an outward status symbol when it was meant to be a sign of an inward state of relationship with God. The people referred to in Isaiah 58 complained that their fasting seemed to have no effect on God. 'What's the point of worship if nothing happens?' is a question still asked today. God's answer through the prophet makes it clear that, if we may put it this way, they have got the wrong end of the stick. Rather than beating themselves, they should be serving others. Rather than making a spectacle of themselves, they should be living in a way that sets other people free: free from injustice, poverty and homelessness, free from fear and oppression. And the generosity of worshippers is to extend even to their own family (often the most challenging context in which to express the love of God). God, it seems, is concerned with attitude and worship that bears fruit in courageously loving behaviour, not with ostentatious and self-seeking ritual (of whatever kind).

In the Gospel, Jesus takes up the point about parading a sense of godliness. It may make an impression on others; it cuts no ice with God. Fasting is something between the believer and God. It is to be entered into because it is a response to God and deepens the relationship between the believer and God. Its intention will be known directly by God. Its effects on others will come through the behaviour of the one who believes. It is not something to be open about in a way that disfigures one's appearance. Religious observances are not for flaunting.

This leads on to the reminder that earthly things will fade away. There is no point in storing up earthly goods. Our true treasure is to be found in God. There is the one in whom our treasure is secure and our trust rewarded.

Writing to the Corinthians, Paul uses the example of an athlete getting fit through continual training. Those who follow Christ must do the same. We need goals to aim at. Our goal must not be to compete with others to show how good we are but to keep single-mindedly to God's way. It is God who will be our 'prize'. And, like Paul, we need to practise what we preach (whatever form our 'preaching' might take). Just before the verses set for Ash Wednesday, Paul has been emphasizing his freedom. It is a freedom to be used wisely. It is a freedom to be used with appropriate constraint. It is a freedom to be used on behalf of others as well as for ourselves.

This passage is a reminder that Lent is a season for growth and development—for a deepening of understanding and a more effective and generous outworking of faith. Christian discipleship is about learning, not display.

*Liberating God,*
*free us from wrong-headed religion and ritual,*
*from self-indulgence and self-deceit,*
*that we may share the joy of your freedom*
*in unbinding those who live in darkness*
*and in the shadow of death.*

# A suggested worship activity for Lent and Holy Week

1. Take two small tree branches (if possible, saved from the Christmas tree, see page 47), strip any foliage and secure loosely (for example, with string) in the form of a cross. Put in a suitable place in one of the main rooms of the house.

2. At some stage during each Sunday in Lent, either attach to the cross or place very close to it an expression of the world's suffering and sin, for example a newspaper cutting, a picture, a poem (produced by others or yourself), a symbolic object (a stone for hardness, a feather for vulnerability... ).

3. As someone brings the item to the cross, a prayer should be said (perhaps one included in this book for the particular Sunday).

4. During Holy Week, the action could be repeated each day until Maundy Thursday.

5. On Good Friday, as the prayer is said, all the objects should be removed as a symbolic sign that on the cross Jesus takes into himself and takes away the sin and the hurt of the world.

6. On the Saturday of Holy Week, collect greenery and flowers for use on Easter Day.

# Lent 1

## Collect

Almighty God,
whose Son Jesus Christ fasted forty days in the wilderness,
and was tempted as we are, yet without sin:
give us grace to discipline ourselves
in obedience to your Spirit;
and, as you know our weakness,
so may we know your power to save;
through Jesus Christ our Lord.

### *Psalms 119.1-8; 91.1-12*

## Old Testament *Genesis 4.1-10 NEB*

Adam lay with his wife Eve, and she conceived and gave birth to Cain. She
said, 'With the help of the Lord I have brought a man into being.' Afterwards
she had another child, his brother Abel. Abel was a shepherd and Cain a tiller
of the soil. The day came when Cain brought some of the produce of the soil
as a gift to the Lord; and Abel brought some of the first-born of his flock, the
fat portions of them. The Lord received Abel and his gift with favour; but
Cain and his gift he did not receive. Cain was very angry and his face fell.
Then the Lord said to Cain, 'Why are you so angry and cast down?

If you do well, you are accepted;
if not, sin is a demon crouching at the door.
It shall be eager for you, and you will be mastered by it.'

Cain said to his brother Abel, 'Let us go into the open country.' While they
were there, Cain attacked his brother Abel and murdered him. Then the Lord
said to Cain, 'Where is your brother Abel?' Cain answered, 'I do not know.
Am I my brother's keeper?' The Lord said, 'What have you done? Hark! your
brother's blood that has been shed is crying out to me from the ground.'

## New Testament *Hebrews 4.12-end RSV*

The word of God is living and active, sharper than any two-edged sword,
piercing to the division of soul and spirit, of joints and marrow, and
discerning the thoughts and intentions of the heart. And before him no
creature is hidden, but all are open and laid bare to the eyes of him with
whom we have to do.

Since then we have a great high priest who has passed through the
heavens, Jesus, the Son of God, let us hold fast our confession. For we have
not a high priest who is unable to sympathize with our weaknesses, but one

who in every respect has been tempted as we are, yet without sinning. Let us then with confidence draw near to the throne of grace, that we may receive mercy and find grace to help in time of need.

## Gospel *Luke 4.1-13 RSV*

Jesus, full of the Holy Spirit, returned from the Jordan, and was led by the Spirit for forty days in the wilderness, tempted by the devil. And he ate nothing in those days; and when they were ended, he was hungry. The devil said to him, 'If you are the Son of God, command this stone to become bread.' And Jesus answered him, 'It is written, "Man shall not live by bread alone." '
And then the devil took him up, and showed him all the kingdoms of the world in a moment of time, and said to him, 'To you I will give all this authority and their glory; for it has been delivered to me, and I give it to whom I will. If you, then, will worship me, it shall all be yours.' And Jesus answered him, 'It is written,
"You shall worship the Lord your God,
and him only shall you serve." '

And he took him to Jerusalem, and set him on the pinnacle of the temple, and said to him, 'If you are the Son of God, throw yourself down from here; for it is written,
"He will give his angels charge of you," and
"On their hands they will bear you up,
lest you strike your foot against a stone." '

And Jesus answered him, 'It is said, "You shall not tempt the Lord your God." '

And when the devil had ended every temptation, he departed from him until an opportune time.

# God's way through in the face of human irresponsibility

*He will cover you with his wings*
*and you will be safe under his feathers,*
*his faithfulness will be your shield and defence. (Ps 91.4)*

Temptation can take many forms. It can focus on our strengths as well as on our weaknesses. Always, its end is to pull us away from God's best. Cain illustrates this in no uncertain terms. His story has a powerful and continuing resonance with human experience. We are not told why the Lord refused Cain's offering but it seems clear from the man's response that all was not well with his inner life. His reaction to perceived criticism, rejection, favouritism. and injustice, though taken to extremes, is not unfamiliar. Jealousy, burning rage, the disowning of personal responsibility—these tempting phenomena are still very much with us. Whether on an individual or a corporate level, their effects can be just as devastating. 'Crouching' sin is not slow to take every opportunity. Within this context, it is interesting to note the dialogue between the Lord and Cain; part of a divine/human dialogue that started in Eden, continues right through the scriptures and has not yet fallen silent. In this exchange, questions play a significant part (on both sides). From Cain comes the first human question—a petulant and uncaring evasion of guilt. From God comes a telling sequel to his primal question of humanity. After the Fall he asks, 'Where are you?' After the first murder he asks, 'Where is your brother?'

It is this searching word of God that is highlighted in Sunday's passage from Hebrews. The opening sentences of the extract are a chilling reminder that absolutely nothing can be hidden from the one to whom we have to give account. The story of failure in Eden is very much present here, and the writer of Hebrews means us to take its implications very seriously indeed. But, effective preacher that he is, he has exposed hard truth in order to emphasize the power of an even deeper reality. Though, before God, we are stripped of all pretence, with our imperfections laid bare, we have nothing to fear. Despite our parlous state, we can approach God's presence not in terror but with 'confidence' (the word has the sense of boldness, total frankness, freedom of speech). Liberated from the need to put on an act, we can be ourselves with God and be assured of receiving his mercy and grace. The reason we can be utterly confident lies in the nature of God. Here is a God who, rather than deploring and punishing our condition, enters into it, feeling the full force of temptation and human frailty. God knows. That throwaway phrase is in fact near the heart of the gospel. At tremendous cost to himself, God knows; God understands; God cares. Out of that knowing, God can bring mighty help.

This truth is reinforced by Luke's account of the temptation of Jesus in the wilderness. Though the devil did the tempting, it was God's Spirit who put Jesus in the way of it. No divine prerogative is exercised here. In a lonely and trying situation, faithfulness to God's best way is severely tested. Crucial to the struggle is the issue of power. Where is it located and how is it to be expressed? In a variation on the dialogue theme, scripture plays a key role in the debate. Even the devil uses it. The difference in Jesus' case is that a living and active relationship with God informs his perception of the sacred texts. Unlike Adam, unlike God's rebellious people in the wilderness, Jesus stays true to the purposes of God. His commitment holds firm. But, as Luke points out, the devil does not give up easily. Jesus is to fight with him again.

*Searching God,*
*you question our motives*
*and lay bare all we try to hide.*
*As in Jesus you know our condition,*
*deal gently with our failings.*

# Lent 2

## Collect

Lord God Almighty,
grant your people grace
to withstand the temptations of the world, the flesh, and the devil,
and with pure hearts and minds
to follow you, the only God;
through Jesus Christ our Lord.

## Psalms 119.33-40; 18.18-26

## Old Testament *Genesis 7.17-end RSV*

The flood continued forty days upon the earth; and the waters increased, and
bore up the ark, and it rose high above the earth. The waters prevailed and
increased greatly upon the earth; and the ark floated on the face of the waters.
And the waters prevailed so mightily upon the earth that all the high
mountains under the whole heaven were covered; the waters prevailed above
the mountains, covering them fifteen cubits deep. And all flesh died that
moved upon the earth, birds, cattle, beasts, all swarming creatures that swarm
upon the earth, and every man; everything on the dry land in whose nostrils
was the breath of life died. He blotted out every living thing that was upon
the face of the ground, man and animals and creeping things and birds of the
air; they were blotted out from the earth. Only Noah was left, and those that
were with him in the ark. And the waters prevailed upon the earth a hundred
and fifty days.

## New Testament *1 John 3.1-10 NEB*

How great is the love that the Father has shown to us! We were called God's
children, and such we are; and the reason why the godless world does not
recognize us is that it has not known him. Here and now, dear friends, we
are God's children; what we shall be has not yet been disclosed, but we
know that when it is disclosed we shall be like him, because we shall see him
as he is. Everyone who has this hope before him purifies himself, as Christ is
pure.

To commit sin is to break God's law: sin, in fact, is lawlessness. Christ
appeared, as you know, to do away with sin, and there is no sin in him. No
man therefore who dwells in him is a sinner; the sinner has not seen him and
does no know him.

My children, do not be misled: it is the man who does right who is
righteous, as God is righteous; the man who sins is a child of the devil, for the

devil has been a sinner from the first; and the Son of God appeared for the very purpose of undoing the devil's work.

A child of God does not commit sin, because the divine seed remains in him; he cannot be a sinner, because he is God's child. That is the distinction between the children of God and the children of the devil: no one who does not do right is God's child, nor is anyone who does not love his brother.

## Gospel *Matthew 12.22-32 NEB*

They brought Jesus to a man who was possessed; he was blind and dumb; and Jesus cured him, restoring both speech and sight. The bystanders were all amazed, and the word went round: 'Can this be the Son of David?' But when the Pharisees heard it they said, 'It is only Beelzebub prince of devils that this man drives the devils out.'

He knew what was in their minds; so he said to them, 'Every kingdom divided against itself goes to ruin; and no town, no household, that is divided against itself can stand. And if it is Satan who casts out Satan, Satan is divided against himself; how then can his kingdom stand? And if it is by Beelzebub that I cast out devils, by whom do your own people drive them out? If this is your argument, they themselves will refute you. But if it is by the Spirit of God that I drive out the devils, then be sure the kingdom of God has already come upon you.

'Or again, how can anyone break into a strong man's house and make off with his goods, unless he has first tied the strong man up before ransacking the house?

'He who is not with me is against me, and he who does not gather with me scatters.

'And so I tell you this: no sin, no slander, is beyond forgiveness of men, except slander spoken against the Spirit, and that will not be forgiven. Any man who speaks a word against the Son of Man will be forgiven; but if anyone speaks against the Holy Spirit, for him there is no forgiveness, either in this age or in the age to come.'

# The battle against evil

*He reached down from on high and took me,*
*he drew me out of the great waters.*
*They confronted me in the day of my calamity,*
*but the Lord was my upholder. (Ps 18.19-20)*

How is evil to be dealt with? Sunday's readings give us some challenging perspectives on this perennial problem. The story of the Flood suggests one responsive strategy: blot out the badness. God is so appalled by the wickedness manifesting itself in creation that he decides to reverse the creative process. A bold experiment had gone wrong. Its consequences had to be eliminated. Yet this is not the whole story. God, it seems, cannot bring himself to make a full end of the things he has brought to life. Representatives of all living beings are saved from destruction. And after the Flood, there is still an earth for them to inhabit. So we learn that, though God abhors evil, there is a divine impulse towards salvation rather than obliteration.

For the writer of Sunday's Epistle, that impulse has taken shape in the form of Christ, the Son of God. The sinless Christ has taken on the machinations of the devil and prevailed. He has carried out the will of his Father, that sin should lose its stranglehold. Those born of God can enter even now into that inheritance. As God's children, they can share God's life and character, as expressed in Christ. Indeed, they carry God's creative life ('seed') within them. They should take care not to destroy it. Children of God should lead godly lives, of which active love will be the keynote. If it be thought that 'John' is a little premature in his ruling out of sin in God's children, he is surely right to stress that evil begets evil. That cycle of negativity is broken only by the courageous intervention of goodness.

In the Gospel reading, negativity springs from a surprising source. It comes not from the godless but from those entrusted with spiritual leadership, whose responsibility it was to interpret the things of God. It is ironic that the crowds who witness a mighty work of Jesus get nearer to the truth than their teachers. But the failure of the Pharisees is far more serious than mere lack of recognition. They wilfully ascribe the ministry of Jesus to the dark power of the prince of demons. The healing work of God's Spirit they assign to Satan. That is akin to blasphemy, according to their own religious code a mortal sin (cf Matthew 26.65f). It is in this particular context that we should understand the fearful words about sin against the Holy Spirit. They are a stark warning, designed to open the eyes of the spiritually blind. If these leaders of God's people persist in their perversity, they will shut out the possibility of forgiveness. They will not even see the need for it. Evil will have its way with them.

He on whom God's Spirit rests (Matthew 12.18) takes this fierce clash with his opponents as an opportunity to stress the weakness of their argument and his superior strength in relation to the power of evil. In typically vivid parabolic style, Jesus makes it clear that Satan is fighting a losing battle. Yet the stronger one will not emerge unscathed from the conflict. In overcoming evil he will himself be bound and humiliated. The wounds will go deep and the scars will be permanent. Such is the commitment of God to a wayward creation.

*God of truth,*
*blot out our badness,*
*unlock our blindness,*
*and open us up*
*to your creative life within us.*

# Lent 3

## Collect

Almighty God,
whose most dear Son went not up to joy but first he suffered pain,
and entered not into glory before he was crucified:
mercifully grant that we, walking in the way of the cross,
may find it none other than the way of life and peace;
through Jesus Christ our Lord.

### Psalms 119.97-104; 115.1-7

## Old Testament *Genesis 12.1-9 TEV*

The Lord said to Abram, 'Leave your native land, your relatives, and your
father's home, and go to a country that I am going to show you. I will give
you many descendants, and they will become a great nation. I will bless you
and make your name famous, so that you will be a blessing.
I will bless those who bless you,
But I will curse those who curse you.
And through you I will bless all the nations.'
  When Abram was seventy-five years old, he started out from Haran, as the
Lord had told him to do; and Lot went with him. Abram took his wife Sarai,
his nephew Lot, and all the wealth and all the slaves they had acquired in
Haran, and they started out for the land of Canaan.
  When they arrived in Canaan, Abram travelled through the land until he
came to the sacred tree of Moreh, and the holy place at Shechem. (At that time
the Canaanites were still living in the land.) The Lord appeared to Abram and
said to him, 'This is the country that I am going to give to your descendants.'
The Abram built an altar there to the Lord, who had appeared to him. After
that, he moved on south to the hill-country east of Bethel and set up his camp
between Bethel on the west and Ai on the east. There also he built an altar
and worshipped the Lord. Then he moved on from place to place, going
towards the southern part of Canaan.

## New Testament *1 Peter 2.19-end TEV*

God will bless you for this, if you endure the pain of undeserved suffering
because you are conscious of his will. For what credit is there if you endure
the beatings you deserve for having done wrong? But if you endure suffering
even when you have done right, God will bless you for it. It was to this that
God called you, for Christ himself suffered for you and left you an example,
so that you would follow in his steps. He committed no sin, and no one ever

heard a lie come from his lips. When he was insulted, he did not answer back with an insult; when he suffered, he did not threaten, but placed his hopes in God, the righteous Judge. Christ himself carried our sins in his body to the cross, so that we might die to sin and live for righteousness. It is by his wounds that you have been healed. You were like sheep that had lost their way, but now you have been brought back to follow the Shepherd and Keeper of your souls.

## Gospel *Matthew 16.13-end JB*

When Jesus came to the region of Caesarea Philippi he put this question to his disciples, 'Who do people say the Son of Man is?' And they said, 'Some say he is John the Baptist, some Elijah, and others Jeremiah or one of the prophets.' 'But you,' he said, 'who do you say I am?' Then Simon Peter spoke up, 'You are the Christ,' he said, 'the Son of the living God.' Jesus replied, 'Simon son of Jonah, you are a happy man! Because it was not flesh and blood that revealed this to you but my Father in heaven. So I now say to you: You are Peter and on this rock I will build my Church. And the gates of the underworld can never hold out against it. I will give you the keys of the kingdom of heaven: whatever you bind on earth shall be considered bound in heaven; whatever you loose on earth shall be considered loosed in heaven.' Then he gave the disciples strict orders not to tell anyone that he was the Christ.

From that time Jesus began to make it clear to his disciples that he was destined to go to Jerusalem and suffer grievously at the hands of the elders and chief priests and scribes, to be put to death and to be raised up on the third day. Then, taking him aside, Peter started to remonstrate with him. 'Heaven preserve you, Lord;' he said, 'this must not happen to you.' But he turned and said to Peter, 'Get behind me, Satan! You are an obstacle in my path, because the way you think is not God's way but man's.'

Then Jesus said to his disciples, 'If anyone wants to be a follower of mine, let him renounce himself and take up his cross and follow me. For anyone who wants to save his life will lose it; but anyone who loses his life for my sake will find it. What, then, will a man gain if he wins the whole world and ruins his life? Or what has a man to offer in exchange for his life?

'For the Son of Man is going to come in the glory of his Father with his angels, and, when he does, he will reward each one according to his behaviour. I tell you solemnly, there are some of these standing here who will not taste death before they see the Son of Man coming with his kingdom.'

# Suffering for the sake of truth

*Not to us, O Lord, not to us,*
*but to your name give the glory,*
*for the sake of your faithfulness and your loving-kindness. (Ps 115.1)*

Following the leading of God is a risky thing to do. All too often it can seem a mixed blessing. Always, it presents a critical challenge. To that, Sunday's readings bear telling witness. Abram's obedient journey into the unknown opened up great opportunities. It was accompanied by divine promises which stretched both faith and imagination. Yet there was a distinctly hard edge to this vision. The familiar had to be left behind. Roots had to be pulled up; security abandoned. Nor was the journey a catalogue of joyful fulfilment. It required effort and constant mobility. As the narrative develops beyond our set passage, it becomes apparent that the promise was by no means fully realized. All this is a powerful paradigm of many a journey of faith. But Abram's story has far more than personal significance. It points to the purposes of God for humanity (blessing) and for the people of God (recipient and agent of blessing). Such a plan and methodology cannot avoid the human realities of disappointment, frustration, failure and pain. It places a premium on faithfulness and hope. Rather than immediate gratification, it demands a keen sense of the welfare of those who come after. It finds its focal expression in the person and vocation of Jesus.

It is Jesus who embodies God's great enterprise of blessing. As Matthew's version of Caesarea Philippi so heavily underlines, here indeed is God's chosen one. Yet God's choice will be the death of him. And his disciples must follow him along the path of the passion. Only so will true life and glory be discovered and ministered. That was a lesson Peter had to learn from bitter experience. At this stage of the journey, his authentic insight was still clouded by other ways of seeing. So it has been and is for countless subsequent followers of Christ. Taking the challenge of Jesus seriously means engaging painfully with the dark side of the world—and of oneself. In God's truth, there is no alternative.

Some of the implications of that are spelt out in Sunday's Epistle. The passage is addressed specifically to household servants (1 Peter 5.18) but it relates very directly to any servant of God. Christ's example in facing 'undeserved suffering' is not just a cause for admiration. It is an example to follow. But to leave it there might well be a recipe for despair. Happily, there is more. The suffering of Jesus is not only exemplary, it is redemptive. The writer of 1 Peter draws on Isaiah 53 to try to convey the significance of a lived experience. The agony of Jesus absorbs our sins. The wounds of Jesus minister our healing. So we are set free and encouraged to live for

God. We may also know that the Jesus who has been through so much for us is our 'Shepherd and Keeper', the one who has our best interests at heart, the one we can trust utterly. Risky our discipleship may be, but it releases blessing beyond words.

*Painstaking God,*
*in our unrootedness, hold us,*
*in our wrestling with darkness, calm us*
*and by the wounds of Jesus, heal us.*

# Lent 4

## Collect

Almighty Father,
whose Son was revealed in majesty before he suffered death upon the cross:
give us faith to perceive his glory,
that we may be strengthened to suffer with him
and be changed into his likeness, from glory to glory;
who is alive and reigns with you and the Holy Spirit,
one God, now and for ever.

*Psalms 119.153-160; 18.27-38*

## Old Testament *Exodus 3.1-16 JB*

Moses was looking after the flock of Jethro, his father-in-law, priest of Midian.
He led his flock to the far side of the wilderness and came to Horeb, the
mountain of God. There an angel of the Lord appeared to him in the shape of
a flame of fire, coming from the middle of a bush. Moses looked; there was
the bush blazing but it was not being burnt up. 'I must go and look at this
strange sight,' Moses said, 'and see why the bush is not burnt.' Now the Lord
saw him go forward to look, and God called to him from the middle of the
bush, 'Moses, Moses!', he said. 'Here I am', he answered. `Come no nearer',
he said. 'Take off your shoes, for the place on which you stand is holy ground.
I am the God of your father,' he said, 'the God of Abraham, the God of Isaac,
and the God of Jacob.' At this Moses covered his face, afraid to look at God.

## New Testament *2 Peter 1.16-19 NEB*

It was not on tales artfully spun that we relied when we told you of the
power of our Lord Jesus Christ and his coming; we saw him with our own
eyes in majesty, when at the hands of God the Father he was invested with
honour and glory, and there came to him from the sublime Presence a voice
which said: 'This is my Son, by Beloved, on whom my favour rests.' This
voice from heaven we ourselves heard; when it came, we were with him on
the sacred mountain.

All this only confirms for us the message of the prophets, to which you
will do well to attend, because it is like a lamp shining in a murky place, until
the day breaks and the morning star rises to illuminate your minds.

# Gospel *Matthew 17.1-13 NEB*

Jesus took Peter, James, and John the brother of James, and led them up a high mountain where they were alone; and in their presence he was transfigured; his face shone like the sun, and his clothes became white as the light. And they saw Moses and Elijah appear, conversing with him. Then Peter spoke: 'Lord,' he said, 'how good it is that we are here! If you wish it, I will make three shelters here, one for you, one for Moses, and one for Elijah.' While he was still speaking, a bright cloud suddenly overshadowed them, and a voice called from the cloud: 'This is my Son, my Beloved, on whom my favour rests; listen to him.' At the sound of the voice the disciples fell on their faces in terror. Jesus then came up to them, touched them, and said, 'Stand up; do not be afraid.' And when they raised their eyes they saw no one, but only Jesus.

On their way down from the mountain, Jesus enjoined them not to tell anyone of the vision until the Son of Man had been raised from the dead. The disciples put a question to him: 'Why then do our teachers say that Elijah must come first?' He replied, 'Yes, Elijah will come and set everything right. But I tell you that Elijah has already come, and they failed to recognize him, and worked their will upon him; and in the same way the Son of Man is to suffer at their hands.' Then the disciples understood that he meant John the Baptist.

# The transforming power of God

*You light my lamp. O Lord my God,*
*you make my darkness to be bright. (Ps 18.30)*

Things aren't always what they seem. There are moments when the veil is lifted, when the mundane opens up its mysteries, when the hidden truth shines through. So it was for Moses and for three privileged disciples of Jesus. And in both cases, their brief glimpses of glory were the prelude to times of testing hardship, confusion and suffering. Exposure to the glory of God carries with it considerable risk: not that of destruction by holiness, but of participation in God's passion for humankind. Transfiguration is not divine self-display. It discloses the reality of God's involvement with the world. It invites responsive commitment to God's work of salvation. That means pain in the service of joy.

Moses was going about his work when he encountered the fire of God's presence. At first he was curious. Such a peculiar phenomenon had to be investigated. When he realizes its significance, interest turns to fear. To look at God was a dangerous privilege (compare Exodus 33:20). Yet when we follow this episode through, beyond the limits of Sunday's reading, we discover that God's object in the meeting was not to immobilize Moses with terror but to recruit him for a campaign of liberation. This proves to be a less than easy task. It is not achieved without lengthy dialogue and divine concession. The glory of God is not coercive. It leaves plenty of room for argument and protest. Its awesomeness is integrated with decidedly down-to-earth exchange. Such paradoxical glory finds its focal expression in the incarnation. So it is that on the 'high mountain' referred to in the Gospel it is not a natural feature that is transfigured but a human being.

The strange experience of the Transfiguration is recorded in all three Synoptic Gospels. Its message permeates the writing of the Fourth Evangelist. It is one of the few pre-Holy Week events in the life of Jesus to be clearly alluded to outside the Gospels (so, Sunday's Epistle). What it illuminates is the significance of Jesus as the fulfilment of God's saving purpose for the world. Moses, reluctant recruit though he was, came to epitomize God's care and provision for his people through the exodus to the Promised Land. By Moses came the gift of the Law, framework for a living relationship with a living God. Elijah, forthright prophet of God, was expected to reappear on earth, signalling the coming of the Messiah. Both Moses and Elijah stood out for God. They ministered God's will, often at great personal cost. In this, they pointed to Jesus. But it is Jesus alone who is definitive radiance of God's glory, the one who exceeds (and challenges) the longings and expectations of the ages.

Matthew's account of the transfiguration has a distinctive feature which highlights the coming together of earth and heaven in the person of Jesus. The overwhelmed disciples fall on their faces in terror. But Jesus comes to them, touches them and urges them to stand up and not be afraid. There, in short compass, is the character and mission of Emmanuel, God with us. It will cost him his life.

*Transfigured Christ,*
*radiance of God's glory,*
*touch us in our fear,*
*hold us to our rule of life,*
*and empower us to proclaim your truth.*

# *Lent 5*

## Collect

Most merciful God,
who by the death and resurrection of your Son Jesus Christ
delivered and saved mankind:
grant that by faith in him who suffered on the cross,
we may triumph in the power of his victory;
through Jesus Christ our Lord.

### *Psalms 76.1-9; 22.23-29*

## Old Testament *Jeremiah 31.31-34 NEB*

The time is coming, says the Lord, when I will make a new covenant with
Israel and Judah. It will not be like the covenant I made with their forefathers
when I took them by the hand and led them out of Egypt. Although they
broke my covenant, I was patient with them, says the Lord. But this is the
covenant which I will make with Israel after those days, says the Lord; I will
set my law within them and write it on their hearts; I will become their God
and they shall become my people. No longer need they teach one another to
know the Lord; all of them, high and low alike, shall know me, says the Lord,
for I will forgive their wrongdoing and remember their sin no more.

## New Testament *Hebrews 9.11-14 JB*

Now Christ has come, as the high priest of all the blessings which were to
come. He has passed through the greater, the more perfect tent, which is
better than the one made by men's hands because it is not of this created
order; and he has entered the sanctuary once and for all, taking with him not
the blood of goats and bull calves, but his own blood, having won an eternal
redemption for us. The blood of goats and bulls and the ashes of a heifer are
sprinkled on those who have incurred defilement and they restore the
holiness of their outward lives; how much more effectively the blood of
Christ, who offered himself as the perfect sacrifice to God through the eternal
Spirit, can purify our inner self from dead actions so that we do our service to
the living God.

# Gospel *Mark 10.32-45 NEB*

Jesus and his disciples were on the road, going up to Jerusalem, Jesus leading the way; and the disciples were filled with awe, while those who followed behind were afraid. He took the Twelve aside and began to tell them what was to happen to him. 'We are now going to Jerusalem,' he said; 'and the Son of Man will be given up to the chief priests and the doctors of the law; they will condemn him to death and hand him over to the foreign power. He will be mocked and spat upon, flogged and killed; and three days afterwards, he will rise again.'

James and John, the sons of Zebedee, approached him and said, 'Master, we should like you to do us a favour.' 'What is it you want me to do?' he asked. They answered, 'Grant us the right to sit in state with you, one at your right and the other at your left.' Jesus said to them, 'You do not understand what you are asking. Can you drink the cup that I drink, or be baptized with the baptism I am baptized with?' 'We can', they answered. Jesus said, 'The cup that I drink you shall drink, and the baptism I am baptized with shall be your baptism; but to sit at my right or left is not for me to grant; it is for those to whom is has already been assigned.'

When the other ten heard this, they were indignant with James and John. Jesus called them to him and said, 'You know that in the world the recognized rulers lord it over their subjects, and their great men make them feel the weight of authority. That is not the way with you; among you, whoever wants to be great must be your servant, and whoever wants to be first must be the willing slave of all. For even the Son of Man did not come to be served but to serve, and to give up his life as a ransom for many.'

# Giving and demanding everything

*I will tell of your name to my brethren,
in the midst of the congregation will I praise you. (Ps 22.23)*

Sunday's readings take us to the heart of the matter. Relating to the living God is not defined by external observance or ritual propriety. Nor is it a passport to status and power. Rather, it involves the risky intimacy of knowing and being known. It both gives and demands everything.

The new covenant prophesied in Jeremiah will establish a bonding far deeper than the 'hand-holding' of the exodus. God's people will 'know' him at the level of profound personal relationship. The behaviour God desires will be ingrained in their hearts, that is, in the motivating core of their being. As such, it will be discovered rather than taught. And a powerful incentive to this discovery will be the experience of radical forgiveness. This promise is for everyone, from the least to the greatest. It is a promise to inspire confidence, for God himself undertakes to bring it to pass. It is instructive to recollect that this prophecy was first spoken to a devastated and humiliated people caught in the consequences of their faithlessness. The faithful God, in his mercy, comes to where we are.

The writer of Hebrews is in no doubt about that truth. For him, the new covenant has been decisively inaugurated in and through Jesus (see especially 8.1—10.25). The blood sealing this covenant is the blood of Christ. And Christ is the Son spoken of in the opening sentence of the Epistle (1.1-4), the one in whom can be seen the very imprint of God. Though the imagery used in much of Hebrews has a particular Jewish context, its underlying message is an essential word at all times and in all places. In Jesus, and at tremendous cost, God has opened up his life to sinful humanity. With staggering humility and determination, he has shared our condition, feeling the force of its negativity. Through it all, he invites us to know him; to enter into a direct relationship which will bring deep cleansing and deeper joy, whilst at the same time calling us to sacrificial service.

The episode recorded in the Gospel reading indicates what a challenge this privileged relationship can be. Jesus is 'on the way' to Jerusalem, moving steadfastly towards the greatest crisis of his life. His very demeanour stirs up awe and fear in his followers. But for two of his closest disciples, neither that atmosphere nor the less than coded warnings of impending tragedy are sufficient counters to seductive ambition. For them (as for many) relationship is something to be exploited as a means of advancement. The lure of personal glory makes them hear what they want to hear, prompting arrogant rudeness. Jesus, who in human terms must have found their behaviour acutely hurtful, nonetheless uses the episode as a teaching opportunity. What he has to say about the nature of true greatness needs to be taken into the heart of the Church's life. All too often, it remains in the pulpit or within the confines of piety, places which in their own way are no more than status symbols until those occupying them risk being touched by the living God, who lays down his life.

*Loving God,*
*you write your covenant in our hearts,*
*and seal it with the blood of Christ.*
*May we know something of the cost*
*of responding to your amazing love.*

# *Palm Sunday*

## Collect

Almighty and everlasting God,
who in your tender love towards mankind
   sent your Son our Saviour Jesus Christ
to take upon him our flesh
and to suffer death upon the cross:
grant that we may follow the example of his patience and humility,
and also be made partakers of his resurrection;
through Jesus Christ our Lord.

### *Psalms 22.1-11; 69.1-9 or 24; 45.1-7*

## Old Testament *Isaiah 50.4-9a NEB*

The Lord God has given me
the tongue of a teacher
and skill to console the weary
with a word in the morning;
he sharpened my hearing
that I might listen like one who is taught.
The Lord God opened my ears
and I did not disobey or turn back in defiance.
I offered my back to the lash,
and let my beard be plucked from my chin,
I did not hide my face from spitting and insult;
but the Lord God stands by to help me;
therefore no insult can wound me.
I have set my face like flint, for I know that I shall not be put to shame,
because one who will clear my name is at my side.
Who dare argue against me? Let us confront one another.
Who will dispute my cause? Let him come forward.
The Lord God will help me; who then can prove me guilty?

## New Testament *Philippians 2.5-11 NEB*

Let your bearing towards one another arise out of your life in Christ Jesus.
For the divine nature was his from the first; yet he did not think to snatch at
equality with God, but made himself nothing, assuming the nature of a slave.
Bearing the human likeness, revealed in human shape, he humbled himself,
and in obedience accepted even death—death on a cross. Therefore God
raised him to the heights and bestowed on him the name above all names,

that at the name of Jesus every knee should bow—in heaven, on earth, and in the depths—and every tongue confess, 'Jesus Christ is Lord', to the glory of God the Father.

## Gospel *Mark 14.32—15.41 RSV*

Jesus and his disciples went to a place which was called Gethsemane . . .

And he said, 'Abba, Father, all things are possible to you; remove this cup from me; yet not what I will, but what you will.' And he came and found them sleeping, and he said to Peter, 'Simon, are you asleep? Could you not watch one hour? Watch and pray that you may not enter into temptation; the spirit indeed is willing, but the flesh is weak.' And again he went away and prayed, saying the same words. And again he came and found them sleeping, for their eyes were very heavy; and they did not know what to answer him. And he came a third time, and said to them, 'Are you still sleeping and taking your rest? It is enough; the hour has come; the Son of Man is betrayed into the hands of sinners. Rise, let us be going; see, my betrayer is at hand.'

And immediately, while he was still speaking, Judas came, one of the twelve, and with him a crowd with swords and clubs, from the chief priests and the scribes and the elders. Now the betrayer had given them a sign, saying, 'The one I shall kiss is the man; seize him and lead him away safely.' And when he came, he went up to him at once, and said, 'Master!' And kissed him. And they laid hands on him and seized him . . .

And they led Jesus to the high priest; and all the chief priests and the elders and the scribes were assembled. And Peter had followed him at a distance, right into the courtyard of the high priest; and he was sitting with the guards, and warming himself at the fire. Now the chief priests and the whole council sought testimony against Jesus to put him to death; but they found none. For many bore false witness against him, and their witness did not agree. And some stood up and bore false witness against him, saying, 'We heard him say, "I will destroy this temple that is made with hands, and in three days I will build another, not made with hands."' Yet not even so did their testimony agree. And the high priest stood up in the midst, and asked Jesus, 'Have you no answer to make? What is it that these men testify against you?' But he was silent and made no answer. Again the high priest asked him, 'Are you the Christ, the Son of the Blessed?' And Jesus said, 'I am; and you will see the Son of Man sitting at the right hand of Power, and coming with the clouds of heaven.' And the high priest tore his mantle, and said, 'Why do we still need witnesses? You have heard his blasphemy. What is your decision?' And they all condemned him as deserving death. And some began to spit on him, and to cover his face, and to strike him, saying to him, 'Prophesy!' And the guards received him with blows. . .

And as soon as it was morning the chief priests, with the elders and scribes, and the whole council held a consultation; and they bound Jesus and led him away and delivered him to Pilate. And Pilate asked him, 'Are you the King of the Jews?' And he answered him, 'You have said so.' And the chief priests accused him of many things. And Pilate again asked him, 'Have you no answer to make? See how many charges they bring against you.' But Jesus made no further answer, so that Pilate wondered.

Now at the feast he used to release for them any one prisoner whom they asked. And among the rebels in prison, who had committed murder in the insurrection, there was a man called Barabbas. And the crowd came up and began to ask Pilate to do as he was wont to do for them. And he answered them, 'Do you want me to release for you the King of the Jews?' For he perceived that it was out of envy that the chief priests had delivered him up. But the chief priests stirred up the crowd to have him release for them Barabbas instead. And Pilate again said to them, 'Then what shall I do with the man whom you call the King of the Jews?' And they cried out again, 'Crucify him.' And Pilate said to them, 'Why, what evil has he done?' But they shouted all the more, 'Crucify him.' So Pilate, wishing to satisfy the crowd, released for them Barabbas; and having scourged Jesus, he delivered him to be crucified . . .

And it was the third hour, when they crucified him. And the inscription of the charge against him read, 'The King of the Jews.' And with him they crucified two robbers, one on his right and one on his left. And those who passed by derided him, wagging their heads, and saying, 'Aha! You who would destroy the temple and build it in three days, save yourself, and come down from the cross!' So also the chief priests mocked him to one another with the scribes, saying, 'He saved others; he cannot save himself. Let the Christ, the King of Israel, come down now from the cross, that we may see and believe.' Those who were crucified with him also reviled him.

And when the sixth hour had come, there was darkness over the whole land until the ninth hour. And at the ninth hour Jesus cried with a loud voice, 'Eloi, Eloi, lama sabach-thani?' which means, 'My God, my God, why have you forsaken me?' And some of the bystanders hearing it said, 'Behold, he is calling Elijah.' And one ran and, filling a sponge full of vinegar, put it on a reed and gave it to him to drink, saying, 'Wait, let us see whether Elijah will come to take him down.' And Jesus uttered a loud cry, and breathed his last. And the curtain of the temple was torn in two, from top to bottom. And when the centurion, who stood facing him, saw that he thus breathed his last, he said, 'Truly this man was a son of God!'

## *The heart of the matter*

*For your sake have I suffered reproach,*
*and shame has covered my face. (Ps 69.7)*

Ever since Christmas, the Gospel has been the controlling reading. This Sunday we reach the longest Gospel reading of the year—and the most telling. Fittingly, the awful climax of Jesus' short life is placed in a context of servanthood.

Isaiah's Servant figure is a teacher, an encourager and a listener. He is obedient. He is willing to suffer. He is convinced that God will vindicate him, whatever happens. That makes him determined to do God's work as God's servant, ready to depend on God for justification. Little wonder that people have seen this Servant figure as pointing to Jesus.

Paul underlines the need for genuine servanthood in the lives of those who seek to follow Jesus the Servant. We are to be servants of others because we are servants of the one who 'made himself nothing'. Paul may well have been using words that his readers would know, a hymn celebrating the wonder of incarnation. It led to the cross of shame. But, as our liturgy reminds us, the tree of shame became the tree of glory.

Mark's passion narrative draws us into this strange mystery. The Evangelist is both master storyteller and telling theologian. At this stage in his writing he shows a stark restraint which strengthens the impact of what he describes. At every level of being, Jesus is progressively stripped bare until, at the end, we are faced with a figure who is utterly alone, utterly desolate, crying out in the darkness. Where, now, is 'the good news of Jesus Christ' (Mark 1.1)? Paradoxically, the very grimness of the situation is the beginning of hope. Throughout his Gospel, Mark has hinted at the more than human significance of Jesus. An atmosphere of awe and wonder has been pervasive, as has the question, 'Who is this?', whether spelt out or implicit. At 14.61f, the truth emerges more blatantly than ever before. Jesus breaks his tantalizing silence to acknowledge messianic status (though notice how quickly the enigmatic Son of Man imagery returns). Yet as we look at this dramatic confrontation, the impression is reinforced that there is more to this figure than meets the eye. It takes a Gentile outsider, one carrying out his cruel duty, one with no history of discipleship, to lead us into deeper truth. In a God-forsaken and humiliated human being, and in the way that he dies, the centurion perceives the presence of God. God has indeed rent asunder the veil hiding his glory. What is revealed is what the world cries out for. Here is a God who goes through hell, with us and for us.

*Servant of God,*
*may we follow you in making ourselves nothing,*
*that those who know nothing of you*
*may come to perceive your glory.*

Note: Because of constraints on space, the Gospel reading has been abridged. Readers are encouraged to ponder on the full reading as set out in their own Bibles.

# Good Friday

## Collect

Almighty Father,
look with mercy on this your family
for which our Lord Jesus Christ was content to be betrayed
and given up into the hands of wicked men
and to suffer death upon the cross;
who is alive and glorified and with you and the Holy Spirit,
one God, now and for ever.

### Psalms 22.14-22; 69.17-23

## Old Testament *Isaiah 52.13—53 end TEV*

The Lord says, 'My servant will succeed in his task; he will be highly honoured.
Many people were shocked when they saw him;
he was so disfigured that he hardly looked human.
But how many nations will marvel at him,
and kings will be speechless with amazement.
They will see and understand something they had never known.'
The people reply, 'Who would have believed what we now report?
Who could have seen the Lord's hand in this?
It was the will of the Lord that his servant
should grow like a plant taking root in dry ground.
He had no dignity or beauty to make us take notice of him.
There was nothing attractive about him, nothing that would draw us to him.
We despised him and rejected him; he endured suffering and pain.
No one would even look at him—we ignored him as if he were nothing.
But he endured the suffering that should have been ours,
the pain that we should have borne.
All the while we thought that his suffering was punishment sent by God.
But because of our sins he was wounded, beaten because of the evil we did.
We are healed by the punishment he suffered,
made whole by the blows he received.
All of us were like sheep that were lost, each of us going his own way.
But the Lord made the punishment fall on him, the punishment all of us deserved.
He was treated harshly, but endured it humbly; he never said a word.
Like a lamb about to be slaughtered,
Like a sheep about to be sheared, he never said a word.
He was arrested and sentenced and led off to die, and no one cared about his fate.
He was put to death for the sins of our people.

He was placed in a grave with evil men, he was buried with the rich,
even though he had never committed a crime or ever told a lie.'
The Lord says, 'It was my will that he should suffer;
his death was a sacrifice to bring forgiveness.
And so he will see his descendants; he will live a long life,
and through him my purpose will succeed.
After a life of suffering, he will again have joy;
he will know that he did not suffer in vain.
My devoted servant, with whom I am pleased,
will bear the punishment of many and for his sake I will forgive them.
And so I will give him a place of honour, a place among great and powerful men.
He willingly gave his life and shared the fate of evil men.
He took the place of many sinners and prayed that they might be forgiven.'

## New Testament *Hebrews 4.14-16; 5.7-9 NEB*

Since we have a great high priest who has passed through the heavens, Jesus
the Son of God, let us hold fast to the religion we profess. For ours is not a
high priest unable to sympathize with our weaknesses, but one who, because
of his likeness to us, has been tested every way, only without sin. Let us
therefore boldly approach the throne of our gracious God, where we may
receive mercy and in his grace find timely help.

In the days of his earthly life Jesus offered up prayers and petitions, with
loud cries and tears, to God who was able to deliver him from the grave.
Because of his humble submission his prayer was heard: son though he was,
he learned obedience in the school of suffering, and, once perfected, became
the source of eternal salvation for all who obey him.

## Gospel *John 18.1—19.37 JB*

Jesus left the city with his disciples and crossed the Kedron valley. There was
a garden there, and he went into it with his disciples. Judas the traitor knew
the place well, since Jesus had often met his disciples there, and he brought
the cohort to this place together with a detachment of guards sent by the chief
priests and the Pharisees, all with lanterns and torches and weapons.
Knowing everything that was going to happen to him, Jesus then came
forward and said, 'Who are you looking for?' They answered, 'Jesus the
Nazarene.' He said, 'I am he.' Now Judas the traitor was standing among
them. When Jesus said, 'I am he', they moved back and fell to the ground . . .

So Pilate went back into the Praetorium and called Jesus to him. 'Are you
the king of the Jews?' he asked. Jesus replied, 'Do you ask this of your own
accord, or have others spoken to you about me?' Pilate answered, 'Am I a
Jew? It is your own people and the chief priests who have handed you over to
me: what have you done?' Jesus replied, 'Mine is not a kingdom of this world;
if my kingdom were of this world, my men would have fought to prevent my

being surrendered to the Jews. But my kingdom is not of this kind.' 'So you are a king then?', said Pilate. 'It is you who say it', answered Jesus. 'Yes, I am a king. I was born for this, I came into the world for this: to bear witness to the truth; and all who are on the side of truth listen to my voice.' 'Truth?', said Pilate, 'What is that?'; and with that he went out again to the Jews and said, 'I find no case against him . . .

'We have a Law', the Jews replied, 'and according to that Law he ought to die, because he has claimed to be the Son of God.'. . .

In the end Pilate handed him over to them to be crucified.

They then took charge of Jesus, and carrying his own cross he went out of the city to the place of the skull or, as it was called in Hebrew, Golgotha, where they crucified him with two others, one on either side with Jesus in the middle. Pilate wrote out a notice and had it fixed to the cross; it ran: 'Jesus the Nazarene, King of the Jews.' . . .

Jesus knew that everything had now been completed, and to fulfil the scripture perfectly he said: 'I am thirsty.'

A jar full of vinegar stood there, so putting a sponge soaked in the vinegar on a hyssop stick they held it up to his mouth. After Jesus had taken the vinegar he said, 'It is accomplished'; and bowing his head he gave up his spirit.

## *The shame and the glory: God's great enterprise of love*

*Hear me, O Lord, as your loving-kindness is good, turn to me as your compassion is great.* (Ps 69.17)

This most solemn day of the Christian year opens up the extremity of God's love for us. With all its pain and anguish and gross injustice, this Friday is, in the profoundest sense, *good*. It tells us that there is no hell where God cannot reach us, no hell from which God cannot rescue us. It tells us that God is with us and for us, at all times and in all places, even in the most awful of situations.

For the suffering servant of God we encounter in today's reading from Isaiah, trusting in the good purposes of God must have been an exceedingly hard thing to do. It is not surprising that, from earliest Christian times, the experience of this mysterious figure has been seen as pointing to that of Jesus. Here is someone who is misunderstood, misrepresented and cruelly mistreated. Here is someone who is a silent victim of the prejudice, sin and projected guilt of many others. Just as humankind cannot bear too much reality (as T.S. Eliot put it), so humankind cannot bear too much goodness. It is far too threatening. It has to be discredited and, all too often, destroyed. Yet the good servant takes all this, bearing the sin of many and its dire consequences, that through his innocent suffering, people may be opened up to deep healing and a new way of life. Such cleansing and renewal are what God desires. For the faithful servant who so painfully realizes God's desire, there is to be (in a way that is not spelt out) vindication and high honour. Even more fulfilling, he will somehow see the fruitful outcome of his travail.

Such was ultimately the case for Jesus. But first the full horror of condemnation and crucifixion had to be endured. Nonetheless, John the Evangelist perceives the powerful truth that the passion itself demonstrates the majesty of the rejected one, the one who is no less than God's Word made flesh. The 'lifting up' of this servant at Golgotha, which in human terms looks like the epitome of shame, is in fact the manifestation of God's glory and, for all people, the greatest sign of hope (cf 1.1-14; 12.20-36). Here, in the midst of humiliation and pain, the light of the world shines at its brightest and is not extinguished. So, in John's account, there is no mention of that 'darkness over all the land' which is such a telling feature of the other Gospel passion narratives. Before Pilate and on the cross is a victorious king, whose sovereignty is not of this world and whose inherent divine authority causes even the armed guards who would arrest him to fall back on to the ground. This servant king carries his own cross (there is no reference to Simon of Cyrene), and in dying lets out a great cry of triumph. The hour has come, and Jesus recognizes it for what it is: *God's moment*—the accomplishment of God's great enterprise of love (3.16-17).

The reading from Hebrews reminds us (in very strong language) of the cost and consequences of this enterprise. Faced with grim and terminal suffering, Jesus responded like the full-blooded human being he was. With loud cries and tears, he begged God to save him. He was neither masochist nor stoic. The prospect of death appalled him. And his raw honesty is described as 'reverence'—prime example of that boldness with which we are encouraged to approach the presence of God. For at the throne of grace, we find a God who offers mercy and help, not from a patronizing distance but from a position of inner understanding. There we find Jesus, raised from the dead, made like us in every respect, yet also the very self-expression of God. There we discover that God knows—because God himself has been there.

*God of all goodness,*
*by the hell and victory of the cross*
*embolden us to come to you*
*with our loud cries and tears,*
*to receive mercy and help*
*in time of need.*

Note: Because of constraints on space, the Gospel reading has been abridged. Readers are encouraged to ponder on the full reading as set out in their own Bibles.

# *Easter Day*

## Collect

Lord of all life and power,
who through the mighty resurrection of your Son
overcame the old order of sin and death
to make all things new in him:
grant that we, being dead to sin
and alive to you in Jesus Christ,
may reign with him in glory;
to whom with you and the Holy Spirit
be praise and honour, glory and might,
now and in all eternity.

Almighty God,
who through your only-begotten Son Jesus Christ
overcame death and opened to us the gate of everlasting life:
we humbly beseech you that,
as by your special grace going before us
you put into our minds good desires,
so by your continued help
we may bring them to good effect;
through Jesus Christ our Lord,
who is alive and reigns with you and the Holy Spirit,
one God, now and for ever.

### *Psalms 118.14-24; 114; Easter Anthems; Te Deum.*

## Old Testament *Isaiah 12 RSV*

You will say in that day:
'I will give thanks to you, O Lord,
for though you were angry with me,
your anger turned away,
and you comforted me.
'Behold, God is my salvation;
I will trust, and will not be afraid;
for the Lord God is my strength and my song,
and he has become my salvation.'
With joy you will draw water from the wells of salvation.
And you will say in that day:
'Give thanks to the Lord,

call upon his name;
make known his deeds among the nations,
proclaim that his name is exalted.
'Sing praises to the Lord, for he has done gloriously;
let this be known in all the earth.
Shout, and sing for joy, O inhabitant of Zion,
for great in your midst is the Holy One of Israel.'

## New Testament *Colossians 3.1-11 RSV*

If you have been raised with Christ, seek the things that are above, where Christ is, seated at the right hand of God. Set your minds on things that are above, not on things that are on earth. For you have died, and your life is hid with Christ in God. When Christ who is our life appears, then you also will appear with him in glory.

Put to death therefore what is earthly in you: immorality, impurity, passion, evil desire, and covetousness, which is idolatry. On account of these the wrath of God is coming. In these you once walked, when you lived in them. But now put them all way: anger, wrath, malice, slander, and foul talk from your mouth. Do not lie to one another, seeing that you have put off the old nature with its practices and have put on the new nature, which is being renewed in knowledge after the image of its creator. Hence there cannot be Greek and Jew, circumcised and uncircumcised, barbarian, Scythian, slave, free man, but Christ is all, and in all.

## Gospel *Mark 16.1-8 NEB*

When the Sabbath was over, Mary of Magdala, Mary the mother of James, and Salome brought aromatic oils intending to go and anoint Jesus; and very early on the Sunday morning, just after sunrise, they came to the tomb. They were wondering among themselves who would roll away the stone for them from the entrance to the tomb, when they looked up and saw that the stone, huge as it was, had been rolled back already. They went into the tomb, where they saw a youth sitting on the right-hand side, wearing a white robe; and they were dumbfounded. But he said to them, 'Fear nothing; you are looking for Jesus of Nazareth, who was crucified. He has been raised again; he is not here; look, there is the place where they laid him. But go and give this message to his disciples and Peter: "He is going on before you into Galilee; there you will see him, as he told you." ' Then they went out and ran away from the tomb, beside themselves with terror. They said nothing to anybody, for they were afraid.

# Experiencing the life-changing power of God's searing love

*Tremble O earth at the presence of the Lord,*
*at the presence of the God of Jacob,*
*who turned the rock into a pool of water,*
*and the flint-stone into a welling spring. (Ps 114.7-8)*

The resurrection of Jesus vibrates with the saving power of God. Shrouded in mystery, it releases new possibilities beyond imagining. It is, indeed, 'the day of the Lord'. Yet here is no day of vengeance after the horror of Calvary. Here is Calvary's consummation: the offer of radical new beginning from the God who, out of boundless love, goes to hell and back (and has the scars to prove it).

The prophet Isaiah perceived something of the character of this extraordinary God. Continuing his oracle about the coming great 'shoot… of Jesse' (11.1ff), he looks forward to God's decisive act of salvation. The language he uses to describe this recalls the exodus experience of the people of God (see especially Exodus 15), as well as the sentiments of a good many psalms. Joy is the keynote. Thanksgiving and proclamation are the consequences. The deliverance of God is to be celebrated and shared. The world needs to know about it.

But God's truth can be overwhelming, as Mark's version of Easter morning makes clear. Throughout Mark's Gospel, Jesus (though decidedly down-to-earth) arouses feelings of awe and fear. The question, 'Who is this?', permeates the narrative. Seeking an answer involves an exploration of faith. So it is also with the Easter Christ. In this Gospel (which in all likelihood ends at 16.8) there is no firsthand appearance of the risen Lord. The affirmation of his resurrection has to be accepted on trust and acted on in faith. It is through the exercise of faithful discipleship that his broken followers will 'see' him. By daring to believe, they will discover that their rejection of Jesus by no means issues in his rejection of them. (And in this connection, we note the poignant singling out of Peter). Such challenge and hope faced the first recipients of Mark's Gospel, perhaps in a context of severe testing. They face us still, whatever our condition. As the women at the tomb no doubt came to realize, the terror of God is not something to flee from. Entered into, however hesitantly, it becomes a life-changing experience of God's searing love.

That is not an experience to be kept secret. As Paul knew well (not without cost to himself) the risen Lord holds together all humanity, of whatever race, background or status. The world cries out for the proclamation of that truth. It will be recognized more effectively when the lives of the proclaimers begin to express the character and attitudes of a reconciling God. In the healing light of the God of Easter, we should seriously take heed to ourselves.

*God of new beginnings,*
*free us from the fear of change.*
*May our experience of Easter*
*so change our lives*
*that they express your boundless love.*

## A suggested worship activity for Easter Day

## (This builds on the activity for Lent and Holy Week)

1. All present join in decorating the bare wooden cross with greenery and fresh flowers.

2. A candle is lit nearby.
One person proclaims: *Alleluia! Christ is risen!*
All respond: *He is risen indeed! Alleluia!*

3. A prayer is said (perhaps the one above).

# Easter 1

## Collect

Almighty Father,
who in your great mercy made glad the disciples
    with the sight of the risen Lord:
give us such knowledge of his presence with us,
that we may be strengthened and sustained by his risen life
and serve you continually in righteousness and truth;
through Jesus Christ our Lord.

### *Psalms 145.1-12; 34.1-10*

## Old Testament *Exodus 16.2-15 NEB*

The Israelites complained to Moses and Aaron in the wilderness and said, 'If only we had died at the Lord's hand in Egypt, where we sat round the fleshpots and had plenty of bread to eat! But you have brought us out into this wilderness to let this whole assembly starve to death.' The Lord said to Moses, 'I will rain down bread from heaven for you. Each day the people shall go out and gather a day's supply, so that I can put them to the test and see whether they will follow my instructions or not. But on the sixth day, when they prepare what they bring in, it shall be twice as much as they have gathered on other days.' Moses and Aaron then said to all the Israelites, 'In the evening you will know that it was the Lord who brought you out of Egypt, and in the morning you will see the glory of the Lord, because he has heeded your complaints against him; it is not against us that you bring your complaints; we are nothing.' 'You shall know this', Moses said, 'when the Lord, in answer to your complaints, gives you flesh to eat in the evening, and in the morning bread in plenty. What are we? It is against the Lord that you bring your complaints, and not against us.'

Moses told Aaron to say to the whole community of Israel, 'Come into the presence of the Lord, for he has heeded your complaints.' While Aaron was speaking to the community of the Israelites, they looked towards the wilderness, and there was the glory of the Lord appearing in the cloud. The Lord spoke to Moses and said, 'I have heard the complaints of the Israelites. Say to them, "Between dusk and dark you will have flesh to eat and in the morning bread in plenty. You shall know that I the Lord am your God."'

That evening a flock of quails flew in and settled all over the camp, and in the morning a fall of dew lay all around it. When the dew had gone, there in the wilderness, fine flakes appeared, fine as hoar-frost on the ground. When the Israelites saw it, they said to one another, 'What is that?', because they did not know what it was. Moses said to them 'That is the bread which the Lord has given you to eat.'

## New Testament *1 Corinthians 15.53-end NEB*

This perishable being must be clothed with the imperishable, and what is mortal must be clothed with immortality. And when our mortality has been clothed with immortality, then the saying of Scripture will come true: 'Death is swallowed up; victory is won!' 'O Death, where is your victory? O Death, where is your sting?' The sting of death is sin, and sin gains its power from the law; but, God be praised, he gives us the victory through our Lord Jesus Christ.

Therefore, my beloved brothers, stand firm and immoveable, and work for the Lord always, work without limit, since you know that in the Lord your labour cannot be lost.

## Gospel *John 6.32-40 JB*

Jesus said,
'I tell you most solemnly,
it was not Moses who gave you bread from heaven,
it is my Father who gives you the bread from heaven,
the true bread;
for the bread of God
is that which comes from heaven
and gives life to the world.'
'Sir,' the people said, 'give us that bread always.'
Jesus answered,
'I am the bread of life.
He who comes to me will never be hungry;
he who believes in me will never thirst.
But, as I have told you,
you can see me and still you do not believe.
All that the Father gives me will come to me,
and whoever comes to me
I shall not turn him away;
because I have come from heaven
not to do my own will,
but to do the will of the one who sent me.
Now the will of him who sent me
is that I should lose nothing
of all that he has given to me,
and that I should raise it up on the last day.
Yes, it is my Father's will

that whoever sees the Son and believes in him
shall have eternal life,
and that I shall raise him up on the last day.'

## *Strength and sustenance*

*O taste and see that the Lord is good,*
*happy the one who hides in him! (Ps 34.8)*

After the euphoria of the exodus comes the resentful complaining. The
ecstatic praise of Exodus 15 quickly turns sour when the going gets hard
(16.2ff). God's mighty work of salvation is thrown back in his face. Slavery
(its oppressive reality soon forgotten) is preferable to the testing challenge
of the wilderness. Life after liberation is not the undiluted joy the people of
God expected. Surely salvation should not hurt so much. Moses and Aaron
are right in their response. The Israelites' criticism, though under cover of
an attack on their leaders, is actually directed against God: the God who,
having rescued them, has apparently left them to perish. But they have a
crucial lesson to learn about this God. His provision for them is not
confined to occasional spectacular acts. Day by day, he attends to their basic
needs. The God of salvation is there always, and always at work, even
when things seem bleak.

Recognizing such a God is a matter of trusting relationship. It is possible
to see, yet not to believe. So it is for those who enter into dialogue with
Jesus after they have been wonderfully provided for on a mountain (John
6:1-15). Some had begun to gain an insight (14-15). But they had not gone
nearly far enough. The *real* wonder is not the bread they have eaten but the
living human being who has distributed it. This is the one sent from the
Father to bring humanity to joyous fulfilment. This is the one who
incarnates the very life of God. And all who turn to him can share that life
for ever. It is a comprehensive offer. It is for 'the world', for 'whoever' will
receive it. No one coming to Jesus will be turned away. To such a one, all
the resources of God are available. For 'the bread of life' is not perishable
manna but God's gift of himself. It is a gift that costs him dearly. Yet,
though it is there for the taking, it is all too often denied, taken lightly or
ignored; even by the people of God, who have not lost their habit of
complaining.

In the Easter mystery, God's life breaks out in a way that redeems human
experience of both life and death. Like Paul, we know only too well the
reality of sin. It is a fact of our lives. It is made the more powerful when we
realize how far we fall short of God's high standards—and how powerless
we are to bridge the gap. We also cannot avoid the reality of death, much as

we try. When the truth of our condition is acknowledged, despair beckons. There is, however, a greater truth. God in Jesus Christ has broken the crushing, debilitating power of sin, perfectionism and death. So we are given the freedom and motivation to work on perseveringly for the Lord. Whatever the circumstances in which we travail, God will make sure that our labour is not in vain. As the Collect puts it, we shall be 'strengthened and sustained', even when euphoria is but a distant dream.

*Bountiful God,*
*you provide for us even as we turn away or grumble.*
*May we graciously accept all you give us*
*in Jesus, bread of life*
*and conqueror of death.*

# Easter 2

## Collect

God of peace,
who brought again from the dead our Lord Jesus Christ,
that great shepherd of the sheep,
by the blood of the eternal covenant:
make us perfect in every good work to do your will,
and work in us that which is well-pleasing in your sight;
through Jesus Christ our Lord.

## Psalms 111; 23

## Old Testament *Ezekiel 34.7-16 NEB*

You shepherds, hear the words of the Lord. As surely as I live, says the Lord
God, because my sheep are ravaged by wild beasts and have become their
prey for lack of a shepherd, because my shepherds have not asked after the
sheep but have cared only for themselves and not for the sheep—therefore,
you shepherds, hear the words of the Lord. These are the words of the Lord
God: I am against the shepherds and will demand my sheep from them. I will
dismiss those shepherds: they shall care only for themselves no longer; I will
rescue my sheep from their jaws, and they shall feed on them no more.

For these are the words of the Lord God: Now I myself will ask after my
sheep and go in search of them. As a shepherd goes in search of his sheep
when his flock is dispersed all around him, so I will go in search of my sheep
and rescue them, no matter where they were scattered in dark and cloudy
days. I will bring them out from every nation, gather them in from other
lands, and lead them home to their own soil. I will graze them on the
mountains of Israel, by her streams and in all her green fields. I will feed them
on good grazing-ground, and their pasture shall be the high mountains of
Israel. There they will rest, there in good pasture, and find rich grazing on the
mountains of Israel. I myself will tend my flock, I myself pen them in their
fold, says the Lord God. I will search for the lost, recover the straggler,
bandage the hurt, strengthen the sick, leave the healthy and strong to play,
and give them their proper food.

## New Testament *1 Peter 5.1-11 NEB*

I appeal to the elders of your community, as a fellow-elder and a witness of
Christ's sufferings, and also a partaker in the splendour that is to be
revealed. Tend that flock of God whose shepherds you are, and do it, not
under compulsion, but of your own free will, as God would have it; not for

gain but out of sheer devotion; not tyrannizing over those who are allotted to your care, but setting an example to the flock. And then, when the Head Shepherd appears, you will receive for your own the unfading garland of glory.

In the same way you younger men must be subordinate to your elders. Indeed, all of you should wrap yourselves in the garment of humility towards each other, because God sets his face against the arrogant but favours the humble. Humble yourselves then under God's mighty hand, and he will lift you up in due time. Cast all your cares on him, for you are his charge.

Awake! be on the alert! Your enemy the devil, like a roaring lion, prowls round looking for someone to devour. Stand up to him, firm in faith, and remember that your brother Christians are going through the same kinds of suffering while they are in the world. And the God of all grace, who called you into his eternal glory in Christ, will himself, after your brief suffering, restore, establish, and strengthen you on a firm foundation. He holds dominion for ever and ever. Amen.

## Gospel *John 10.7-16 NEB*

Jesus said, 'In truth, in very truth I tell you, I am the door of the sheepfold. The sheep paid no heed to any who came before me, for these were all thieves and robbers. I am the door; anyone who comes into the fold through me shall be safe. He shall go in and out and shall find pasturage.

'The thief comes only to steal, to kill, to destroy; I have come that men may have life, and may have it in all its fullness. I am the good shepherd; the good shepherd lays down his life for the sheep. The hireling, when he sees the wolf coming, abandons the sheep and runs away, because he is no shepherd and the sheep are not his. Then the wolf harries the flock and scatters the sheep. The man runs away because he is a hireling and cares nothing for the sheep.

'I am the good shepherd; I know my own sheep and my sheep know me—as the Father knows me and I know the Father—and I lay down my life for the sheep. But there are other sheep of mine, not belonging to this fold, whom I must bring in; and they too will listen to my voice. There will then be one flock, one shepherd.'

# Shepherding as it was meant to be

*He will refresh my soul,*
*and guide me in right pathways for his name's sake. (Ps 23.3)*

The readings for 'Good Shepherd Sunday' provide a timely opportunity to consider the nature of leadership in the context of the people of God.

In the Jewish scriptures, the metaphor of shepherding had its focus in government rather than pastoral care. The shepherd was the king. But he derived his authority to govern from the delegated power of God, Israel's true ruler (cf Psalm 80 and Jeremiah 23.1-6, which has strong similarities with Ezekiel 34). During the crisis of the Babylonian exile, Ezekiel makes it clear that, on God's part, delegation does not mean abdication. In a withering invective, the leaders of God's people come under severe judgment for their self-interest and gross dereliction of duty. Because of their failure, those for whom they were responsible under God have suffered grievously and are, quite literally, scattered abroad. The time for direct rule has arrived. What is said here about the leadership of God is well worth pondering. It is passionately concerned for people's welfare. It is pro-active in its approach to the lost and the helpless. In such cases, God does not leave them to help themselves. He spares no effort on their behalf. But his care for them, and for all, is appropriate. It enables them to be themselves, in the most conducive of conditions. Neither domination nor *laissez-faire*, God's leading is empowerment at its best.

Ezekiel's prophecy finds its fulfilment in Jesus, as the Fourth Evangelist so eloquently discerns. This 'good shepherd' is more than the promised Davidic Messiah (Ezekiel 34.23f). He is the enfleshment of God's own rule. Through him who is also 'the door' can be found both ultimate security and ultimate freedom. As shepherd, his authority rests on relationship rather than ruling, on the intimacy of love-knowledge rather than exercise of power. He knows his sheep personally—and is responsively known. But this does not lead to cosy exclusivism. The divine shepherd has a heartfelt mission to bring outsiders into the safety and delight of his pasture. Whether the existing sheep make them welcome is another matter!

The leadership of the good shepherd has, of course, a further dimension. In saving and protecting his sheep, he is prepared to set aside his own interests, he is prepared even to die. His commitment to the flock is total. And that indeed is the death of him. It is one of the profoundest insights of John's Gospel that the good shepherd is also 'the lamb of God' (1.29). And according to Johannine chronology the shepherd lays down his life at the very time that Passover lambs are being slain in the temple.

Such is the daunting example set before Christian leaders in Sunday's Epistle. But encouragement comes with the promise of God's grace and the assurance that leaders also matter to God. Sufferings are shared. But so is the sign of glory.

*Shepherd of your people,*
*in your concern for our welfare*
*you enable us to be truly ourselves.*
*Help us bring others to know your care*
*and to delight in your commitment.*

# Easter 3

## Collect

Almighty God, whose Son Jesus Christ is the resurrection
and the life of all who put their trust in him:
raise us, we pray, from the death of sin to the life of righteousness;
that we may seek the things which are above,
where he reigns with you and the Holy Spirit,
one God, now and for ever.

### *Psalms 16; 30*

## Old Testament *1 Kings 17.17-end TEV*

The son of the widow in Zarephath fell ill; he got worse and worse, and
finally he died. She said to Elijah, 'Man of God, why did you do this to me?
Did you come here to remind God of my sins and so cause my son's death?'

'Give the boy to me,' Elijah said. He took the boy from her arms, carried
him upstairs to the room where he was staying, and laid him on the bed.
Then he prayed aloud, 'O Lord my God, why have you done such a terrible
thing to this widow? She has been kind enough to take care of me, and now
you kill her son!' Then Elijah stretched himself out on the boy three times and
prayed, 'O Lord my God, restore this child to life!' The Lord answered Elijah's
prayer; the child started breathing again and revived.

Elijah took the boy back downstairs to his mother and said to her, 'Look,
your son is alive!'

She answered, 'Now I know that you are a man of God and that the Lord
really speaks through you!'

## New Testament *Colossians 3.1-11 NEB*

Were you not raised to life with Christ? Then aspire to the realm above, where
Christ is, seated at the right hand of God, and let your thoughts dwell on that
higher realm, not on this earthly life. I repeat, you died; and now your life lies
hidden with Christ in God. When Christ, who is our life, is manifested, then
you too will be manifested with him in glory.

Then put to death those parts of you which belong to the earth—
fornication, indecency, lust, foul cravings, and the ruthless greed which is
nothing less than idolatry. Because of these, God's dreadful judgement is
impending; and in the life you once lived these are the ways you yourselves
followed. But now you must yourselves lay aside all anger, passion, malice,
cursing, filthy talk—have done with them! Stop lying to one another, now that
you have discarded the old nature with its deeds and have put on the new

nature, which is being constantly renewed in the image of its Creator and brought to know God. There is no question here of Greek and Jew, circumcised and uncircumcised, barbarian, Scythian, slave and freeman; but Christ is all, and is in all.

## Gospel *John 11.17-27 NEB*

On his arrival Jesus found that Lazarus had already been four days in the tomb. Bethany was just under two miles from Jerusalem, and many of the people had come from the city to Martha and Mary to condole with them on their brother's death. As soon as she heard that Jesus was on his way, Martha went to meet him, while Mary stayed at home.

Martha said to Jesus, 'If you had been here, sir, my brother would not have died. Even now I know that whatever you ask of God, God will grant to you.' Jesus said, 'Your brother will rise again.' 'I know that he will rise again,' said Martha, 'at the resurrection on the last day.' Jesus said, 'I am the resurrection and I am life. If a man has faith in me, even though he die, he shall come to life; and no one who is alive and has faith shall ever die. Do you believe this?' 'Lord, I do,' she answered; 'I now believe that you are the Messiah, the Son of God who was to come into the world.'

# Why does God let people die?

*O Lord my God I cried to you,*
*and you have made me whole. (Ps 30.2)*

When Paul urged the Colossians to 'aspire to the realm above' he was not advocating some form of heavenly escapism. He wanted them to face the reality of their sin with the reality of Christ's death and resurrection. Out of that painful encounter should come re-creation; a renewed humanity in living relationship with the living God. But such a God-ward focus will mean constant struggle as well as constant renewal. Exposure to God shows up what is not of God. And in Christ, that has to be addressed. Looking to heaven is not a comfortable option.

And the struggle is not just with sin, as Sunday's other two readings so graphically illustrate. Human experience throws up many questions—questions of the heart as well as of the mind, not least for the believer. Why this cruel suffering? Why has God allowed it? Where was God when it happened? The widow of Zarapheth resorts to a then conventional answer which has by no means vanished from the scene. The death of her son is the punishing judgment of God on her sins. Yet there is healthy anger rather than acceptance in her challenge to Elijah. It is a challenge Elijah has no hesitation in taking up with God. Without any pious ceremony, he confronts God directly and critically with the question, 'Why?' Then, instead of dwelling on his anger, he calls on God to redeem the situation, doing all in his power to cooperate. So life comes out of death.

Much later, Martha takes the same forthright approach. Jesus had failed to respond to the urgent plea she and her sister had sent to him. Though he had helped others, he had not come to the aid of his friends. Lazarus had died. When at last (but too late) Jesus does put in an appearance, Martha flouts convention and goes out to face him with her questioning grief. She does not mince her words. But (like Elijah with God) neither does she hold back her continuing faith in his power. Such determined honesty opens up a dialogue profound in its theological significance and startling in its context: an unauthorized male teacher conversing publicly with a woman about the things of God. Truth breaks through wherever there is openness to God. It is not confined to any 'proper channels'. Martha's directness elicits from Jesus a self-revelation which has meaning far beyond its immediate setting. From Jesus flows the power of God to bring life where life has been destroyed. Jesus' directness elicits from Martha a confession of faith to rival that of Peter, recorded in the Synoptics. And her words are born out of suffering.

Neither the widow, nor Elijah, nor Martha are given definitive answers to their questions. Yet, in deep distress, they have come to know God better.

It is raw honesty and tenacious faith that provide the key. They open doors into heaven.

*Living God,*
*you make all things new.*
*As we struggle with the death of loved ones,*
*honour our honest questioning*
*with faith that opens doors into heaven.*

# Easter 4

## Collect

Almighty God,
who alone can bring order
to the unruly wills and passions of sinful men:
give us grace, to love what you command
and to desire what you promise,
that in all the changes and chances of this world,
our hearts may surely there be fixed
where lasting joys be found;
through Jesus Christ our Lord.

## *Psalms 33.1-12; 37.23-32*

## Old Testament *Proverbs 4.10-19 RSV*

Hear, my son, and accept my words
that the years of your life may be many.
I have taught you the way of wisdom;
I have led you in the paths of uprightness.
When you walk, your step will not be hampered;
and if you run, you will not stumble.
Keep hold of instruction, do not let go;
guard her, for she is your life.
Do not enter the path of the wicked,
and do not walk in the way of evil men.
Avoid it; do not go on it; turn away from it and pass on.
For they cannot sleep unless they have done wrong;
they are robbed of sleep unless they have made someone stumble.
For they eat the bread of wickedness
and drink the wine of violence.
But the path of the righteous is like the light of dawn,
which shines brighter and brighter until full day.
The way of the wicked is like deep darkness;
they do not know over what they stumble.

## New Testament *2 Corinthians 4.13—5.5 NEB*

Scripture says, 'I believed, and therefore I spoke out', and we too, in the same
spirit of faith, believe and therefore speak out; for we know that he who
raised the Lord Jesus to life will with Jesus raise us too, and bring us to his
presence, and you with us. Indeed, it is for your sake that all things are

ordered, so that, as the abounding grace of God is shared by more and more, the greater may be the chorus of thanksgiving that ascends to the glory of God.

No wonder we do not lose heart! Though our outward humanity is in decay, yet day by day we are inwardly renewed. Our troubles are slight and short-lived; and their outcome an eternal glory which outweighs them far. Meanwhile our eyes are fixed, not on the things that are seen, but on the things that are unseen: for what is seen passes away; what is unseen is eternal. For we know that if the earthly frame that houses us today should be demolished, we possess a building which God has provided—a house not made by human hands, eternal, and in heaven. In this present body we do indeed groan; we yearn to have our heavenly habitation put on over this one—in the hope that, being thus clothed, we shall not find ourselves naked. We groan indeed, we who are enclosed within this earthly frame; we are oppressed because we do not want to have the old body stripped off. Rather our desire is to have the new body put on over it, so that our mortal part may be absorbed into life immortal. God himself has shaped us for this very end; and as a pledge of it he has given us the Spirit.

## Gospel *John 14.1-11 NEB*

Jesus said, 'Set your troubled hearts at rest. Trust in God always; trust also in me. There are many dwelling-paces in my Father's house; if it were not so I should have told you; for I am going there on purpose to prepare a place for you. And if I go and prepare a place for you, I shall come again and receive you to myself, so that where I am you may be also; and my way there is known to you.' Thomas said, 'Lord, we do not know where you are going, so how can we know the way?' Jesus replied, 'I am the way; I am the truth and I am life; no one comes to the Father except my me.

If you knew me you would know my Father too. From now on you do know him; you have seen him.' Philip said to him, 'Lord, show us the Father and we ask no more.' Jesus answered, 'Have I been all this time with you, Philip, and you still do not know me? Anyone who has seen me has seen the Father. Then how can you say, "Show us the Father"? Do you not believe that I am in the Father, and the Father in me? I am not myself the source of the words I speak to you: it is the Father who dwells in me doing his own work. Believe me when I say that I am in the Father and the Father in me; or else accept the evidence of the deeds themselves.'

# On the way to the Way

*The mouth of the righteous utters wisdom,*
*and his tongue speaks what is right.*
*The law of his God is in his heart,*
*and his footsteps will not slip. (Ps 37.31-32)*

The people of God should always be a people on the move. Such, at least, is the biblical testimony. The scriptures are full of journeying, be it territorial or spiritual (it is often both). Faith is a pilgrimage, a risky adventure involving pain and perseverance as well as joyful discovery. Static it can never be, for 'walking in the way of the Lord' means entering into relationship with the living and active God. That is true even in the keeping of God's commandments (see Psalm 119).

With the aid of an experienced guide, the youth addressed in the Proverbs reading has embarked on 'the way of wisdom'. Provided he heeds those who know better, keeping to the path of righteousness and avoiding the path of wickedness, all will go well with him. His progress will be unhindered. Light will shine on him in abundance. It is a very polarized, optimistic interpretation of how life's journey will be for those who are obedient to God's claims. Typical of much wisdom teaching (in the ancient Near East generally, as well as in Jewish tradition) it has not disappeared from popular consciousness. A good life should be rewarded, a bad life punished. Yet even at the time, this easy equation did not go unchallenged, as the book of Job so powerfully testifies. The reality of life too often seems to fly in the face of such pious conviction.

For Job, the way through to a deeper understanding was in a devastating meeting with God. In a different context, so it was for the disciples of Jesus. At festival time, they had arrived in Jerusalem, the goal and focus of pilgrimage. Yet it was now for them a place of disturbance, fear and confusion. Where was their leader taking them—and why did he speak in such riddles? The way ahead looked heavy with tragedy rather than triumph. Here, in Jesus, was a young man who had certainly kept to 'the paths of uprightness'. Yet it looked ominously as if the years of his life were not to be many. Where then, in this time of crisis, was God to be found? The answer of the Johannine Jesus repays much prayerful exploration. The way into the presence of God, the way which opens up the life and truth of God is not a code of practice but a person; a person whose manner of living and dying expresses the very heart of God (compare Hebrews 10.19-23 for a fruitful parallel). Trusting this person, whatever the circumstances, means journeying with the God whose love has the will and the power to redeem all the negativity in the world. 'Believe me', says Jesus, 'or else accept the evidence of the deeds themselves'. The greatest of those deeds is the raising of Jesus from the dead. Accepting in faith the truth of that great work moves us on towards the end for which God made us. That, as Paul confidently reminds the Corinthians, is the consummation of our humanity, the fulfilling of all our potential in the eternal life of God. Not only should that arouse profound thanksgiving. It is also something to shout about on the way.

*God of our life,*
*uphold us on our way,*
*that we may know for ourselves*
*the truth of the risen Christ.*

# *Easter 5*

## Collect

Almighty and everlasting God,
you are always more ready to hear than we to pray
and give more than either we desire or deserve.
Pour down upon us the abundance of your mercy,
forgiving us those things of which our conscience is afraid
and giving us those good things which we are not worthy to ask
save through the merits and mediation
of Jesus Christ your Son our Lord.

### *Psalms 84; 15*

## Old Testament *Deuteronomy 34 RSV*

Moses went up from the plains of Moab to Mount Nebo, to the top of Pisgah, which is opposite Jericho. And the Lord showed him all the land, Gilead as far as Dan, all Naphtali, the land of Ephraim and Manasseh, all the land of Judah as far as the Western Sea, the Negeb, and the Plain, that is, the valley of Jericho the city of palm trees, as far as Zoar. And the Lord said to him, 'This is the land of which I swore to Abraham, to Isaac, and to Jacob, "I will give it to your descendants." I have let you see it with your eyes, but you shall not go over there.' So Moses the servant of the Lord died there in the land of Moab, according to the word of the Lord, and he buried him in the valley in the land of Moab opposite Beth-peor; but no man knows the place of his burial to this day. Moses was a hundred and twenty years old when he died; his eye was not dim, nor his natural force abated. And the people of Israel wept for Moses in the plains of Moab thirty days; then the days of weeping and mourning for Moses were ended.

And Joshua the son of Nun was full of the spirit of wisdom, for Moses had laid his hands upon him; so the people of Israel obeyed him, and did as the Lord commanded Moses. And there has not arisen a prophet since in Israel like Moses, whom the Lord knew face to face, none like him for all the signs and the wonders which the Lord sent him to do in the land of Egypt, to Pharaoh and to all his servants and to all his land, and for all the mighty power and all the great and terrible deeds which Moses wrought in the sight of all Israel.

## New Testament *Romans 8.28-end RSV*

We know that in everything God works for good with those who love him, who are called according to his purpose. For those whom he foreknew he also predestined to be conformed to the image of his Son, in order that he night be the first-born among many brethren. And those whom he predestined he also called; and those whom he called he also justified; and those whom he justified he also glorified.

What then shall we say to this? If God is for us, who is against us? He who did not spare his own Son but gave him up for us all, will he not also give us all things with him? Who shall bring any charge against God's elect? It is God who justifies; who is to condemn? Is it Christ Jesus, who died, yes, who was raised from the dead, who is at the right hand of God, who indeed intercedes for us? Who shall separate us from the love of Christ? Shall tribulation, or distress, or persecution, or famine, or nakedness, or peril, or sword? As it is written,

'For your sake we are being killed all the day long;
we are regarded as sheep to be slaughtered.'

No, in all these things we are more than conquerors through him who loved us. For I am sure that neither death, nor life, nor angels, nor principalities, nor things present, nor things to come, nor powers, nor height, nor depth, nor anything else in all creation, will be able to separate us from the love of God in Christ Jesus our Lord.

## Gospel *John 16.12-24 NRB*

Jesus said, 'There is still much that I could say to you, but the burden would be too great for you now. However, when he comes who is the Spirit of truth, he will guide you into all the truth; for he will not speak on his own authority, but will tell only what he hears; and he will make known to you the things that are coming. He will glorify me, for everything that he makes known to you he will draw from what is mine. All that the Father has is mine, and that is why I said, "Everything that he makes known to you he will draw from what is mine."

'A little while, and you see me no more; again a little while, and you will see me.' Some of his disciples said to one another, 'What does he mean by this: "A little while, and you will not see me, and again a little while, and you will see me", and by this: "Because I am going to my Father"?' So they asked, 'What is this "little while" that he speaks of? We do not know what he means.'

Jesus knew that they were wanting to question him, and he said, 'Are you discussing what I said: "A little while, and you will not see me, and again a little while, and you will see me"? In very truth I tell you, you will weep and mourn, but the world will be glad. But though you will be plunged in grief, your grief will be turned to joy. A woman in labour is in pain because her time has come; but when the child is born she forgets the anguish in her joy that a man has been born into the world. So it is with you: for the moment you are sad at heart; but I shall see you again, and then you will be joyful, and no one shall rob you of your joy. When that day comes you will ask nothing of me. In very truth I tell you, if you ask the Father for anything in my name, he will give it you. So far you have asked nothing in my name. Ask and you will receive, that your joy may be complete.'

## Struggling with the truth

*Lord, who may abide in your tabernacle,*
*or who may dwell upon your holy hill? (Ps 15.1)*

As so often, the writer of the Fourth Gospel is concerned with truth. The Spirit who is to come is the Spirit of truth. This Spirit will open up to the disciples the truth that is at present hidden from them: hidden because at the moment they are in no state to face up to it. Even what Jesus then chooses to disclose needs unpacking. The truth of God is not always obvious. It is apprehended more effectively by experience than by abstract intellect. Yet what Jesus explains in striking imagery, he tells them 'in very truth'. They are suffering birth-pangs; they are on the point of the delivery of new life, new joy. In enjoying that new life, they will be enabled to ask and receive. But there will be much to learn, and that includes recognizing that any approach to the Father has to be through and in the person (name) of Jesus. Divine truth is not propositional but personal. It gets to the heart of things. It is about relationship.

Moses had struggled with truth. After much travail, the exodus had been born in joyful deliverance. But the experience had turned sour. People grumbled and would rather have the bondage of slavery than the tribulations that seemed to come with freedom. Leadership of God's people can often seem a thankless task. At the end, Moses is granted a broad vision of the promised land, seeing it from afar. But it is not to be his to enjoy. Where he went and where he rested remained a mystery, as with the going up of Jesus. But the writer of Deuteronomy recognized that Moses had known truth, for he was someone 'the Lord knew face to face'. Through that open, sometimes stormy, relationship, energized by God's 'spirit of wisdom', much had been achieved.

Wrestling with truth leads Paul to pose many questions. In Sunday's passage from Romans, the questions are in reality strong affirmations of faith. Rhetorically, they underline Paul's fundamental conviction (tested in his own turbulent life) that God's love can be utterly relied upon at all times and in all places. In that steadfast redemptive love is the basis for the believer's victory over adverse circumstances. But hard questions remain, some of them thrown up by Paul's own confident assertions. The vexed issue of predestination has caused not a little havoc in the Church. If we are to take Paul seriously, we must still grapple with his meaning, planted firmly, as it seems to be, in God's foreknowledge. And what of unbelievers? There are crucial theological questions here that cry out for exploration. They are more than academic. That is a truth creatively perceived by Julian of Norwich. Out of revelatory anguish and long years of reflection on God's love, there emerged for Julian a profound word of encouragement from the Lord. In the mysterious providence of God and through much heartache, 'All shall be well, and all shall be well, and all manner of thing shall be well'. That is a fitting nutshell exegesis of this Sunday's readings.

*God of truth,*
*make us expectant of new life,*
*ready to receive whatever you give,*
*in confident reliance on your love.*

# Ascension Day

## Collect

Almighty God,
as we believe your only-begotten Son our Lord Jesus Christ
to have ascended into the heavens,
so may we also in heart and mind thither ascend
and with him continually dwell;
who is alive and reigns with you and the Holy Spirit,
one God, now and for ever.

## *Psalms 8; 21.1-7*

## Old Testament *Daniel 7.9-14 RSV*

As I looked,
thrones were placed
and one that was ancient of days took his seat;
his raiment was white as snow,
and the hair of his head like pure wool;
his throne was fiery flames,
its wheels were burning fire.
A stream of fire issued and came forth from before him;
a thousand thousands served him,
and ten thousand times ten thousand stood before him;
the court sat in judgement,
and the books were opened.
I looked then because of the sound of the great words which the horn was
speaking. And as I looked, the beast was slain, and its body destroyed and
given over to be burned with fire. As for the rest of the beasts, their dominion
was taken away, but their lives were prolonged for a season and a time.
I saw in the night visions,
and behold, with the clouds of heaven there came one like a son of man, and
he came to the Ancient of Days and was presented before him.
And to him was given dominion and glory and kingdom,
that all peoples, nations, and languages should serve him;
his kingdom is an everlasting dominion
which shall not pass away,
and his kingdom one that shall not be destroyed.

# New Testament *Acts 1.1-11 TEV*

Dear Theophilus: In my first book I wrote about all the things that Jesus did and taught from the time he began his work until the day he was taken up to heaven. Before he was taken up, he gave instructions by the power of the Holy Spirit to the men he had chosen as his apostles. For forty days after his death he appeared to them many times in ways that proved beyond doubt that he was alive. They saw him, and he talked with them about the Kingdom of God. And when they came together, he gave them this order: 'Do not leave Jerusalem, but wait for the gift I told you about, the gift my Father promised. John baptized with water, but in a few days you will be baptized with the Holy Spirit.'

When the apostles met together with Jesus, they asked him, 'Lord, will you at this time give the Kingdom back to Israel?'

Jesus said to them, 'The times and occasions are set by my Father's own authority, and it is not for you to know when they will be. But when the Holy Spirit comes upon you, you will be filled with power, and you will be witnesses for me in Jerusalem, in all Judaea and Samaria, and to the ends of the earth.' After saying this, he was taken up to heaven as they watched him, and a cloud hid him from their sight.

They still had their eyes fixed on the sky as he went away, when two men dressed in white suddenly stood beside them and said, 'Galileans, why are you standing there looking up at the sky? This Jesus, who was taken from you into heaven, will come back in the same way that you saw him go to heaven.'

# Gospel *Matthew 28.16-end JB*

The eleven disciples set out for Galilee, to the mountain where Jesus had arranged to meet them. When they saw him they fell down before him, though some hesitated. Jesus came up and spoke to them. He said, 'All authority in heaven and on earth has been given to me. Go, therefore, make disciples of all the nations; baptize them in the name of the Father and of the Son and of the Holy Spirit, and teach them to observe all the commands I gave you. And know that I am with you always; yes, to the end of time.'

# Commissioned to witness to the vindicated Jesus

*The king shall rejoice in your strength, O Lord,*
*he shall exult in your salvation. (Ps 21.1)*

The two New Testament readings set for Ascension Day give us accounts of what seems to have been the last conversation Jesus had with the eleven before he went from them. Both readings make the point that Jesus was with them. Both speak of the disciples going out and witnessing for him throughout the world. But there are differences.

Matthew's Gospel describes the eleven as disciples; Luke's account in the Acts of the Apostles speaks of those Jesus had chosen as his apostles. Matthew has the meeting taking place on a mountain in Galilee. Luke has the meeting in Jerusalem or perhaps just outside it. Matthew's Gospel has Jesus telling the eleven to make disciples, to baptize people, to teach them in and with his authority. Luke has Jesus giving them instructions in the power of the Holy Spirit, urging them to look forward to the same power that will come on them when they are baptized with the Holy Spirit, power that will enable them to go out and witness.

The different accounts offer us a range of perspectives on the significance of Christ's departure from the physical constraints of human existence. The Gospel suggests that after the Resurrection, the disciples were not quite sure about their relationship with Jesus. The Acts reading suggests that they were still unclear as to what it all meant. In the light of the trauma they had been through, this is not at all surprising.

The risen Christ had to restore and encourage his erstwhile followers—to lift them out of their failure, confusion and misguided hopes, so that they could share the true character of God's good news with a needy world. He does this in Galilee, where their discipleship had first begun. He does this in Jerusalem, where their discipleship had confronted its greatest crisis, plumbed the depths of failure and despair, only to meet with the seemingly impossible on the first day of the week. In each place, Jesus calls for a renewed and daring commitment which will take them far from where they are, both physically and spiritually. And, though removed from their sight, he will be with them. With his presence, and the power of the Holy Spirit, they can go out into the world with confidence. But, as the Acts passage reminds us, the Spirit's power is not to be taken for granted. It is a gift to be given when the time is right.

All this still has much to say to present-day followers of Jesus as together they share the commission entrusted to the first disciples.

The reading from Daniel gives us a mysterious picture of the heavenly court sitting in judgment. Dominion and glory and kingdom are given to the strange figure of the son of man who comes before the Ancient of Days. Whatever Daniel had in mind, Christian tradition has sought to identify this strange figure with the one who seems to have called himself 'Son of man'. And his ascension confirms him as vindicated and enthroned as Christ the King.

*God of vindication,*
*as you lifted Jesus to great honour,*
*and drew his disciples out of desolation,*
*lift us to new confidence*
*to live in the power of your Spirit.*

# The Sunday after Ascension Day

## Collect

Eternal God, the King of Glory,
you have exalted your only Son
with great triumph to your kingdom in heaven.
Leave us not comfortless,
but send your Holy Spirit to strengthen us
and exalt us to the place
where Christ is gone before,
and where with you and the Holy Spirit
he is worshipped and glorified,
now and for ever.

## *Psalms 24; 47*

## Old Testament *2 Kings 2.1-15 NEB*

The time came when the Lord would take Elijah up to heaven in a whirlwind. Elijah and Elisha left Gilgal, and Elijah said to Elisha, 'Stay here; for the Lord has sent me to Bethel.' But Elisha said, 'As the Lord lives, your life upon it, I will not leave you.' So they went down country to Bethel. There a company of prophets came out to Elisha and said to him, 'Do you know that the Lord is going to take your lord and master from you today?' 'I do know', he replied; 'say no more.' The Elijah said to him, 'Stay here, Elisha; for the Lord has sent me to Jericho.' But he replied, 'As the Lord lives, your life upon it, I will not leave you.' So they went to Jericho. There a company of prophets came up to Elisha and said to him, 'Do you know that the Lord is going to take your lord and master from you today?' 'I do know', he said; 'say no more.' Then Elijah said to him, 'Stay here; for the Lord has sent me to the Jordan.' The other replied, 'As the Lord lives, your life upon it, I will not leave you.' So the two of them went on.

Fifty of the prophets followed them, and stood watching from a distance as the two of them stopped by the Jordan. Elijah took his cloak, rolled it up and struck the water with it. The water divided to right and left, and they both crossed over on dry ground. While they were crossing, Elijah said to Elisha, 'Tell me what I can do for you before I am taken from you.' Elisha said, 'Let me inherit a double share of your spirit.' 'You have asked a hard thing,' said Elijah. 'If you see me taken from you, may your wish be granted; if you do not, it shall not be granted.' They went on, talking as they went, and suddenly there appeared chariots of fire and horses of fire, which separated them one from the other, and Elijah was carried up in the whirlwind to heaven. When Elisha saw it, he cried, 'My father, my father, the chariots and the horsemen of Israel!', and he saw him no more. Then he took hold of his mantle and rent it in two, and he picked up the cloak which had fallen from Elijah, and came back and stood on the bank of the Jordan. There he too struck water with Elijah's cloak and said, 'Where is the Lord the God of Elijah?' When he struck the water, it was again divided to right and left, and he crossed over. The prophets from Jericho, who were watching, saw him and said, 'The spirit of Elijah has settled on Elisha.'

## New Testament *Ephesians 4.1-13 NEB*

I entreat you,—I, a prisoner for the Lord's sake: as God has called you, live up to your calling. Be humble always and gentle, and patient too. Be forbearing with one another and charitable. Spare no effort to make fast with bonds of peace the unity which the Spirit gives. There is one body and one Spirit, as there is also one hope held out in God's call to you; one Lord, one faith, one baptism; one God and Father of all, who is over all and through all and in all.

But each of us has been given his gift, his due portion of Christ's bounty. Therefore Scripture says:

'He ascended into the heights
with captives in his train;
he gave gifts to men.'

Now, the word 'ascended' implies that he also descended to the lowest level, down to the very earth. He who descended is no other than he who ascended far above all heavens, so that he might fill the universe. And these were his gifts: some to be apostles, some prophets, some evangelists, some pastors and teachers, to equip God's people for work in his service, to the building up of the body of Christ. So shall we all at last attain to the unity inherent in our faith and our knowledge of the Son of God—to mature manhood, measured by nothing less than the full stature of Christ.

## Gospel *Luke 24.45-end JB*

Jesus opened the disciples' minds to understand the scriptures, and he said to them, 'So you see how it is written that the Christ would suffer and on the third day rise from the dead, and that, in his name, repentance for the forgiveness of sins would be preached to all the nations, beginning from Jerusalem. You are witnesses to this.

'And now I am sending down to you what the Father has promised. Stay in the city then, until you are clothed with the power from on high.'

Then he took them out as far as the outskirts of Bethany, and lifting up his hands he blessed them. Now as he blessed them, he withdrew from them and was carried up to heaven. They worshipped him and then went back to Jerusalem full of joy; and they were continually in the Temple praising God.

## *Living up to our calling*

*O clap your hands all you peoples,*
*and cry aloud to God with shouts of joy. (Ps 47.1)*

'Live up to your calling'. That exhortation to the Ephesians resonates through all three of Sunday's readings. Elisha has clearly served his prophetic apprenticeship well (cf 1 Kings 19.16-21). He is both determined and ready to take on his master Elijah's mantle. Indeed, he actively pursues his vocation. And after Elijah's somewhat dramatic departure, Elisha's authenticity as successor is demonstrated by his first solo action as a prophet. Now he has met the conditions and the time is right, his bold request to inherit Elijah's prophetic power is emphatically granted. Divine calling combined with human co-operation has realized God's purpose.

So, too, the disciples of Jesus must respond positively to the urging of God if the message of salvation is to be proclaimed throughout the world. In Luke's compressed account of Easter/Ascension (see his extended version in Acts 1.1-14) he stresses that God is vocation's source and resource. It is God who calls and commissions, in accordance with the great divine plan of redemption (a theme of some moment in Luke's theology). Understanding and empowering for the task are both divine gifts, not human achievements. In this case, those gifts have not been eagerly sought. The group of people visited by the risen Christ (more than the Eleven, as 24.33 makes clear) are in a state of shock—confused and fearful to say the least. Yet they are called to be what they truly are: witnesses; witnesses of the truth in all its wonder and its shame. How typical of the Easter God to call those who are forgiven failures to get across the liberating gospel of forgiveness. In a very real sense, these broken disciples have been raised to new life by the uncondemning risen Lord. Creative response has been evoked. How, then, could Luke's Gospel not end, as it began, on a note of sheer joy?

For the writer of Ephesians, Christian vocation is to be seen as part of God's cosmic purpose, set forth in Christ, 'to unite all things in him, things in heaven and things on earth' (1.10). But involvement in this great mystery has very down-to-earth implications for the way Christians live and behave. God's people must live up to their calling, however much it costs, remembering that they have all the resources of God to draw on. The Epistle highlights how generous God is in the bestowal of gifts. It also stresses that divine prodigality has a purpose. Gifts are given by the ascended Christ who knows full well the depths of the human condition. These gifts are designed to bring out the best in people and so enable the Church to grow into its identity and vocation—the effective manifestation of the saving presence of Christ. The challenge is that, in Christ, we become what we already have the potential to be.

*God of Ascension,*
*help us to make the most of all you give us,*
*that in witnessing to your truth*
*we may draw out the best in others,*
*and so become what we are called to be.*

# *Pentecost*

## Collect

Almighty God,
who on the day of Pentecost
sent your Holy Spirit to the disciples
with the wind from heaven and in tongues of flame,
filling them with joy and boldness to preach the Gospel:
send us out in the power of the same Spirit
to witness to your truth
and to draw all men to the fire of your love;
through Jesus Christ our Lord.

### *Psalms 122; 36.5-10*

## Old Testament *Genesis 11.1-9 NEB*

Once upon a time all the world spoke a single language and used the same words. As men journeyed in the east, they came upon a plain in the land of Shinar and settled there. They said to one another, 'Come, let us make bricks and bake them hard'; they used bricks for stone and bitumen for mortar. 'Come,' they said, 'let us build ourselves a city and a tower with its top in the heavens, and make a name for ourselves; or we shall be dispersed all over the earth.' Then the Lord came down to see the city and tower which mortal men had built, and he said, 'Here they are, one people with a single language, and now they have started to do this; henceforward nothing they have a mind to do will be beyond their reach. Come, let us go down there and confuse their speech, so that they will not understand what they say to one another.' So the Lord dispersed them from there all over the earth, and they left off building the city. That is why it is called Babel, because the Lord there made a babble of language of all the world; from that place the Lord scattered men all over the face of the earth.

## New Testament *Acts 2.1-21 RSV*

When the day of Pentecost had come, the disciples were all together in one place. And suddenly a sound came from heaven like the rush of a mighty wind, and it filled all the house where they were sitting. And there appeared to them tongues as of fire, distributed and resting on each one of them. And they were all filled with the Holy Spirit and began to speak in other tongues, as the Spirit gave them utterance.

Now there were dwelling in Jerusalem Jews, devout men from every nation under heaven. And at this sound the multitude came together, and they were bewildered, because each one heard them speaking in his own language. And they were amazed and wondered, saying, 'Are not all these who are speaking Galileans? And how is it that we hear, each of us in his own native language? Parthians and Medes and Elamites and residents of Mesopotamia, Judaea and Cappadocia, Pontus and Asia, Phrygia and Pamphylia, Egypt and the parts of Libya belonging to Cyrene, and visitors from Rome, both Jews and proselytes, Cretans and Arabians, we hear them telling in our own tongues the mighty works of God.' And all were amazed and perplexed, saying to one another, 'What does this mean?' But others mocking said, 'They are filled with new wine.'

But Peter, standing with the eleven, lifted up his voice and addressed them, 'Men of Judaea and all who dwell in Jerusalem, let this be known to you, and give ear to my words. For these men are not drunk, as you suppose, since it is only the third hour of the day; but this is what was spoken by the prophet Joel:

'And in the last days it shall be, God declares,
that I will pour out my Spirit upon all flesh,
and your sons and your daughters shall prophesy,
and your young men shall see visions,
and your old men shall dream dreams;
yea, and on my menservants and my maidservants in those days
I will pour out my Spirit; and they shall prophesy.
And I will show wonders in the heaven above
and signs on the earth beneath,
blood, and fire, and vapour of smoke;
the sun shall be turned into darkness
and the moon into blood,
before the day of the Lord comes,
the great and manifest day.
And it shall be that whoever calls on the name of the Lord shall be saved.'

## Gospel *John 14.15-26 JB*

Jesus said,
'If you love me you will keep my commandments.
'I shall ask the Father,
and he will give you another Advocate
to be with you for ever,
that Spirit of truth
whom the world can never receive
since it nether sees nor knows him;
but you know him,
because he is with you, he is in you.
I will not leave you orphans;

I will come back to you.
In a short time the world will no longer see me;
but you will see me,
because I live and you will live.
On that day
you will understand that I am in my Father
and you in me and I in you.
Anybody who receives my commandments and keeps them
will be one who loves me;
and anybody who loves me will be loved by my Father,
and I shall love him and show myself to him.'

Judas—this was not Judas Iscariot—said to him, 'Lord, what is all this about? Do you intend to show yourself to us and not to the world?' Jesus replied:

'If anyone loves me he will keep my word,
and my Father will love him,
and we shall come to him
and make our home with him.
Those who do not love me do not keep my words.
And my word is not my own:
it is the word of the one who sent me.
I have said these things to you
while still with you;
but the Advocate, the Holy Spirit,
whom the Father will send in my name,
will teach you everything
and remind you of all I have said to you.'

## *Communicating truth*

*For with you is the well of life,*
*and in your light shall we see light. (Ps 36.9)*

One of the most telling features of the Bible is that the God it presents cannot easily be packaged. A rich variety of (often clashing) imagery is used of God in trying to express the inexpressible. Through the scriptures, we encounter different perceptions of God which defy facile harmonization. That is as it should be, if God really is God. We do well to remind ourselves that the only place where God will be pinned down is, briefly, on a cross.

The readings set for Pentecost underline the dynamic diversity of the one God. The Babel narrative tells of a God distinctly threatened by a humanity determined to overreach itself. So he uses his power to divide and rule. As a theological reflection on the existence of many languages, we may feel this story leaves something to be desired. It is so delightfully anthropomorphic in its expression (and so easy to locate in the annals of human power games) that we might begin to suspect there is not a little projection at work. Nonetheless, here is a God who can be understood in human terms. He is not so far distant as to be beyond comprehension; and human beings have the capacity to reach out towards him.

The God of the scriptures is most definitely a communicator, even when he is warning people to keep to their side of the boundary (as in the alternative reading from Exodus 19). In the Acts passage the lines of communication are decisively opened rather than closed by the Spirit of God. God's language transcends all the shortcomings and barriers of human speech. It speaks directly to all, whatever their background or circumstance. And it excites response. God speaks not just to arouse interest but to offer salvation.

The disciples were gathered in Jerusalem at the time of that festival which celebrated the giving of the Law on Sinai, with all the dramatic phenomena that accompanied it. The giving of God's Spirit is no less dramatic and of far deeper significance. It signals the realization of that for which the Law was intended—a living relationship with a living God; sometimes unpredictable and breathtaking but always profoundly personal.

What Jesus says about the Spirit in the Last Discourses of John's Gospel leaves us in no doubt as to the personal character of the Advocate. The Spirit of Pentecost is expressed by Luke as a mighty empowering force. The Helper promised by the Johannine Jesus is one who will be a stimulating companion and teacher. We are also reminded by the Gospel passage that this Spirit of truth is the one who continues the ministry of Jesus and is the gift of the Father. As so often in the Fourth Gospel, we are being invited to ponder on the mystery of who God is and how God works. Even the Word made flesh stirs up questions rather than providing easy answers.

*God of communication,*
*your voice is heard throughout the world.*
*May we know your living Spirit*
*as companion and teacher,*
*encourager and guide.*

# Trinity Sunday

## Collect

Almighty and everlasting God,
you have given us your servants grace,
by the confession of a true faith
to acknowledge the glory of the eternal Trinity,
and in the power of the divine Majesty to worship the Unity.
Keep us steadfast in this faith,
that we may evermore be defended from all adversities;
through Jesus Christ our Lord,
who is alive and reigns with you and the Holy Spirit,
one God, now and for ever.

Almighty and eternal God
you have revealed yourself as Father, Son and Holy Spirit,
and live and reign in the perfect unity of love.
Hold us firm in this faith,
that we may know you in all your ways
and evermore rejoice in your eternal glory,
who are three Persons in one God, now and for ever.

## Psalms 93; 97

## Old Testament *Isaiah 6.1-8 RSV*

In the year that King Uzziah died I saw the Lord sitting upon a throne, high and lifted up; and his train filled the temple. Above him stood the seraphim; each had six wings: with two he covered his face, and with two he covered his feet, and with two he flew. And one called to another and said:

'Holy, holy, holy is the Lord of hosts;
the whole earth is full of his glory.'

And the foundations of the thresholds shook at the voice of him who called, and the house was filled with smoke. And I said: 'Woe is me! For I am lost; for I am a man of unclean lips, and I dwell in the midst of a people of unclean lips; for my eyes have seen the King, the Lord of hosts!'

Then flew one of the seraphim to me, having in his hand a burning coal which he had taken with tongs from the altar. And he touched my mouth, and said: 'Behold, this has touched your lips; your guilt is taken away, and your sin forgiven.' And I heard the voice of the Lord saying, 'Whom shall I send, and who will go for us?' Then I said, 'Here I am! Send me.'

# New Testament *Ephesians 1.3-15 NEB*

Praise be to the God and Father of our Lord Jesus Christ, who has bestowed on us in Christ every spiritual blessing in the heavenly realms. In Christ he chose us before the world was founded, to be dedicated, to be without blemish in his sight, to be full of love; and he destined us—such was his will and pleasure—to be accepted as his sons through Jesus Christ, in order that the glory of his gracious gift, so graciously bestowed on us in his Beloved, might redound to his praise. For in Christ our release is secured and our sins are forgiven through the shedding of his blood. Therein lies the richness of God's free grace lavished upon us, imparting full wisdom and insight. He has made known to us his hidden purpose—such was his will and pleasure determined beforehand in Christ—to be put into effect when the time was ripe; namely, that the universe, all in heaven and on earth, might be brought into a unity in Christ.

In Christ indeed we have been given our share in the heritage, as was decreed in his design whose purpose is everywhere at work. For it was his will that we, who were the first to set our hope on Christ, should cause his glory to be praised. And you too, when you had heard the message of the truth, the good news of your salvation, and had believed it, became incorporate in Christ and received the seal of the promised Holy Spirit; and that Spirit is the pledge that we shall enter upon our heritage, when God has redeemed what is his own, to his praise and glory.

# Gospel *John 14.8-17 JB*

Philip said to Jesus, 'Lord, let us see the Father and then we shall be satisfied.'
'Have I been with you all this time, Philip,' said Jesus to him, 'and you still do not know me?
'To have seen me is to have seen the Father,
so how can you say, "Let us see the Father"?
Do you not believe
that I am in the Father and the Father is in me?
The words I say to you I do not speak as from myself:
it is the Father, living in me, who is doing this work.
You must believe me when I say
that I am in the Father and the Father is in me;
believe it on the evidence of this work, if for no other reason.
I tell you most solemnly,
whoever believes in me
will perform the same works as I do myself,
he will perform even greater works,
because I am going to the Father.
Whatever you ask for in my name I will do,
so that the Father may be glorified in the Son.

If you ask for anything in my name,
I will do it.
If you love me you will keep my commandments.
I shall ask the Father,
and he will give you another Advocate
to be with you for ever,
that Spirit of truth
whom the world can never receive
since it nether sees nor knows him;
but you know him,
because he is with you, he is in you.'

## Mystery, revelation and relationship intertwined

*Clouds and darkness are round about him,*
*righteousness and justice are the foundation of his throne.*
*Light dawns for the righteous,*
*and joy for the true of heart. (Ps 97.2, 11)*

The God we worship is a God of mystery and of relationship. So testify the
three readings set for Trinity Sunday. Isaiah's dramatic vision in the temple
is of a God far greater than the impressive structure built to accommodate
his glory. The train of his garment alone 'filled the temple'. His glory fills
'the whole earth'. The God Isaiah encounters is awesome in splendour and
perfect in holiness. He is a God who both reveals and hides himself. Isaiah
sees and hears the Lord, yet the Lord's appearance is carefully covered.
Revelation is very much on God's terms. Neither is Isaiah granted this
privileged vision as a spectacular spiritual experience *per se*. It has distinctly
sobering implications both for the prophet and for the whole people of
God. The message with which Isaiah's cleansed lips are entrusted is a hard
one. It is to do with radical judgment (6.9-13). God, it seems, cares
passionately enough about the condition of his people to do something
about it. Holy though he be, he is not, after all, a separatist God. Even in
the context of heaven, it would appear that God does not dwell in isolation.
Quite apart from the strange seraphim, there is the tantalizing use of the
first person plural in verse 8. Is it merely rhetorical, emphasizing God's
majesty? Does it relate to some kind of heavenly council (cf 1 Kings 22.19;
Job 1.6)? Or is it one of those 'hints and guesses' that prompt us to ask
deeper questions of the divine Being (cf Genesis 1.26)?

The passage from Ephesians takes us further into both mystery and
relationship. The God portrayed here is purposeful and positive, actively

working out 'his will and pleasure' in respect of all creation. Yet the divine work is not easy to fathom, a fact underlined by the use of the word 'mystery' in verse 9 (obscured in the NEB translation). Its character and direction are nonetheless disclosed to those who have been set free by the saving work of Christ. It is that experience of salvation which points to the heart of the matter. Such experience awakens the perceptive faculties to God's determined and costly longing: to sum up all things in Christ. And Christ, declares this Epistle, was in relationship with God as Father from before the foundation of the world. Knowing this is a fruit of faith, not a work of reason. It is a truth to be explored, not least in the context of worship. It is a truth in which the Holy Spirit is closely involved.

As John's Gospel so powerfully insists, divine truth is personal. It is essentially to do with relationship. It calls for responsive trust, for the risk of intimate knowing. Father, Son and Spirit of truth may be baffling in terms of doctrinal arrangement, but the real mystery is encountered in giving oneself over to a God whose interaction of love bursts all boundaries. To borrow George Herbert's phrase about prayer, in coming humbly to this God, we may discover in the depths 'something understood'.

*God of mystery,*
*draw us nearer to you.*
*God of relationship,*
*draw us nearer to each other.*
*God in Trinity,*
*draw us into deeper understanding*
*through your gift of faith*
*and the outpouring of your love.*

# Pentecost 2

## Collect

Almighty and everlasting God,
by whose Spirit the whole body of the Church is governed and sanctified:
hear our prayer which we offer for all your faithful people;
that each in his vocation and ministry
may serve you in holiness and truth
to the glory of your name;
through our Lord and Saviour Jesus Christ.

## *Psalms 95.1-7; 135.1-6*

## Old Testament *2 Samuel 7.4-16 NEB*

The word of the Lord came to Nathan: 'Go and say to David my servant, "This is the word of the Lord: Are you the man to build me a house to dwell in? Down to this day I have never dwelt in a house since I brought Israel up from Egypt; I made my journey in a tent and a tabernacle. Wherever I journeyed with Israel, did I ever ask any of the judges whom I appointed shepherds of my people Israel why they had not built me a house of cedar?" Then say this to my servant David: "This is the word of the Lord of Hosts: I took you from the pastures, and from following the sheep, to be a prince over my people Israel. I have been with you wherever you have gone, and have destroyed all the enemies in your path. I will make you a great name among the great ones of the earth. I will assign a place for my people Israel; there I will plant them, and they shall dwell in their own land. They shall be disturbed no more, never again shall wicked men oppress them as they did in the past, ever since the time when I appointed judges over Israel my people; and I will give you peace from all your enemies. The Lord has told you that he would build up your royal house. When your life ends and you rest with your forefathers, I will set up one of your family, one of your own children, to succeed you and I will establish his kingdom. It is he who shall build a house in honour of my name, and I will establish his royal throne for ever. I will be his father, and he shall be my son. When he does wrong, I will punish him as any father might, and not spare the rod. My love will never be withdrawn from him as I withdrew it from Saul, whom I removed from your path. Your family shall be established and your kingdom shall stand for all time in my sight, and your throne shall be established for ever."'

## New Testament *Acts 2.37-end NEB*

When the crowd heard this they were cut to the heart, and said to Peter and the apostles, 'Friends, what are we to do?' 'Repent,' said Peter, 'repent and be baptized, every one of you, in the name of Jesus the Messiah for the forgiveness of your sins; and you will receive the gift of the Holy Spirit. For the promise is to you, and to your children, and to all who are far away, everyone whom the Lord our God may call.'

In these and many other words he pressed his case and pleaded with them: 'Save yourselves', he said, 'from this crooked age.' Then those who accepted his word were baptized, and some three thousand were added to their number that day.

They met constantly to hear the apostles teach, and to share the common life, to break bread, and to pray. A sense of awe was everywhere, and many marvels and signs were brought about through the apostles. All whose faith had drawn them together held everything in common; they would sell their property and possessions and make a general distribution as the need of each required. With one mind they kept up their daily attendance at the temple, and, breaking bread in private houses, shared their meals with unaffected joy, as they praised God and enjoyed the favour of the whole people. And day by day the Lord added to their number those whom he was saving.

## Gospel *Luke 14.15-24 NEB*

One of the company said to Jesus, 'Happy the man who shall sit at the feast in the kingdom of God!' Jesus answered, 'A man was giving a big dinner party and had sent out many invitations. At dinner-time he sent his servant with a message for his guests, "Please come, everything is now ready." They began one and all to excuse themselves. The first said, "I have bought a piece of land, and I must go and look over it; please accept my apologies." The second said, "I have bought five yoke of oxen, and I am on my way to try them out; please accept my apologies." The next said, "I have just got married and for that reason I cannot come." When the servant came back he reported this to his master. The master of the house was angry and said to him, "Go out quickly into the streets and alleys of the town, and bring me in the poor, the crippled, the blind, and the lame." The servant said, "Sir, your orders have been carried out and there is still room." The master replied, "Go out on to the highways and along the hedgerows and make them come in; I want my house to be full. I tell you that not one of those who were invited shall taste my banquet." '

# Responding to God appropriately

*I know that the Lord is great,*
*and that our Lord is above all gods.*
*(Ps 135.5)*

What are we to do about God? What does God want of us? In their different ways, all Sunday's readings face us with these searching questions. They also challenge us to respond.

Aware of the great contrast between his own lavish 'house', a royal palace, and the tent that housed the ark of the Lord, David had wanted to build something more fitting for God. Nathan had effectively given him permission, because it seemed that God was with David in all things (2 Samuel 7.1-3). But 'that night' the true substance of God's word for David comes to Nathan. Even God's prophet has to have his assumptions challenged. It is at this point that the extract from 2 Samuel begins. David is presuming too much. Certainly God has been with the king, and God will continue to look after his people Israel, blessing David's family as the royal house. But David must not assume that because he has been blessed thus far he therefore knows God's mind in all things. For God's good reasons, it is David's son who will have the task of building a house for God's name. No kind of spiritual privilege or status dispenses with the imperative to listen honestly for God's unexpected word. Nor does it excuse from the duty of obedient response.

Those deeply affected by Peter's Pentecost outpouring make no assumptions. The overwhelming nature of their experience impels them to search for an appropriate response. 'What are we to do?' is a cry that comes from the heart. The answering challenge demands a radical change in outlook and lifestyle, one which will surely test the reality of their commitment. Yet for these converts, the way of sacrifice proves to be the way of joy. In giving and sharing, learning and worshipping, they discover and proclaim the God who is good news indeed.

The only sacrifice required of the prospective guests in the Gospel parable is to take the trouble to turn up at a dinner-party. Their excuses are not entirely convincing. Who would invest in land without first checking it out? Hospitality spurned (and therefore in the culture of the time profoundly insulted), the host sets about filling his house with the disadvantaged and marginalized; with those undesirables popularly considered as being on the edge of God's mercy; with those whose only responsive repayment could be their sheer enjoyment of the feast. The context of this parable (14.1-14) points up its shocking power. Respectable religious leaders, the guardians of the things of God, are so blinded by convention and status that they fail even to recognize God's gracious invitation when it comes. How tragic that commitment to preconceived notions can block out the liberating joy of God.

*God of challenge,*
*may we listen for your word,*
*respond to your demands,*
*and refuse the temptation*
*to put our wishes before yours.*

# Pentecost 3

## Collect

Lord God our Father,
through our Saviour Jesus Christ
you have assured mankind of eternal life
and in baptism have made us one with him.
Deliver us from the death of sin
and raise us to new life in your love,
in the fellowship of the Holy Spirit,
by the grace of our Lord Jesus Christ.

## *Psalms 44.1-9; 150*

## Old Testament *Deuteronomy 8.11-end NEB*

Take care not to forget the Lord your God and do not fail to keep his
commandments, laws and statutes which I give you on this day. When you
have plenty to eat and live in fine houses of your own building, when your
herds and flocks increase, and your silver and gold and all your possessions
increase too, do not become proud and forget the Lord your God who
brought you out of Egypt, out of the land of slavery; he led you through the
vast and terrible wilderness infested with poisonous snakes and scorpions, a
thirsty, waterless land, where he caused water to flow from the hard rock; he
fed you in the wilderness on manna which your fathers did not know, to
humble you and test you, and in the end to make you prosper. Nor must you
say to yourselves, 'My own strength and energy have gained me this wealth',
but remember the Lord your God; it is he that gives you strength to become
prosperous, so fulfilling the covenant guaranteed by oath with your
forefathers, as he is doing now.

If you forget the Lord your God and adhere to other gods, worshipping
them and bowing down to them, I give you a solemn warning this day that
you will certainly be destroyed. You will be destroyed because of your
disobedience to the Lord your God, as surely as were the nations whom the
Lord destroyed at your coming.

## New Testament *Acts 4.8-12 NEB*

Peter, filled with the Holy Spirit, said, 'Rulers of the people and elders, if the
question put to us today is about help given to a sick man, and we are asked
by what means he was cured, here is the answer, for all of you and for all the
people of Israel: it was by the name of Jesus Christ of Nazareth, whom you
crucified, whom God raised from the dead; it is by his name that this man

stands here before you fit and well. This Jesus is the stone rejected by the builders which has become the keystone—and you are the builders. There is no salvation in anyone else at all, for there is no other name under heaven granted to men, by which we may receive salvation.'

## Gospel *Luke 8.41-end NEB*

A man appeared—Jairus was his name and he was president of the synagogue. Throwing himself down at Jesus' feet he begged him to come to his house, because he had an only daughter, about twelve years old, who was dying. And while Jesus was on his way he could hardly breathe for the crowds.

Among them was a woman who had suffered from haemorrhages for twelve years; and nobody had been able to cure her. She came up from behind and touched the edge of his cloak, and at once her haemorrhage stopped. Jesus said, 'Who was it that touched me?' All disclaimed it, and Peter and his companions said, 'Master, the crowds are hemming you in and pressing upon you!' But Jesus said, 'Someone did touch me, for I felt that power had gone out from me.' Then the woman, seeing that she was detected, came trembling and fell at his feet. Before all the people she explained why she had touched him and how she had been instantly cured. He said to her, 'My daughter, your faith has cured you. Go in peace.'

While he was still speaking, a man came from the president's house with the message, 'Your daughter is dead; trouble the Rabbi no further.' But Jesus heard, and interposed. 'Do not be afraid,' he said; 'only show faith and she will be well again.' On arrival at the house he allowed no one to go in with him except Peter, John, and James, and the child's father and mother. And all were weeping and lamenting for her. He said, 'Weep no more; she is not dead: she is asleep'; and they only laughed at him, well knowing that she was dead. But Jesus took hold of her hand and called her: 'Get up, my child.' Her spirit returned, she stood up immediately, and he told them to give her something to eat. Her parents were astounded; but he forbade them to tell anyone what had happened.

# The demands and the risks of love

*Praise him for his mighty acts,*
*praise him according to his abundant goodness. (Ps 150.2)*

God's love is such that it allows the possibility of rejection. Past experience of that love can readily be forgotten in perceived self-sufficiency. Success, fine living, prosperity—all these factors can be taken as signs of God's blessing, leading to thanksgiving and responsible stewardship. They can also be taken as signs of human achievement. God can easily be pushed out of the picture. This is the sense of the warning given in Sunday's reading from Deuteronomy. There the emphasis is on the covenant relationship that exists between God and the people of Israel. A covenant carries with it responsibilities as well as privileges. God takes his responsibilities very seriously. If God's people fail to do likewise, they will experience the awful consequences of cutting themselves off from God's love and empowering. The decision is theirs.

The richness of God's blessing is enfleshed in Jesus. Here, still, acceptance is invited rather than forced. Refusal is a genuine option, as the extract from Acts makes clear. It begins as Peter and John are under arrest for proclaiming in Jesus the resurrection from the dead. This proclamation had been reinforced in action when many in the temple had witnessed the healing of a lame beggar. Peter is answering the question, 'By what power or by what name did you do this?' He confirms that the power lies in the 'name', that is the person of Jesus. Jesus is God's key to saving health. Those who have rejected Jesus (including the rulers and elders to whom Peter is responding) have in fact rejected God.

Though he is a ruler of the synagogue, Jairus turns to Jesus in the desperation of his need. His only daughter is dying. In extremity he abandons his dignity and throws himself at the feet of an unauthorized teacher. Love breaks down all barriers. And love wins through, despite the mocking unbelief of those mourning the child's death. The anguished faith of Jairus issues in blessing. So also for the woman with the issue of blood. Her long years of illness, compounded by the ostracizing uncleanness it entailed, come to their end in an act of great courage. By touching this man, she risks his wrath and further rejection. Yet what results is not just cure but healing acceptance and affirmation of worth. How deeply the address, 'My daughter', must have registered.

How wholesome and transforming is the love of God. And how much it demands of him. To reject it is both our loss and his.

*God of compassion,*
*you show your power in healing.*
*Give us courage to come to you,*
*for ourselves and for others.*

# Pentecost 4

## Collect

Almighty God,
you have broken the tyranny of sin
and have sent the Spirit of your Son into our hearts
whereby we call you Father.
Give us grace to dedicate our freedom to your service,
that all mankind may be brought to the glorious liberty of the sons of God;
through Jesus Christ our Lord.

## *Psalms 63.1-9; 67*

## Old Testament *Isaiah 63.7-14 RSV*

I will recount the steadfast love of the Lord,
the praises of the Lord,
according to all that the Lord has granted us,
and the great goodness to the house of Israel
which he has granted them according to his mercy,
according to the abundance of his steadfast love.
For he said, Surely they are my people,
sons who will not deal falsely;
and he became their Saviour.
In all their affliction he was afflicted,
and the angel of his presence saved them;
in his love and in his pity he redeemed them;
he lifted them up and carried them all the days of old.

But they rebelled
and grieved his holy Spirit;
therefore he turned to be their enemy,
and himself fought against them.
Then he remembered the days of old,
of Moses his servant.
Where is he who brought up out of the sea
the shepherds of his flock?
Where is he who put in the midst of them
his holy Spirit,
who caused his glorious arm
to go at the right hand of Moses,
who divided the waters before them

to make for himself an everlasting name,
who led them through the depths?
Like a horse in the desert,
they did not stumble.
Like cattle that go down into the valley,
the Spirit of the Lord gave them rest.
So you lead your people,
to make for yourself a glorious name.

## New Testament *Acts 8.26-38 JB*

The angel of the Lord spoke to Philip saying, 'Be ready to set out at noon along the road that goes from Jerusalem down to Gaza, the desert road.' So he set off on his journey. Now it happened than Ethiopian had been on pilgrimage to Jerusalem; he was a eunuch and an officer at the court of the kandake, or queen, of Ethiopia, and was in fact her chief treasurer. He was now on his way home; and as he sat in his chariot he was reading the prophet Isaiah. The Spirit said to Philip, 'Go up and meet that chariot.' When Philip ran up, he heard him reading Isaiah the prophet and asked, 'Do you understand what you are reading?' 'How can I', he replied, 'unless I have someone to guide me?' So he invited Philip to get in and sit by his side. Now the passage of scripture he was reading was this:
'Like a sheep that is led to the slaughter-house,
like a lamb that is dumb in front of its shearers,
like these he never opens his mouth.
He has been humiliated and has no one to defend him.
Who will ever talk about his descendants,
since his life on earth has been cut short!'
    The eunuch turned to Philip and said, 'Tell me, is the prophet referring to himself or someone else?' Starting, therefore, with this text of scripture Philip proceeded to explain the Good News of Jesus to him.
    Further along the road they came to some water, and the eunuch said, 'Look, there is some water here; is there anything to stop me being baptized?' He ordered the chariot to stop, then Philip and the eunuch both went down into the water and Philip baptized him.

## Gospel *Luke 15.1-10 RSV*

Now the tax collectors and sinners were all drawing near to hear Jesus. And the Pharisees and the scribes murmured, saying, 'This man receives sinners and eats with them.'
    So he told them this parable: 'What man of you, having a hundred sheep, if he has lost one of them, does not leave the ninety-nine in the wilderness, and go after the one which is lost, until he finds it? And when he has found it, he lays it on his shoulders, rejoicing. And when he comes home, he calls together

his friends and his neighbours, saying to them, "Rejoice with me, for I have found my sheep which was lost." Even so, I tell you, there will be more joy in heaven over one sinner who repents than over ninety-nine righteous persons who need no repentance.

'Or what woman, having ten silver coins, if she loses one coin, does not light a lamp and sweep the house and seek diligently until she finds it? And when she has found it, she calls together her friends and neighbours, saying, "Rejoice with me, for I have found the coin which I had lost." Even so, I tell you, there is joy before the angels of God over one sinner who repents.'

## *Reaching out to those on the edge*

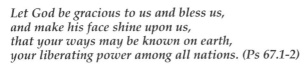

*Let God be gracious to us and bless us,*
*and make his face shine upon us,*
*that your ways may be known on earth,*
*your liberating power among all nations. (Ps 67.1-2)*

Mission involves being available and being sent—and sometimes being amazed at the results. Philip was clearly someone of discernment. He was prepared to listen to what God was saying to him. He was prepared to be where God wanted him—and at short notice. He was also a pastor and teacher. Not only did he know the good news; he knew how best to share it and explain it, beginning from where the Ethiopian was (in more than one sense). Philip was prepared to take the enquirer seriously and this led to an intensive preparation for something neither of them could have foreseen. After his baptism, the eunuch goes on his way rejoicing (Acts 8.39). Interestingly, we hear nothing of any post-baptismal follow-up. In God's economy, Philip's task has been completed.

Jesus' task included searching out God's lost ones. It got him into serious trouble with the religious powers-that-be, who took a very negative view of his mixing with the riff-raff of society. His responsive stories of the man searching for his missing sheep and the woman sweeping single-mindedly to find her lost coin say a good deal about what he counted as important. The wilderness does not sound immediately inviting. But there the bulk of the sheep were left—in confidence that for the time being they could look after themselves. It was the lost sheep which had to have priority. So it was with the lost coin. A full-scale search was instituted. Other things—and other people—had to wait.

If these are parables of the kingdom, then the God suggested by the man and woman is not exclusively concerned with those who already belong. Indeed, it seems that priority is given to the lapsed, the strayed, and, by extension, to those who don't yet realize that God loves them. God is prepared to go to great lengths to find them and bring them to where they belong. What joy when, being found, they turn to come home with the God who has sought them out.

It is all part of the outworking of the steadfast love of the Lord, recounted in the passage from Isaiah. In love, the Lord suffers whenever and wherever his people suffer. Even when he is grieved by their turning against him, he brings to mind what has gone before and the promises he made to his people. And remembering unlocks action as he tends to their needs. This God is passionately committed. This God will work against all the odds to bring the lost to the joy of heaven. This divine shepherd will thus become the sacrificial lamb.

*Caring God,*
*help us to look out for your lost ones,*
*to share your good news with them,*
*and to bring them to know you.*

# Pentecost 5

## Collect

Almighty God,
you show to those who are in error the light of your truth,
that they may return to the way of righteousness.
May we and all who have been admitted to the fellowship of Christ's religion
reject those things which are contrary to our profession
and follow all such things as are agreeable to the same;
through Jesus Christ our Lord.

## Psalms 119.57-64; 119.89-96

## Old Testament *Ruth 1.8-17, 22 NEB*

Naomi said to her two daughters-in-law, 'Go back, both of you, to your mothers' homes. May the Lord keep faith with you, as you have kept faith with the dead and with me; and may he grant each of you security in the home of a new husband.' She kissed them and they wept aloud. Then they said to her, 'We will return with you to your own people.' But Naomi said, 'Go back, my daughters. Why should you go with me? Am I likely to bear any more sons to be husbands for you? Go back, my daughters, go. I am too old to marry again. But even if I could say that I had hope of a child, if I were to marry this night and if I were to bear sons, would you then wait until they grew up? Would you then refrain from marrying? No, no, my daughters, my lot is more bitter than yours, because the Lord has been against me.' At this they wept again. Then Orpah kissed her mother-in-law and returned to her people, but Ruth clung to her.

'You see,' said Naomi, 'your sister-in-law has gone back to her people and her gods; go back with her.' 'Do not urge me to go back and desert you,' Ruth answered. 'Where you go, I will go, and where you stay, I will stay. Your people shall be my people, and your God my God. Where you die, I will die, and there I will be buried. I swear a solemn oath before the Lord your God: nothing but death shall divide us.'

This is how Naomi's daughter-in-law, Ruth the Moabitess, returned with her from the Moabite country. The barley harvest was beginning when they arrived in Bethlehem.

# New Testament *Acts 11.4-18 NEB*

Peter began by laying before those who were of Jewish birth the facts as they had happened.

'I was in the city of Joppa', he said, 'at prayer; and while in a trance I had a vision: a thing was coming down that looked like a great sheet of sail-cloth, slung by the four corners and lowered from the sky till it reached me. I looked intently to make out what was in it and I saw four-footed creatures of the earth, wild beasts, and things that crawl or fly. Then I heard a voice saying to me, "Up, Peter, kill and eat." But I said, "No, Lord, no: nothing profane or unclean has even entered my mouth." A voice from heaven answered a second time, "It is not for you to call profane what God counts clean." This happened three times, and then they were all drawn up again into the sky. At that moment three men, who had been sent to me from Caesarea, arrived at the house where I was staying; and the Spirit told me to go with them. My six companions here came with me and we went into the man's house. He told us how he had seen an angel standing in his house who said, "Send to Joppa for Simon also called Peter. He will speak words that will bring salvation to you and all our household." Hardly had I begun speaking, when the Holy Spirit came upon them, just as upon us at the beginning. Then I recalled what the Lord had said: "John baptized with water, but you will be baptized with the Holy Spirit." God gave them no less a gift than he gave us when we put our trust in the Lord Jesus Christ; then how could I possibly stand in God's way?'

When they heard this their doubts were silenced. They gave praise to God and said, 'This means that God has granted life-giving repentance to the Gentiles also.'

# Gospel *Luke 10.1-12 NEB*

The Lord appointed a further seventy-two and sent them on ahead in pairs to every town and place he was going to visit himself. He said to them: 'The crop is heavy, but labourers are scarce; you must therefore beg the owner to send labourers to harvest his crop. Be on your way. And look, I am sending you like lambs among wolves. Carry no purse or pack, and travel barefoot. Exchange no greetings on the road. When you go into a house, let your first words be, "Peace to this house." If there is a man of peace there, your peace will rest upon him; if not, it will return and rest upon you. Stay in that one house, sharing their food and drink; for the worker earns his pay. Do not move from house to house. When you come into a town and they make you welcome, eat the food provided for you; heal the sick there, and say, "The kingdom of God has come close to you." When you enter a town and they do not make you welcome, go out into its streets and say, "The very dust of your town that clings to our feet we wipe off to your shame. Only take note of this: the kingdom of God has come close." I tell you, it will be more bearable for Sodom on the great Day than for that town.'

# Harvesting God's chosen

*Your hands have made me and fashioned me,*
*O give me understanding that I may learn your commandments.*
*(Ps 119.73)*

The reading from Acts sets out the story of one of the great turning-points in the early Church. Peter had been criticized for baptizing people who were not Jews. But Peter had been convinced that he had done what was right. Much to his surprise, he had seen evidence of the Holy Spirit at work in the lives of Gentile people he had been urged to visit. He felt there was no course open to him but to baptize them. The whole incident had been a revelation to him. As it unfolded, his puzzlement as to the meaning of his earlier vision had vanished. The penny had dropped. Either God's rules about profanity had been misunderstood or God was doing a new thing and breaking his own rules.

Peter's graphic account of what had happened undoubtedly shocked his critics. But they were ready to believe that God was doing something startlingly different. And, refreshingly, their reaction was to praise God for it.

The people sent out by Jesus in missionary pairs were told to be prepared for anything, yet to take few physical resources. Those they were to visit would soon make it clear by their behaviour what their attitude to God's new message would be. A welcome was to be honoured by a sharing of the good news in word and deed. A lack of welcome spoke for itself. There was no point in continuing missionary activity in an environment that was hostile and inhospitable. In this case, the proclamation of the kingdom would become a proclamation of judgment.

Ruth was someone prepared for change. She faced the ignominy of being a young widow of a Jew who had married outside his race. A foreign woman like that was hardly likely to receive a warm welcome from those who kept to the Jewish Law. Little wonder that Naomi urges Ruth to go back home and seek a new husband from her own people. But Ruth persists. Her devotion to her mother-in-law has grown deeper than her family roots. As she clings to Naomi, Ruth makes an expression of commitment that is nothing short of an exemplary covenant promise—and this to an embittered woman who blames God for her troubles. Ruth the foreigner is not just ancestress of David; she is the minister of God to a hurting member of God's people. As Naomi returns home, Ruth goes with her to face an uncertain future. At this point, the storyteller makes a comment full of allusive anticipation. The two women arrive back in Bethlehem just as the barley harvest is beginning. That harvest is sign of a fruitful new beginning for Ruth, the faithful outsider.

*God of surprises,*
*help us minister wherever you call us,*
*to the unknown and the unlikely,*
*to hurting members of your people,*
*and to those whose lives you have already changed.*

# Pentecost 6

## Collect

Almighty God,
without you we are not able to please you.
Mercifully grant that your Holy Spirit
may in all things direct and rule our hearts;
through Jesus Christ our Lord.

## Psalms 112; 1

## Old Testament *Micah 6.1-8 RSV*

Hear what the Lord says;
Arise, plead your case before the mountains,
and let the hills hear your voice.
Hear, you mountains, the controversy of the Lord,
and you enduring foundations of the earth;
for the Lord has a controversy with his people,
and he will contend with Israel.
    'O my people, what have I done to you?
In what have I wearied you? Answer me!
For I brought you up from the land of Egypt,
and redeemed you from the house of bondage;
and I sent before you Moses, Aaron, and Miriam.
O my people remember what Balak king of Moab devised,
and what Balaam the son of Beor answered him,
and what happened from Shittim to Gilgal,
that you may know the saving acts of the Lord.'
    'With what shall I come before the Lord,
and bow myself before God on high?
Shall I come before him with burnt offerings,
with calves a year old?
Will the Lord be pleased with thousands of rams,
with ten thousands of rivers of oil?
Shall I give my first-born for my transgression,
the fruit of my body for the sin of my soul?
He has showed you, O man, what is good;
and what does the Lord require of you
but to do justice, and to love kindness,
and to walk humbly with your God?'

# New Testament *Ephesians 4.17-end RSV*

Now this I affirm and testify in the Lord, that you must no longer live as the Gentiles do, in the futility of their minds; they are darkened in their understanding, alienated from the life of God because of the ignorance that is in them, due to their hardness of heart; they have become callous and have given themselves up to licentiousness, greedy to practise every kind of uncleanness. You did not so learn Christ!—assuming that you have heard about him and were taught in him, as the truth is in Jesus. Put off your old nature which belongs to your former manner of life and is corrupt through deceitful lusts, and be renewed in the spirit of your minds, and put on the new nature, created after the likeness of God in true righteousness and holiness.

Therefore, putting away falsehood, let every one speak the truth with his neighbour, for we are members one of another. Be angry but do not sin; do not let the sun go down on your anger, and give no opportunity to the devil. Let the thief no longer steal, but rather let him labour, doing honest work with his hands, so that he may be able to give to those in need. Let no evil talk come out of your mouths, but only such as is good for edifying, as fits the occasion, that it may impart grace to those who hear. And do not grieve the Holy Spirit of God, in whom you were sealed for the day of redemption. Let all bitterness and wrath and anger and clamour and slander be put away from you, with all malice, and be kind to one another, tenderhearted, forgiving one another, as God in Christ forgave you.

# Gospel *Mark 10.46-end NEB*

Jesus and his disciples came to Jericho; and as he was leaving the town, with his disciples and a large crowd, Bartimaeus son of Timaeus, a blind beggar, was seated at the roadside. Hearing that it was Jesus of Nazareth, he began to shout, 'Son of David, Jesus, have pity on me!' Many of the people told him to hold his tongue; but he shouted all the more, 'Son of David, have pity on me.' Jesus stopped and said, 'Call him'; so they called the blind man and said, 'Take heart; stand up; he is calling you.' At that he threw off his cloak, sprang up, and came to Jesus. Jesus said to him, 'What do you want me to do for you?' 'Master,' the blind man answered, 'I want my sight back.' Jesus said to him, 'Go; your faith has cured you.' And at once he recovered his sight and followed him on the road.

# New outlook and new insight

*Light arises in darkness for the upright,
gracious and merciful is the righteous man. (Ps 112.4)*

In differing ways, the readings set for Sunday point to the need for and the way to acquiring a different outlook on life. As he does elsewhere, Paul links a change in inward attitude with a change in outside appearance. He uses the illustration of a change of clothing as a sign of that profound change in outlook that comes to those who have moved from lack of understanding of the true God (characteristic, for instance, of the Gentile way of life) to being in a position of knowing the truth in Christ. Those who have gone through such a change are exhorted to ensure that it is carried through in their everyday behaviour. There is now no place for anger, dishonesty and lies. Resentment and all that flows from it is to be overcome by adopting and holding on to the kind of forgiving attitude that they have learned from Christ; the open, forgiving behaviour that God has in fact shown towards them. What may have seemed natural in the past is no longer appropriate, because it belongs to a past and partial understanding. Now God has called them to new life and new ways.

Some 800 years earlier, God's longing for a change of outlook had been discerned by the prophet Micah. In this case, it is not so much a comparison between those who do not know God and those who claim to know God. Rather, it is an indictment of those who fail to follow through belief with action. Simply going through what is ritually appropriate is a far from adequate response to the God who has called them and redeemed them. Empty ritual counts for nothing, compared with right attitude. Even the possibility of being called on to follow pagan habits of child sacrifice, costly as that would be in personal terms, is far from fulfilling God's requirements. God calls for something radically new: behaving in a God-like way. God calls on people to be dispensers of justice, and to be related to each other in that quality of loving-kindness that marks the covenant relationship between God and his people. God calls for his people to live in humble relationship with him as they travel with their God, rather than to indulge in superficial and ostentatious sacrifice. Faith in action goes much deeper than that.

For Bartimaeus, having a new outlook on life was no mere metaphor. The physical healing he received was the gateway to new life in abundance. As a blind beggar, Bartimaeus would not have been welcome at temple worship. He would hardly have been noticed by people on the streets. Yet his persistent crying out wins the attention of Jesus. When Jesus asks what he can do for Bartimaeus, there is no hesitation. And with sight restored, Bartimaeus follows Jesus on the way.

*God of insight,*
*help us to discern your will for us,*
*that having a new outlook on life*
*we may see you more clearly*
*and follow you more closely.*

# Pentecost 7

## Collect

Lord you have taught us
that all our doings without love are nothing worth.
Send your Holy Spirit
and pour into our hearts that most excellent gift of love,
the true bond of peace and of all virtues,
without which whoever lives is counted dead before you.
Grant this for the sake of your only Son,
Jesus Christ our Lord.

## *Psalms 62; 103.8-18*

## Old Testament *Deuteronomy 10.12—11.1 NEB*

What, O Israel, does the Lord your God ask of you? Only to fear the Lord
your God, to conform to all his ways, to love him and to serve him with all
your heart and soul. This you will do by keeping the commandments of the
Lord and his statutes which I give you this day for your good. To the Lord
your God belong heaven itself, the highest heaven, the earth and everything
in it; yet the Lord cared for your forefathers in his love for them and chose
their descendants after them. Out of all nations you were his chosen people as
you are this day. So now you must circumscribe the foreskin of your hearts
and not be stubborn any more, for the Lord your God is God of gods and
Lord of lords, the great, mighty, and terrible God. He is no respecter of
persons and is not to be bribed; he secures justice for widows and orphans,
and loves the alien who lives among you, giving him food and clothing. You
too must love the alien, for you once lived as aliens in Egypt. You must fear
the Lord your God, serve him, hold fast to him and take your oaths in his
name. He is your praise, your God who has done for you these great and
terrible things which you have seen with your own eyes. When your
forefathers went down into Egypt they were only seventy strong, but now the
Lord your God has made you countless as the stars in the sky.

You shall love the Lord your God and keep for all time the charge he laid
upon you, the statutes, the laws, and the commandments.

# New Testament *Romans 8.1-11 JB*

The reason why those who are in Christ Jesus are not condemned, is that the law of the spirit of life in Christ Jesus has set you free from the law of sin and death. God has done what the Law, because of our unspiritual nature, was unable to do. God dealt with sin by sending his own Son in a body as physical as any sinful body, and in that body God condemned sin. He did this in order that the Law's just demands might be satisfied in us, who behave not as our unspiritual nature but as the spirit dictates.

The unspiritual are interested only in what is unspiritual, but the spiritual are interested in spritual things. It is death to limit oneself to what it unspiritual; life and peace can only come with concern for the spiritual. That is because to limit oneself to what is unspiritual is to be at enmity with God: such a limitation never could and never does submit to God's law. People who are interested only in unspiritual things can never be pleasing to God. Your interests, however, are not in the unspiritual, but in the spiritual, since the Spirit of God has made his home in you. In fact, unless you possessed the Spirit of Christ you would not belong to him. Though your body may be dead it is because of sin, but if Christ is in you then your spirit is life itself because you have been justified; and if the Spirit of him who raised Jesus from the dead is living in you, then he who raised Jesus from the dead will give life to your own mortal bodies through his Spirit living in you.

# Gospel *Mark 12.28-34 NEB*

One of the lawyers, who had been listening to the discussions and had noted how well Jesus answered, came forward and asked him, 'Which commandment is first of all?' Jesus answered, 'The first is, "Hear, O Israel: the Lord our God is the only Lord; love the Lord your God with all your heart, with all your soul, with all your mind, and with all your strength." The second is this: "Love your neighbour as yourself." There is no other commandment greater than these.' The lawyer said to him, 'Well said, Master. You are right in saying that God is one and beside him there is no other. And to love him with all your heart, all your understanding, and all your strength, and to love your neighbour as yourself—that is far more than any burnt offerings or sacrifices.' When Jesus saw how sensibly he answered, he said to him, 'You are not far from the kingdom of God.'

# The demands of passionate love

*The Lord is full of compassion and mercy,*
*slow to anger and of great goodness. (Ps 103.8)*

What kind of God asks for our absolute allegiance? If we consent, what will such total commitment mean? Will it be the ending or the making of us?

Sunday's readings all point in the direction of a relationship which offers enormous potential for creative fulfilment. It is not a relationship of equals, yet one in which God leads the way in self-giving. It works against selfish individualism, whilst affirming the profound worth of the individual. It enters into covenant agreement not to enslave but to provide the best context for liberation. And God's freedom enables people to find their true selves, in such a way that the obligation to look to the good of others becomes not duty but joy. Above all, it is a relationship fired by the passion of God's love.

Divine love does make demands, as the passage from Deuteronomy stresses. The people of God must be totally faithful to their Lord, as he is to them. Yet the commandments they must keep in the process should not be burdensome, for they are designed for the people's good. God is on their side; he is actively for them. 'Great, mighty and terrible' he might be, and the owner of all that is, but he is at the same time the God who cares for his own—and in a down-to-earth way. This God is beyond corruption and favouritism (except in his fierce defence of the disadvantaged). Though for his own purposes he may have chosen and blessed a particular grouping of people, that in no way justifies them in adopting an attitude of arrogant exclusivism. They are to love the outsider in the same way that God does. Such love involves not condescension but committed service.

The service that God has rendered the whole of humanity is highlighted in the opening of the great eighth chapter of the Epistle to the Romans. In his Son, Jesus Christ, God has experienced at first hand the reality of the human situation, infected as it is by the mysterious power of sin. The language of the Jerusalem Bible (selected for the ASB) perhaps obscures the full impact of this. Paul uses the term 'flesh', rather than 'unspiritual' or 'physical'. It is a word which graphically suggests the frailty and mortality of the human condition, and its susceptibility to that which works against the interests of love. In order, as Robert Llewelyn put it, 'to love the hell out of us', God took that hell into himself, felt the full force of it—and shattered its power. Those who give themselves to this God need have no fear of condemnation. Rather, they will enjoy the life-giving infusion of God's Spirit. That will motivate and empower them to be for God as God is for them.

In the days of his flesh, Jesus met an expert in the Jewish Law. It is one of the few occasions when Jesus gives a direct answer to a direct question. The commandment which has primacy is that which requires the people of God (and every member thereof) to love God with all that they are. But Jesus also gives the lawyer more than he asked for. The imperative consequent upon the loving of God is the loving of one's neighbour and oneself. To his great credit—and the approval of Jesus—the questioner perceives the essential truth of the response. God's way of life is not about sacrificial ritual. It is about sacrificial love.

*God of love,*
*help us to love the unlovable outsider*
*and the unlikely neighbour*
*with the passion of that love*
*from which we can never be separated.*

# Pentecost 8

## Collect

Almighty God,
who sent your Holy Spirit to be the life and light of your Church:
open our hearts to the riches of his grace,
that we may bring forth the fruit of the Spirit
in love and joy and peace;
through Jesus Christ our Lord.

## Psalms 25.1-10; 27.1-8

## Old Testament *Ezekiel 37.1-14 JB*

The hand of the Lord was laid on me, and he carried me away by the spirit of the Lord and set me down in the middle of a valley, a valley full of bones. He made me walk up and down among them. There were vast quantities of these bones on the ground the whole length of the valley; and they were quite dried up. He said to me, 'Son of man, can these bones live?' I said, 'You know, Lord God.' He said, 'Prophesy over these bones. Say, "Dry bones, hear the word of the Lord. The Lord God says this to these bones: I am now going to make breath enter you, and you will live. I shall put sinews on you, I shall make flesh grow on you, I shall cover you with skin and give you breath, and you will live; and you will learn that I am the Lord."' I prophesied as I had been ordered. While I was prophesying, there as a noise, a sound of clattering; and the bones joined together. I looked, and saw hat they were covered with sinews; flesh was growing on them and skin was covering them, but there was no breath in them. He said to me, 'Prophesy to the breath; prophesy, son of man. Say to the breath, "The Lord God says this: Come from the four winds, breath; breathe on these dead; let them live!"' I prophesied as he had ordered me, and the breath entered them; they came to life again and stood up on their feet, a great, an immense army.

Then he said, 'Son of man, these bones are the whole House of Israel. They keep saying, "Our bones are dried up, our hope has gone; we are as good as dead." So prophesy. Say to them, "The Lord God says this: I am now going to open your graves; I mean to raise you from your graves, my people, and lead you back to the soil of Israel. And you will know that I am the Lord, when I open your graves and raise you from your graves, my people. And I shall put my spirit in you, and you will live, and I shall resettle you on your own soil; and you will know that I, the Lord, have said and done this—it is the Lord God who speaks."'

# New Testament *1 Corinthians 12.4-13 NEB*

There are varieties of gifts, but the same Spirit. There are varieties of service, but the same Lord. There are many forms of work, but all of them, in all men, are the work of the same God. In each of us the Spirit is manifested in one particular way, for some useful purpose. One man, through the Spirit, has the gift of wise speech, while another, by the power of the same Spirit, can put the deepest knowledge into words. Another, by the same Spirit, is granted faith; another by the one Spirit, gifts of healing, and another miraculous powers; another has the gift of prophecy, and another ability to distinguish true spirits from false; yet another has the gift of ecstatic utterance of different kinds, and another the ability to interpret it. But all these gifts are the work of one and the same Spirit, distributing them separately to each individual at will.

For Christ is like a single body with its many limbs and organs, which, many as they are, together make up one body. For indeed we were all brought into one body by baptism, in the one Spirit, whether we are Jews or Greeks, whether slaves or free men, and that one Holy Spirit was poured out for all of us to drink.

## Gospel *Luke 6.27-38 NEB*

Jesus said: 'To you who hear me I say: Love your enemies; do good to those who hate you; bless those who curse you; pray for those who treat you spitefully. When a man hits you on the cheek, offer him the other cheek too; when a man takes your coat, let him have your shirt as well. Give to everyone who asks you; when a man takes what is yours, do not demand it back. Treat others as you would like them to treat you.

'If you love only those who love you, what credit is that to you? Even sinners love those who love them. Again, if you do good only to those who do good to you, what credit is that to you? Even sinners do as much. And if you lend only where you expect to be repaid, what credit is that to you? Even sinners lend to each other to be repaid in full. But you must love your enemies and do good; and lend without expecting any return; and you will have a rich reward: you will be sons of the Most High, because he himself is kind to the ungrateful and wicked. Be compassionate as your Father is compassionate.

'Pass no judgement, and you will not be judged; do not condemn, and you will not be condemned; acquit, and you will be acquitted; give, and gifts will be given to you. Good measure, pressed down, shaken together, and running over, will be poured into your lap; for whatever measure you deal out to others will be dealt to you in return.'

# The transforming Spirit of God

*The Lord is my light and my salvation,*
*whom then shall I fear?*
*The Lord is the strength of my life,*
*of whom shall I be afraid? (Ps 27.1)*

The Spirit of God brings vitality, hope, variety, community—and radical challenge. Such is the telling testimony of Sunday's readings.

To say the least, the prophet Ezekiel had some interesting visionary experiences. In one of his most memorable, the valley of dry bones, he encounters a God urgent with the promise of new creation for a despairing and exiled people. Out of their deadness, God will make them afresh, will breathe divine life into them, will give them a new genesis, a new beginning. They will stand up with confidence, ready for their journey home under the leadership of their God. Restored and energized, they will acknowledge the power of their Lord and the rightness of his claim to obedience. The breath of God's Spirit will bring transformation.

For the Corinthian Christians, the Spirit's transforming activity had proved intoxicating and not a little bewildering. Human divisiveness and pride had worked their pernicious work. And under the guise of the Spirit's spontaneity, unseemly disorder was undermining corporate worship (compare chapter 14). It may well be that in the whole section we know as chapters 12 to 14, Paul is addressing the specific issue of spiritual gifts because it has been raised with him as a matter for concern in a letter from the church at Corinth. In the Epistle as a whole, there are a number of matters dealt with which seem to be responsive in character and they are all introduced by the same phrase, 'Now concerning... ' (7.1, 25; 8.1; 12.1; 16.1, 12). Here Paul stresses the unifying character of God's Spirit. God's purpose is that all things (and all people) should work together for good. To that end, the divine economy is richly mixed. Diverse gifts are given not to enhance the status and lifestyle of the recipient but to ensure that the community of faith functions effectively and corporately realizes its potential. The life of the one Spirit is for all, regardless of identity or background. The gifts of the one Spirit are many and various, distributed to whomsoever God wills (cf Hebrews 2.4). So the one body of Christ is multi-faceted. But there is a life-blood which should flow unhindered through all the members—and that is incomparably described in chapter 13. It is love.

And therein lies the Spirit's challenge. It is set out baldly by the Lukan Jesus: 'Love your enemies'. Responding to the congenial in warm fellowship is one thing. Offering blessing for curse is quite another. But the children of the Most High must be like their Father; and that means a fundamental, motivating attitude of sacrificial generosity. Selective love will not do. Nor will judgmental self-righteousness. The overflowing good measure of God is free, yet costly. Only the re-creative life of the Spirit can enable us to be its purveyors as well as its beneficiaries.

*Life-giving Spirit,*
*breathe into the dead parts of our beings,*
*unite us in working together for good,*
*and help us to reach out to the uncongenial*
*with warmth and understanding.*

# Pentecost 9

## Collect

Almighty God,
you see that we have no power of ourselves to help ourselves.
Keep us both outwardly in our bodies and inwardly in our souls,
that we may be defended from all adversities
    which may happen to the body,
and from all evil thoughts which may assault and hurt the soul;
through Jesus Christ our Lord.

## Psalms 18.1-7; 18.32-38

## Old Testament *1 Samuel 17.37-50 NEB*

David said to Saul, 'The Lord who saved me from the lion and the bear will save me from this Philistine.' 'Go then,' said Saul; 'and the Lord will be with you.' He put his own tunic on David, placed a bronze helmet on his head and gave him a coat of mail to wear; he then fastened his sword on David over his tunic. But David hesitated, because he had not tried them, and said to Saul, 'I cannot go with these, because I have not tried them.' So he took them off. Then he picked up his sling, chose five smooth stones from the brook and put them in a shepherd's bag which served as his pouch. He walked out to meet the Philistine with his sling in his hand.

The Philistine came on towards David, with his shield-bearer marching ahead; and he looked David up and down and had nothing but contempt for this handsome lad with his ruddy cheeks and bright eyes. He said to David, 'Am I a dog that you come out against me with sticks?' And he swore at him in the name of his god. 'Come on,' he said, 'and I will give your flesh to the birds and the beasts.' David answered, 'You have come against me with sword and spear and dagger, but I have come against you in the name of the Lord of Hosts, the God of the army of Israel which you have defied. The Lord will put you into my power this day; I will kill you and cut your head off and leave your carcass and the carcasses of the Philistines to the birds and the wild beasts; all the world shall know that there is a God in Israel. All those who are gathered here shall see that the Lord saves neither by sword nor spear; the battle is the Lord's, and he will put you all into our power.'

When the Philistine began moving towards him again, David ran quickly to engage him. He put his hand into his bag, took out a stone, slung it, and struck the Philistine in the forehead. The stone sank into his forehead, and he fell flat on his face on the ground. So David proved the victor with his sling and stone; he struck Goliath down and gave him a mortal wound, although he had no sword.

## New Testament 2 *Corinthians 6.3-10 RSV*

In order that our service may not be brought into discredit, we avoid giving offence in anything. As God's servants, we try to recommend ourselves in all circumstances by our steadfast endurance: in distress, hardships, and dire straits; flogged, imprisoned, mobbed; overworked, sleepless, starving. We recommend ourselves by the innocence of our behaviour, our grasp of truth, our patience and kindliness; by gifts of the Holy Spirit, by sincere love, by declaring the truth, by the power of God. We wield the weapons of righteousness in right hand and left. Honour and dishonour, praise and blame, are alike our lot: we are the impostors who speak the truth, the unknown men whom all men know; dying we still live on; disciplined by suffering, we are not done to death; in our sorrows we have always cause for joy; poor ourselves, we bring wealth to many; penniless, we own the world.

## Gospel *Mark 9.14-29 NEB*

When Jesus, with Peter, James, and John came back to the disciples they saw a large crowd surrounding them and lawyers arguing with them. As soon as they saw Jesus the whole crowd were overcome with awe, and they ran forward to welcome him. He asked them, 'What is this argument about?' A man in the crowd spoke up: 'Master, I brought my son to you. He is posessed by a spirit which makes him speechless. Whenever it attacks him, it dashes him to the ground, and he foams at the mouth, grinds his teeth, and goes rigid. I asked your disciples to cast it out, but they failed.' Jesus answered: 'What an unbelieving and perverse generation! How long shall I be with you? How long must I endure you? Bring him to me.' So they brought the boy to him; and as soon as the spirit saw him it threw the boy into convulsions, and he fell on the ground and rolled about foaming at the mouth. Jesus asked his father, 'How long has he been like this?' 'From childhood,' he replied; 'often it has tried to make an end of him by throwing him into the fire or into water. But if it is at all possible for you, take pity on us and help us.' 'If it is possible!' said Jesus. 'Everything is possible to one who has faith.' 'I have faith,' cried the boy's father; 'help me where faith falls short.' Jesus saw then that the crowd was closing in upon them, so he rebuked the unclean spirit. 'Deaf and dumb spirit,' he said, 'I command you, come out of him and never go back!' After crying aloud and racking him fiercely, it came out; and the boy looked like a corpse; in fact, many said, 'He is dead.' But Jesus took his hand and raised him to his feet, and he stood up.

Then Jesus went indoors, and his disciples asked him privately, 'Why could not we cast it out?' He said, 'There is no means of casting out this sort but prayer.'

# Divine disarming

*It is God that girded me with strength,*
*that made my way perfect. (Ps 18.34)*

By the world's standards, God's armoury does not count for much. It is to be dismissed or derided. Yet its force for good is incalculable, and desperately needed in a world full of the destructive weapons of human devising. To the Church's shame, the soldiers of Christ have too often forgotten that truth.

Not so with Paul, intrepid champion of the gospel. He fought God's battles by remaining true to the claims of Christ in a whole range of trying and painful circumstances. Opposition, overwork and stress Paul knew in full measure. Yet his experience of God's good news was stronger than any negatives; and he was determined to share that good news, whatever the personal cost. His weaponry in the struggle consisted not in instruments of coercion but in a (quite literally) godly way of life. The qualities of character Paul identifies are all perfectly expressed in the God of Jesus Christ. For the power of God lies not in the imposition of will but in the exercise of a committed relationship of love. In a human context, the consequence of that is paradox. Like the incarnate God, God's servants will be both loved and hated, lauded and condemned. Their disclosure of truth will surely involve struggle; but the only sense in which it is armed is with divine love. Such love, strangely, has the power to disarm by the sheer intensity of its purity and vulnerability.

In the epic confrontation between David and Goliath, there is also paradox. It is the one who appears to be in the strongest position who is in fact most vulnerable. Pitted against a foolhardy and virtually defenceless youth, the Philistine looks forward (with some disappointment) to annihilating an unworthy opponent. He had reckoned without the involvement of 'the Lord of Hosts' who, in the cause of righteousness, persistently seems to choose the weak to confound the strong. David's confidence in this God proves well-founded (as indeed does his decision to act in a way that for him is tried and tested). Faith bears fruit in victory.

But faith in the saving power of God is no easy option, as many disciples of Jesus have discovered over the ages. Those concerned in the incident described in the Gospel reading are certainly no exception. Faced with a desperate plea for help, they are helpless. The reaction of Mark's Jesus is (as ever) both comfort and challenge. Fresh from his transfiguring experience on the mountain, he takes the situation in hand and effects a dramatic healing. Quite apart from his action, his very presence is awesome. And, as in other cases, he gives vent to feelings of frustration and concomitant rebuke. The people of God should have known God better. The disciples of

Jesus, above all, should have known that faith is about being in touch with a faithful God. It is about relationship; it is about prayer. The one who points the way is, typically, not a privileged insider but 'a man in the crowd'. He cries out in raw honesty, aware both of his own shortcomings and the extremity of his loved one's distress. His directness is the only weapon he needs.

*God of paradox,*
*whose power lies not in a will imposed*
*but in a love committed;*
*give us the confidence to be vulnerable,*
*that in your name we may disarm others.*

# Pentecost 10

## Collect

Father of mankind,
who gave your only-begotten Son
to take upon himself the form of a servant
and to be obedient even to death on a cross:
give us the same mind that was in Christ Jesus
that, sharing his humility,
we may come to be with him in his glory;
who is alive and reigns with you and the Holy Spirit,
one God, now and for ever.

## *Psalms 71.1-8; 73.23-end*

## Old Testament *1 Samuel 24.9-17 (or 1-17) NEB*

(When Saul returned from the pursuit of the Philistines, he learnt that David
was in the wilderness of En-gedi. So he took three thousand men picked from
the whole of Israel and went in search of David and his men to the east of the
Rocks of the Wild Goats. There beside the road were some sheepfolds, and
near by was a cave, at the far end of which David and his men were sitting
concealed. Saul came to the cave and went in to relieve himself. His men said
to David, 'The day has come: the Lord has put your enemy into your hands,
as he promised he would, and you may do what you please with him.' David
said to his men, 'God forbid that I should harm my master, the Lord's
anointed, or lift a finger against him; he is the Lord's anointed.' So David
reproved his men severely and would not let them attack Saul. He himself got
up stealthily and cut off a piece of Saul's cloak; but when he had cut it off, his
conscience smote him. Saul rose, left the cave and went on his way;
whereupon David also came out of the cave and called after Saul, 'My lord
the king!').

When Saul looked round, David prostrated himself in obeisance and said
to him, 'Why do you listen when they say that David is out to do you harm?
Today you can see for yourself that the Lord put you into my power in the
cave; I had a mind to kill you, but no, I spared your life and said, "I cannot lift
a finger against my master, for he the Lord's anointed." Look, my dear lord,
look at this piece of your cloak in my hand. I cut it off, but I did not kill you;
this will show you that I have no thought of violence or treachery against you,
and that I have done you no wrong; yet you are resolved to take my life. May
the Lord judge between us! but though he may take vengeance on you for my
sake, I will never lift my hand against you; "One wrong begets another", as

the old saying goes, yet I will never lift my hand against you. Who has the king of Israel come out against? What are you pursuing? A dead dog, a mere flea. The Lord will be judge and decide between us; let him look into my cause, he will plead for me and will acquit me.'

When David had finished speaking, Saul said, 'Is that you, David my son?', and he wept. Then he said, 'The right is on your side, not mine; you have treated me so well, I have treated you so badly.'

## New Testament *Galatians 6.1-10 NEB*

We must not be conceited, challenging one another to rivalry, jealous of one another. If a man should do something wrong, my brothers, on a sudden impulse, you who are endowed with the Spirit must set him right again very gently. Look to yourself, each one of you: you may be tempted too. Help one another to carry these heavy loads, and in this way you will fulfil the law of Christ.

For if a man imagines himself to be somebody, when he is nothing, he is deluding himself. Each man should examine his own conduct for himself; then he can measure his achievement by comparing himself with himself and not with anyone else. For everyone has his own proper burden to bear.

When anyone is under instruction in the faith, he should give his teacher a share of all good things he has.

Make no mistake about this: God is not to be fooled; a man reaps what he sows. If he sows seed in the field of his lower nature, he will reap from it a harvest of corruption, but if he sows in the field of the Spirit, the Spirit will bring him a harvest of eternal life. So let us never tire of doing good, for if we do not slacken our efforts we shall in due time reap our harvest. Therefore, as opportunity offers, let us work for the good of all, especially members of the household of the faith.

## Gospel *Luke 7.36-end JB*

One of the Pharisees invited Jesus to a meal. When he arrived at the Pharisee's house and took his place at table, a woman came in, who had a bad name in the town. She had heard he was dining with the Pharisee and had brought with her an alabaster jar of ointment. She waited behind him at his feet, weeping, and her tears fell on his feet, and she wiped them away with her hair; then she covered his feet with kisses and anointed them with the ointment.

When the Pharisee who had invited him saw this, he said to himself, 'If this man were a prophet, he would know who this woman is that is touching him and what a bad name she has.' Then Jesus took him up and said, 'Simon, I have something to say to you.' 'Speak, Master', was the reply. 'There was once a creditor who had two men in his debt; one owed him five hundred denarii, the other fifty. They were unable to pay, so he pardoned them both.

Which of them will love him more?' 'The one was pardoned more, I suppose', answered Simon. Jesus said, 'You are right.'

Then he turned to the woman. 'Simon,' he said, 'you see this woman? I came into your house, and you poured no water over my feet, but she has poured out her tears over my feet and wiped them away with her hair. You gave me no kiss, but she has been covering my feet with kisses ever since I came in. You did not anoint my head with oil, but she has anointed my feet with ointment. For this reason I tell you that her sins, her many sins, must have been forgiven her, or she would not have shown such great love. It is the man who is forgiven little who shows little love.' Then he said to her, 'Your sins are forgiven.' Those who were with him at table began to say to themselves, 'Who is this man, that he even forgives sins?' But he said to the woman, 'Your faith has saved you; go in peace.'

## Towards right relationships

*Nevertheless I am always with you,*
*for you hold me by my right hand. (Ps 73.23)*

The way we behave towards other people should reflect and express the character of God. That is a tall order. Our own woefully inadequate resources cannot attain to it. We need the transforming influence of the Spirit of God. Yet we also need to put effort into the task. Godly relationships have to be worked at.

That was certainly true for David. He 'had a mind to kill' Saul; to seize the opportunity of destroying one who sought to destroy him. The king, David's former patron and friend, now deranged with jealousy, was no longer the leader the people needed or wanted. It might have been a service to dispose of him, particularly as it seemed the Lord had put him into David's power. Yet David decided to break the vicious cycle of vengeance. He perceived that meeting evil with evil begets more evil. It is for the Lord to judge. And with the Lord there is mercy.

Within the Christian community, that same principle applies. So Paul urges the Galatians to eschew the poisonous attractions of pride, jealousy and a competitive spirit. Such attitudes are deadly enemies of the Church's well-being. They feed a judgmental self-righteousness which can only harm both recipient and perpetrator. Paul therefore bids the Galatian believers (and us) to recall an evident truth: No one is perfect. No one is immune from the pull of sin—not even the most committed of Christians. Our response to the failure of another is critical. Any attempt to bring the trespasser to repentance should be undertaken in the context of a keen awareness of our own need for forgiveness. It should also be done 'very gently' and only under the impetus of the Spirit of God. Indeed, it is the Spirit's motivation and resourcing which should permeate the whole of a believer's approach to life. Then that life will bear fruit in doing good—something far removed from the corrupting lure of condescending do-gooding. Self-awareness and mutual understanding born of openness to God should be at the heart of our behaviour and relationships.

There seems to have been a distinct lack of any such qualities in the Pharisee who invited Jesus to a meal. Whatever the reason for his invitation, it was not that Simon regarded Jesus as a valued guest. Jesus was not even offered the normal courtesies of hospitality. At this table, he was an object of curiosity and judgment. It is a woman of low reputation who shows up the real truth. The host and his companions are so enclosed in their preconceived notions of holiness that they fail to perceive the primacy of God's forgiving love. Such love calls forth an answering love which breaks down the barriers built by human fear and pride. It releases a heartfelt joy which exposes the very heart of God. Therein lies salvation.

*Christ, our true wisdom,*
*grant that whenever we have a mind to act*
*we may be so mindful of you,*
*that we shun what is hurtful*
*and hold to what is wholesome.*

# Pentecost 11

## Collect

Almighty Father,
whose Son Jesus Christ has taught us
that what we do for the least of our brethren we do also for him;
give us the will to be the servant of others as he was the servant of all,
who gave up his life and died for us,
but is alive and reigns with you and the Holy Spirit,
one God, now and for ever.

## Psalms 31.21-end; 40.1-7

## Old Testament *1 Chronicles 29.1-9 NEB*

King David said to the whole assembly, 'My son Solomon is the one chosen
by God, Solomon alone, a boy of tender years; and this is a great work, for it
is a palace not for man but for the Lord God. Now to the best of my strength I
have made ready for the house of my God gold for the gold work, silver for
the silver, bronze for the bronze, iron for the iron, and wood for the
woodwork, together with cornelian and other gems for setting, stones for
mosaic work, precious stones of every sort, and marble in plenty. Further,
because I delight in the house of my God, I give my own private store of gold
and silver for the house of my God—over and above all the store which I
have collected for the sanctuary—namely three thousand talents of gold, gold
from Ophir, and seven thousand talents of fine silver for overlaying the walls
of the buildings, for providing gold for the gold work, silver for the silver,
and for any work to be done by skilled craftsmen. Now who is willing to give
with open hand to the Lord today?'

Then the heads of families, the officers administering the tribes of Israel,
the officers over units of a thousand and a hundred, and the officers in charge
of the king's service, responded willingly and gave for the work of the house
of God five thousand talents of gold, ten thousand darics, ten thousand
talents of silver, eighteen thousand talents of bronze, and a hundred thousand
talents of iron. Further, those who possessed precious stones gave them to the
treasury of the house of the Lord, into the charge of Jehiel the Gershonite. The
people rejoiced at this willing response, because in the loyalty of their hearts
they had given willingly to the Lord.

## New Testament *Philippians 1.1-11 NEB*

From Paul and Timothy, servants of Christ Jesus, to all those of God's people, incorporate in Christ Jesus, who live at Philippi, including their bishops and deacons.

Grace to you and peace from God our Father and the Lord Jesus Christ.

I thank my God whenever I think of you; and when I pray for you all, my prayers are always joyful, because of the part you have taken in the work of the Gospel from the first day until now. Of one thing I am certain: the One who started the good work in you will bring it to completion by the Day of Christ Jesus. It is indeed only right that I should feel like this about you all, because you hold me in such affection, and because, when I lie in prison or appear in the dock to vouch for the truth of the Gospel, you all share in the privilege that is mine. God knows how I long for you all, with the deep yearning of Christ Jesus himself. And this is my prayer, that your love may grow richer and richer in knowledge and insight of every kind, and may thus bring you the gift of true discrimination. Then on the Day of Christ you will be flawless and without blame, reaping the full harvest of righteousness that comes through Jesus Christ, to the glory and praise of God.

## Gospel *Matthew 20.1-16 NEB*

Jesus said to his disciples, 'The kingdom of Heaven is like this. There was once a landowner who went out early one morning to hire labourers for his vineyard; and after agreeing to pay them the usual day's wage he sent them off to work. Going out three hours later he saw some more men standing idle in the market-place. "Go and join the others in the vineyard," he said, "and I will pay you a fair wage"; so off they went. At midday he went out again, and at three in the afternoon, and made the same arrangement as before. An hour before sunset he went out and found another group standing there; so he said to them, "Why are you standing about like this all day with nothing to do?" "Because no one has hired us", they replied; so he told them, "Go and join the others in the vineyard." When evening fell, the owner of the vineyard said to his steward, "Call the labourers and give them their pay, beginning with those who came last and ending with the first." Those who had started work an hour before sunset came forward, and were paid the full day's wage. When it was the turn of the men who had come first, they expected something extra, but were paid the same amount as the others. As they took it, they grumbled at their employer: "These late-comers have done only one hour's work, yet you have put them on a level with us, who have sweated the whole day long in the blazing sun!" The owner turned to one of them and said, "My friend, I am not being unfair to you. You agreed on the usual wage for the day, did you not? Take your pay and go home. I choose to pay the last man the same as you. Surely I am free to do what I like with my own money. Why be jealous because I am kind?" Thus will the last be first, and the first last.'

# Incorrigible generosity

*He has put a new song in my mouth,*
*even a song of thanksgiving to our God. (Ps 40.3)*

Actions speak louder than words. And they say many things, both positive and negative. Sunday's readings show how 'the serving community' (Sunday's theme) might express its service. In each case, how people respond to God is of critical importance for the way they behave.

According to 1 Chronicles, the people of God gave willingly, joyfully and abundantly of their material wealth to provide for a house worthy of their Lord. Proper honouring of the majesty of God counted more than their own treasure-stores. It has to be said that their earthly king had been decidedly up-front in his exhortation and example. David had made it clear that, as well as accumulating precious raw materials, he had also contributed from his own personal resources. So he challenges others to be as open-handed in their generosity. As in this case, such overt leading from the front can prove highly effective. But it clearly also carries its dangers, not least overbearing pride, and the inducing of guilt, resentment and rebellion. It is interesting to set alongside this narrative the little episode concerning donations to the temple treasury recorded in Mark 12.41-44.

The assembly addressed by David rejoiced that they had expressed their commitment to God by giving of their substance to beautify a place of worship. Those who in the Gospel parable bore the heat and burden of the day were certainly not rejoicing. They had laboured long in trying circumstances, but those who had come late to the task had been given exactly the same payment. To many hearers of the story, then, surely, as well as now, the complainants seem to have had a fair point. But this is not a story about social justice and conditions of employment. It is about God's economy. It is about divine, sovereign love, which itself freely and painfully gives all, that joy may abound. This is the love we are called to share, for ourselves and with others. God is incorrigibly generous. Are his servants?

The Philippian Christians were undoubtedly generous-hearted. Their support and cooperation meant a great deal to Paul. And their response to the One who started the good work in them had been to take forward eagerly the work of the gospel. Active love had evoked active love. They are no passive recipients of grace. It is their willingness to act upon the promptings of God that encourages Paul to pray for the continuing enrichment of their love in knowledge, insight and true discrimination. Such qualities are essential for effective service. It is not surprising that it is with the receptive Philippians that Paul shares his own insight into the servanthood of Christ (2.1-11). Participating in the mind and vocation of this divine servant, whilst costing us dear, will release more of God's healing love into a hurting world. That is not just our duty. It is our joy.

*God of extravagance,*
*so enrich our love*
*that we may give with zeal,*
*ready to be spent in your service.*

# Pentecost 12

## Collect

Almighty God,
who called your Church to witness
that you were in Christ reconciling men to yourself:
help us so to proclaim the good news of your love,
that all who hear it may be reconciled to you;
through him who died for us and rose again
and reigns with you and the Holy Spirit,
one God, now and for ever.

### Psalms 96.1-6; 96.7-end

## Old Testament *Micah 4.1-5 RSV*

It shall come to pass in the latter days
that the mountain of the house of the Lord
shall be established as the highest of the mountains,
and shall be raised up above the hills;
and peoples shall flow to it,
and many nations shall come, and say:
'Come, let us go up to the mountain of the Lord,
to the house of the God of Jacob;
that he may teach us his ways
and we may walk in his paths.'
For out of Zion shall go forth the law,
and the word of the Lord from Jerusalem.
He shall judge between many peoples,
and shall decide for strong nations afar off;
and they shall beat their swords into ploughshares,
and their spears into pruning hooks;
nation shall not lift up sword against nation,
neither shall they learn war any more;
but they shall sit every man under his vine
    and under his fig tree,
and none shall make them afraid;
for the mouth of the Lord of hosts has spoken.
For all the peoples walk each in the name of its god,
but we will walk in the name of the Lord our God
for ever and ever.

## New Testament *Acts 17.22-end NEB*

Paul stood up before the Court of Aeropagus and said: 'Men of Athens, I see that in everything that concerns religion you are uncommonly scrupulous. For as I was going round looking at the objects of your worship, I noticed among other things an altar bearing the inscription "To an Unknown God". What you worship but do not know—this is what I now proclaim.

'The God who created the world and everything in it, and who is Lord of heaven and earth, does not live in shrines made by men. It is not because he lacks anything that he accepts service at men's hands, for he is himself the universal giver of life and breath and all else. He created every race of men of one stock, to inhabit the whole earth's surface. He fixed the epochs of their history and the limits of their territory. They were to seek God, and, it might be, touch and find him; though indeed he is not far from each one of us, for in him we live and move, in him we exist; as some of your own poets have said, "We are also his offspring." As God's offspring, then, we ought not to suppose that the deity is like an image in gold or silver or stone, shaped by human craftsmanship and design. As for the times of ignorance, God has overlooked them; but now he commands mankind, all men everywhere, to repent, because he has fixed the day on which he will have the world judged, and justly judged, by a man of his choosing; of this he has given assurance to all by raising him from the dead.'

When they heard about the raising of the dead, some scoffed; and others said, 'We will hear you on this subject some other time.' And so Paul left the assembly. However, some men joined him and became believers, including Dionysius, a member of the Court of Areopagus; also a woman named Damaris, and others besides.

## Gospel *Matthew 5.13-16 JB*

Jesus said, 'You are the salt of the earth. But if salt becomes tasteless, what can make it salty again? It is good for nothing, and can only be thrown out to be trampled underfoot by men.

'You are the light of the world. A city built on a hill-top cannot be hidden. No one lights a lamp to put it under a tub; they put it on the lamp-stand where it shines for everyone in the house. In the same way your light must shine in the sight of men, so that, seeing your good works, they may give the praise to your Father in heaven.'

# Witnessing out of love

*Say among the nations that the Lord is king;*
*he has made the world so firm that it cannot be moved*
*and he shall judge the peoples with equity. (Ps 96.10)*

There are many and various ways of bearing witness to the living God. Sunday's readings highlight some of them.

In the extract from the Sermon the Mount, Jesus tells his hearers that they are like salt. A very little salt can have a significant impact on a large plateful. But it has to be spread and absorbed to do its job, whether of flavouring or preserving. And if it loses its zest, it is useless. The people of God are also like light. Continuing his typically down-to-earth manner of teaching, Jesus emphasizes how ineffective a light is if it is obscured. Here, then, are two perspectives on how the community of faith can reveal the presence of God. One is the way of hidden influence, the other the way of obvious manifestation. Both are to have their end in drawing attention to a praiseworthy God.

In the prophet Micah's vision, God will attract all peoples to himself. He will do so from his base on Mount Zion and through the faithful proclamation of his people. The nations will recognize the blessings and the claims of this God. The 'God of Jacob' will be seen as the God of all the world. People from afar will make pilgrimage to his dwelling, eager for guidance and teaching. And their encounter with this God will lead them to abandon violence and conflict in favour of active peace. So security and confidence will be the order of the day. It is a consummation devoutly to be wished amidst the wars and terrorism of our own age, though we might find the locus of God's earthly dwelling more difficult to identify,

Rather than waiting for people to make a move towards God, Paul is much more pro-active on God's behalf. According to Acts 17.16-21, it is his willingness to be where people are and engage with them there that leads him (not entirely on his own initiative) to his preaching opportunity 'before the Court of Areopagus'. Here he seeks to uncover the truth his hearers had never before realized yet which, he believed, was inherent in their experience. He therefore majors on the transcendence and imminence of the Creator God, making reference to religious ideas and literature which would be familiar to his audience. But, having established common ground, Paul moves on to the specifics of the Christian faith, concentrating on the resurrection of a man of God's choosing. Before Jesus is even named, dissension is provoked. The very claim that someone might be raised from the dead causes some to scoff, others to delay further consideration, and some to pursue the issue to the point of becoming believers. All are free to come to their own decisions.

Behind the differing forms of witness in each of Sunday's readings lies a God who longs to bring out the best in and for humanity. Those who are his witnesses should share his longing.

*God of longing,*
*bring out the best in us,*
*that we may point others to you,*
*through the influence of our lives*
*and by the proclamation of your truth.*

# *Pentecost 13*

## Collect

Lord God,
whose blessed Son our Saviour
gave his back to the smiters
and did not hide his face from shame:
give us grace to endure the sufferings of this present time
with sure confidence in the glory that shall be revealed;
through Jesus Christ our Lord.

## *Psalms 31.1-5; 43*

## Old Testament *Jeremiah 20.7-11a RSV*

O Lord, you have deceived me,
and I was deceived;
you are stronger than I,
and you have prevailed.
I have become a laughingstock all the day;
everyone mocks me.
For whenever I speak, I cry out,
I shout, 'Violence and destruction!'
For the word of the Lord has become for me
a reproach and derision all day long.
If I say, 'I will not mention him,
or speak any more in his name,'
there is in my heart as it were a burning fire
shut up in my bones,
and I am weary with holding it in,
and I cannot.
For I hear many whispering.
Terror is on every side!
'Denounce him! Let us denounce him!'
say all my familiar friends, watching for my fall.
'Perhaps he will be deceived,
then we can overcome him,
and take our revenge on him.'
But the Lord is with me as a dread warrior;
therefore my persecutors will stumble,
and they will not overcome me.

## New Testament *Acts 20.17-35 TEV*

From Miletus Paul sent a message to Ephesus, asking the elders of the church to meet him. When they arrived, he said to them, 'You know how I spent the whole time I was with you, from the first day I arrived in the province of Asia. With all humility and many tears I did my work as the Lord's servant during the hard times that came to me because of the plots of the Jews. You know that I did not hold back anything that would be of help to you as I preached and taught in public and in your homes. To Jews and Gentiles alike I gave solemn warning that they should turn from their sins to God and believe in our Lord Jesus. And now, in obedience to the Holy Spirit I am going to Jerusalem, not knowing what will happen to me there. I only know that in every city the Holy Spirit has warned me that prison and troubles wait for me. But I reckon my own life to be worth nothing to me; I only want to complete my mission and finish the work that the Lord Jesus gave me to do, which is to declare the Good News about the grace of God.

'I have gone about among all of you, preaching the Kingdom of God. And now I know that none of you will ever see me again. So I solemnly declare to you this very day: if any of you should be lost, I am not responsible. For I have not held back from announcing to you the whole purpose of God. So keep watch over yourselves and over all the flock which the Holy Spirit has placed in your care. Be shepherds of the church of God, which he made his own through the death of his Son. I know that after I leave, fierce wolves will come among you, and they will not spare the flock. The time will come when some men from your own group will tell lies to lead the believers away after them. Watch, then, and remember that with many tears, day and night, I taught every one of you for three years.

'And now I commend you to the care of God and to the message of his grace, which is able to build you up and give you the blessings God has for all his people. I have not wanted anyone's silver or gold or clothing. You yourselves know that I have worked with these hands of mine to provide everything that my companions and I have needed. I have shown you in all things that by working hard in this way we must help the weak, remembering the words that the Lord Jesus himself said, "There is more happiness in giving than in receiving." '

## Gospel *Matthew 10.16-22 JB*

Jesus said, 'Remember, I am sending you out like sheep among wolves; so be cunning as serpents and yet as harmless as doves.

'Beware of men: they will hand you over to sanhedrins and scourge you in their synagogues. You will be dragged before governors and kings for my sake, to bear witness before them and the pagans. But when they hand you over, do not worry about how to speak or what to say; what you are to say will be given to you when the time comes; because it is not you who will be speaking; the Spirit of your Father will be speaking in you.

'Brother will betray brother to death, and the father his child; children will rise against their parents and have them put to death. You will be hated by all men on account of my name; but the man who stands firm to the end will be saved.'

## *Determined endurance*

*You are God my refuge, why have you turned me away,*
*why must I go like a mourner*
*because the enemy oppresses me? (Ps 43.2)*

Serving God has never been an easy matter. Suffering of one kind or another seems to crop up again and again. Whatever God's good news is, it is no soft option. Nor does it answer all our questions. If anything, those questions can become even more painful and acute. As Jeremiah discovered, God does sometimes appear more like enemy than friend. At such times, mention of good news seems at best a hollow joke.

In the depths of despair, Jeremiah rails against God—the God whose compulsive calling he cannot escape, yet who has brought him nothing but comprehensive pain. The language is strong. God has seduced him and led him on, betrayed him. All that seemed good has been distorted. Serving God has been his downfall. Even his friends are waiting for him to go over the edge, to put the finishing touches to his destruction. Suffering is even harder to bear when you are mocked and laughed at. Yet, no doubt through gritted teeth, Jeremiah proclaims a faith he cannot feel, a faith which seems to be denied by all the evidence, a faith in a God who will vindicate the faithful and see justice done. This is raw rather then blind faith.

Such faith is needed also by the followers of Jesus. According to Sunday's Gospel reading, Jesus' warnings of what lies ahead are not for the faint-hearted. Physical abuse, betrayal by those one would trust most, obvious hatred and even death: these are the likely outcomes of steadfast witness. The only saving factor—but the one that makes all the difference— is that in any of these situations God is at hand. In particular, those who are called to give account of their faith will be given the right words at the right time. If only people will trust God, his Spirit will take over. Determined endurance will open the way for the salvation of God, though this be through rather than from suffering.

Paul used similar language when he took his leave of the leaders of the church at Ephesus. He had been through 'hard times'—something of a euphemism, judging by what we read elsewhere in Acts. He had worked 'with all humility and many tears'. Yet in spite of warnings, he was determined to go to Jerusalem, knowing that prison and troubles lay before him. His one end was to finish his God-given work: 'to declare the Good News about the grace of God'.

At this critical point, Paul warns that the church at Ephesus will be torn apart if their elders are not watchful. There will be false teachers. The leaders will have to hold fast to their faith and to guard those put in their care, remembering Paul's example. Yet in all this the church has to avoid being inward-looking; it has to be open to people's needs. They will thus come to know the truth of the saying that it is more blessed to give than to receive.

Therein lies a clue. It is in honest relationship with a God who gives his life that good news is to be realized.

*Compulsive God,*
*you lead us on*
*in ways we would not choose.*
*Whatever hardship lies ahead,*
*help us hold on to you.*

# Pentecost 14

## Collect

Lord God,
the protector of all who trust in you,
without whom nothing is strong, nothing is holy:
increase and multiply upon us your mercy,
that you being our ruler and guide,
we may so pass through things temporal
that we finally lose not the things eternal.
Grant this, heavenly Father,
for the sake of Jesus Christ our Lord.

## *Psalms 127; 128*

## Old Testament *Genesis 45.1-15 NEB*

Joseph could no longer control his feelings in front of his attendants, and he
called out, 'Let everyone leave my presence.' So there was nobody present
when Joseph made himself known to this brothers, but so loudly did he
weep that the Egyptians and Pharaoh's household heard him. Joseph said to
his brothers, 'I am Joseph; can my father be still alive?' His brothers were so
dumbfounded at finding themselves face to face with Joseph that they could
not answer. Then Joseph said to his brothers, 'Come closer', and so they
came close. He said, 'I am your brother Joseph whom you sold into Egypt.
Now do not be distressed or take it amiss that you sold me into slavery here;
it was God who sent me ahead of you to save men's lives. For there have
now been two years of famine in the country, and there will be another five
years with neither ploughing nor harvest. God sent me ahead of you to
ensure that you will have descendants on earth, and to preserve you all, a
great band of survivors. So it was not you who sent me here, but God, and
he has made me a father to Pharaoh, and lord over all his household and
ruler of all Egypt. Make haste and go back to my father and give him this
message from his son Joseph: "God has made me lord of all Egypt. Come
down to me; do not delay. You shall live in the land of Goshen and be near
me, you, your sons and your grandsons, your flocks and herds and all that
you have. I will take care of you there, you and your household and all that
you have, and see that you are not reduced to poverty; there are still five
years of famine to come." You can see for yourselves, and so can my brother
Benjamin, that it is Joseph himself who is speaking to you. Tell my father of
all the honour which I enjoy in Egypt, tell him all you have seen, and make
haste to bring him down here.' Then he threw his arms round his brother

Benjamin and wept, and Benjamin too embraced him weeping. He kissed all his brothers and wept over them, and afterwards his brothers talked with him.

## New Testament *Ephesians 3.14-end RSV*

I bow my knees before the Father, from whom every family in heaven and on earth is named, that according to the riches of his glory he may grant you to be strengthened with might through his Spirit in the inner man, and that Christ may dwell in your hearts through faith; that you, being rooted and grounded in love, may have power to comprehend with all the saints what is the breadth and length and height and depth, and to know the love of Christ which surpasses knowledge, that you may be filled with all the fullness of God.

Now to him who by the power at work within us is able to do far more abundantly than all that we ask or think, to him be glory in the church and in Christ Jesus to all generations, for ever and ever. Amen.

## Gospel *Luke 11.1-13 JB*

Jesus was in a certain place praying, and when he had finished one of his disciples said, 'Lord, teach us to pray, just as John taught his disciples.' He said to them, 'Say this when you pray:

"Father, may your name be held holy,
your kingdom come;
give us each day our daily bread,
and forgive us our sins,
for we ourselves forgive each one who is in debt to us.
And do not put us to the test."

He also said to them, 'Suppose one of you has a friend and goes to him in the middle of the night to say, "My friend, lend me three loaves, because a friend of mine on his travels has just arrived at my house and I have nothing to offer him"; and the man answers from inside the house, "Do not bother me. The door is bolted now, and my children and I are in bed; I cannot get up to give it you." I tell you, if the man does not get up and give it him for friendship's sake, persistence will be enough to make him get up and give his friend all he wants.

'So I say to you: Ask, and it will be given to you; search, and you will find; knock, and the door will be opened to you. For the one who asks always receives; the one who searches always finds; the one who knocks will always have the door opened to him. What father among you would hand his son a stone when he asked for bread? Or hand him a snake instead of a fish? Or hand him a scorpion if he asked for an egg? If you then, who are evil, know how to give your children what is good, how much more will the heavenly Father give the Holy Spirit to those who ask him!'

# The challenge of human relationships

*Blessed is everyone who fears the Lord,*
*and walks in the confine of his ways. (Ps 128.1)*

The saying 'Blood is thicker than water' can be used disparagingly. Relationships wrongly used can lead to nepotism and worse. It remains true that blood relationship can be stronger than might be expected, even when that blood is spilt (either literally or metaphorically). Joseph's blood had not been physically spilt (although his brothers had tried to make it look as if it had). Yet in spite of his mistreatment and rejection by his blood relatives, he cannot deny the relationship when there is an opportunity to affirm it. It is for the sake of his father and his family that Joseph opens himself up to his brothers. But it is for their sake and for his own sake too. They need forgiveness. He needs to be able to express honestly the joy of reconciliation with Benjamin and the rest. (Note, however, even at this point how Joseph continues the theme of favouritism which, in his own case, had already caused much heartache.)

In view of the famine, this reunion was timely. And Joseph explains its timing by reference to God's foresight and sovereignty. Nonetheless, it was a very difficult time for the brothers. To be reminded of something for which you need forgiveness is never easy.

Yet that kind of reminder is set at the heart of Luke's version of what we have come to call the Lord's Prayer. It is in the light of our relationship with God that we can pray for our needs to be satisfied and for our sins to be forgiven. It is not a matter of contract; it is a matter of trusting love. And whilst it might be hard indeed to offer real forgiveness, we must always be aware how painful it can be to be on the receiving end, whether for ourselves or for those we seek to forgive. Wholehearted forgiveness is at the heart of hope. It changes things. It transforms relationships. It is at the very heart of God. It is also one of the most difficult things in the world to realize.

Its realization may be encouraged as we take in the meaning of Paul's prayer that we should be strengthened inwardly, in both faith and love. We notice that the prayer is firmly based in relationship. Paul prays to the Father that Christians may know the indwelling of Jesus through the power of God's Spirit. There is a sense here of God acting in relationship: within himself as well as in relationship with humanity. More than this, the prayer is that the love of Christ may be known in such a way that it releases all the fulness of God. Such knowing is far beyond any intellectual dimension. It has to do with the depth of experience. It has to do with the power of God which works on the inside of life to achieve the seemingly impossible. Under the impetus of this God, the enduring challenge of human relationships can be worked together for good.

*God of relationship,*
*you know the bonds of kinship,*
*its strains and its joys.*
*May open-hearted forgiveness*
*release us all to live as one.*

# Pentecost 15

## Collect

Almighty Father,
whose will is to restore all things in your beloved Son, the king of all:
govern the hearts and minds of those in authority,
and bring the families of the nations,
divided and torn apart by the ravages of sin,
to be subject to his just and gentle rule;
who is alive and reigns with you and the Holy Spirit,
one God, now and for ever.

### Psalms 82; 20

## Old Testament *1 Kings 3.4-15 RSV*

King Solomon went to Gibeon to sacrifice there, for that was the great high place; Solomon used to offer a thousand burnt offerings upon that altar. At Gibeon the Lord appeared to Solomon in a dream by night; and God said, 'Ask what I shall give you.' And Solomon said, 'You have shown great and steadfast love to your servant David my father, because he walked before you in faithfulness, in righteousness, and in uprightness of heart towards you; and you have kept for him this great and steadfast love, and have given him a son to sit on his throne this day. And now, O Lord my God, you have made your servant king in place of David my father, although I am but a little child; I do not know how to go out or come in. And your servant is in the midst of your people whom you have chosen, a great people, that cannot be numbered or counted for multitude. Give your servant therefore an understanding mind to govern your people, that I may discern between good and evil; for who is able to govern this your great people?'

It pleased the Lord that Solomon had asked this. And God said to him, 'Because you have asked this, and have not asked for yourself long life or riches or the life of your enemies, but have asked for yourself understanding to discern what is right, behold, I now do according to your word. Behold, I give you a wise and discerning mind, so that none like you has been before you and none like you shall arise after you. I give you also what you have not asked, both riches and honour, so that no other king shall compare with you, all your days. And if you will walk in my ways, keeping my statutes and my commandments, as your father David walked, then I will lengthen your days.'

And Solomon awoke, and behold, it was a dream. Then he came to Jerusalem, and stood before the ark of the covenant of the Lord, and offered up burnt offerings and peace offerings, and made a feast for all his servants.

## New Testament *1 Timothy 2.1-7 NEB*

First of all I urge that petitions, prayers, intercessions, and thanksgivings be offered for all men; for sovereigns and all in high office, that we may lead a tranquil and quiet life in full observance of religion and high standards of morality. Such prayer is right, and approved by God our Saviour, whose will it is that all men should find salvation and come to know the truth. For there is one God, and also one mediator between God and men, Christ Jesus, himself man, who sacrificed himself to win freedom for all mankind, so providing, at the fitting time, proof of the divine purpose; of this I was appointed herald and apostle (this is no lie, but the truth), to instruct the nations in the true faith.

## Gospel *Matthew 14.1-12 NEB*

Reports about Jesus reached the ears of Prince Herod. 'This is John the Baptist,' he said to his attendants; 'John has been raised to life, and that is why these miraculous powers are at work in him.' Now Herod had arrested John, put him in chains, and thrown him into prison, on account of Herodias, his brother Philip's wife; for John had told him: 'You have no right to her.' Herod would have like to put him to death, but he was afraid of the people, in whose eyes John was a prophet. But at his birthday celebrations the daughter of Herodias danced before the guests, and Herod was so delighted that he took an oath to give her anything she cared to ask. Prompted by her mother, she said, 'Give me here on a dish the head of John the Baptist.' The king was distressed when he heard it; but out of regard for his oath and for his guests, he ordered the request to be granted, and had John beheaded in prison. The head was brought in on a dish and given to the girl; and she carried it to her mother. Then John's disciples came and took away the body, and buried it; and they went and told Jesus.

# The use and abuse of power

*May the Lord hear you in the day of trouble,*
*the God of Jacob lift you up to safety. (Ps 20.1)*

Sunday's readings (and Sunday's theme) invite us to grapple with the perennial issue of the use and abuse of power. This is, of course, no academic matter. It is integral to human relationships and the affairs of nations. The exercise of power can bring much that is good. It also has enormous potential for evil and destruction. And where, in all this, is the 'God of power and might'?

Solomon inherited a monarchy that was still, for the people of Israel, a relatively new form of government. The Jewish scriptures reflect an ambiguous attitude towards the institution and its outworking. For some it was a rejection of God's sovereignty (see e.g. 1 Samuel 8:4-22). For others, it was (ideally at least) an extension and expression of God's own rule (see e.g. Psalm 110). Yet, whether monarchy was tolerated or willed by God, it is the clear conviction of Old Testament writers that the monarch owed allegiance to God and must uphold God's standards. The author of Deuteronomy sums this up well, in a passage that seems to point the finger at a great and wise Solomon who did not fully live up to his early promise (Deuteronomy 17:14-20; compare 1 Kings 11). Solomon's prayer (set for Sunday) had seemed to bode well. Instead of taking the tempting opportunity offered him to ask for earthly glory, he acknowledges the primacy of God, the fact that the people of Israel are God's people not his, and his own urgent need of God's resources for the task. He prays for 'an understanding mind' and the gift of discernment. He describes himself as God's 'servant'. His subsequent reign can only be described as glittering, marked by an abundance of material blessing—a veritable golden age. But the relationship between wisdom, power and success is not a straightforward one. Solomon's legacy was not unalloyed well-being for the nation.

At no stage in his career does discerning wisdom seem to have characterized the person and reign of King Herod. A puppet king, accountable to the governing Romans rather than to the people of God (or, it would seem, to God himself), Herod had an eye to his own position and to what those with influence thought of him. Angered at the criticism of his immorality, Herod has had John the Baptist thrown into prison. Nervous of the extent of John's popularity (and fearful for his own standing), he delays execution until a rash oath made in front of influential guests leads to a moment of moral dilemma. The dilemma is quickly resolved by reference to the greater self-interest. John is beheaded. The king breathes again.

The writer of 1 Timothy bids his readers pray for such as Herod and Herod's Roman superiors. Praying constantly for those in secular authority has always been a challenge for Christians, not least in communities which in everyday life know nothing of the freedom Christ's death has won. Yet we are to persist. We are to continue in hope that despite what Sunday's collect terms 'the ravages of sin' (something all too apparent on our television screens), we—and all those for whom we pray—will come to be subject to God's rule. That rule is characterized by justice and gentleness. That rule has at its heart the cross of Jesus Christ. Only there can we begin to understand and experience the paradox and liberation of divine power—and to share its possibilities with a world out of joint.

*God of authority,*
*you share your authority*
*with those who exercise leadership.*
*Give them such understanding and discernment,*
*that they may show your mercy and truth,*
*your righteousness and peace.*

## Collect

Almighty God,
you have taught us through your Son
that love is the fulfilling of the law.
Grant that we may love you with our whole heart
and our neighbours as ourselves;
through Jesus Christ our Lord.

## Psalms 34.1-10; 34.11-18

## Old Testament *Deuteronomy 15.7-11 NEB*

Moses said to all Israel, 'When one of your fellow-countrymen in any of your
settlements in the land which the Lord your God is giving you becomes poor,
do not be hard-hearted or close-fisted with your countryman in his need. Be
open-handed towards him and lend him on pledge as much as he needs. See
that you do not harbour iniquitous thoughts when you find that the seventh
year, the year of remission, is near, and look askance at your needy
countryman and give him nothing. If you do, he will appeal to the Lord
against you, and you will be found guilty of sin. Give freely to him and do
not begrudge him your bounty, because it is for this very bounty that the Lord
your God will bless you in everything that you do or undertake. The poor
will always be with you in the land, and for that reason I command you to be
open-handed with your countrymen, both poor and distressed, in your own
land.'

## New Testament *1 John 4.15-end JB*

If anyone acknowledges that Jesus is the son of God,
God lives in him, and he in God.
We ourselves have known and put our faith in
God's love towards ourselves.
God is love
and anyone who lives in love lives in God,
and God lives in him.
Love will come to its perfection in us
when we can face the day of Judgement without fear;
because even in this world
we have become as he is.
In love there can be no fear,
but fear is driven out by perfect love:

because to fear is to expect punishment,
and anyone who is afraid is still imperfect in love.
We are to love, then,
because he loved us first.
Anyone who says, 'I love God',
and hates his brother,
is a liar,
since a man who does not love the brother that he can see
cannot love God, whom he has never seen.
So this is the commandment that he has given us,
that anyone who loves God must also love his brother.

## Gospel *Luke 16.19-end JB*

Jesus said, 'There was a rich man who used to dress in purple and fine linen
and feast magnificently every day. And at his gate there lay a poor man called
Lazarus, covered with sores, who longed to fill himself with the scraps that
fell from the rich man's table. Dogs even came and licked his sores. Now the
poor man died and was carried away by angels to the bosom of Abraham.
The rich man also died and was buried.

'In his torment in Hades he looked up and saw Abraham a long way off
with Lazarus in his bosom. So he cried out, "Father Abraham, pity me and
send Lazarus to dip the tip of his finger in water and cool my tongue, for I am
in agony in these flames." "My son," Abraham replied, "remember that
during your life good things came your way, just as bad things came the way
of Lazarus. Now he is being comforted here while you are in agony. But that
is not all: between us and you a great gulf has been fixed, to stop anyone, if he
wanted to, crossing from our side to yours, and to stop any crossing from
your side to ours."

'The rich man replied, "Father, I beg you then to send Lazarus to my
father's house, since I have five brothers, to give them warning so that they
do not come to this place of torment too." "They have Moses and the
prophets," said Abraham, "let them listen to them." "Ah no, father
Abraham," said the rich man, "but if someone comes to them from the dead,
they will repent." Then Abraham said to him, "If they will not listen either to
Moses or to the prophets, they will not be convinced even if someone should
rise from the dead."'

# The root of love in action

*The Lord is close to those who are broken-hearted,*
*and the crushed in spirit he saves.*
*(Ps 34.18)*

It is not always easy to believe that genuine open-handedness brings blessing. A generous act unacknowledged or thrown back in one's face can be a cause of lasting bitterness or conflict. Perhaps that is one reason why the Old Testament reading set for Sunday stresses the dangers of hard-heartedness and the bounty of God in blessing those who give freely. This message is in fact a deeply challenging one. Taken seriously, it moves us into a radical examination of our motives and desires. Why do we so often tend towards the 'close-fisted'? Do we need to name the greed and self-interest within us, even as we may deplore it in others? The passage is a challenge, too, in areas such as community giving and community support, for example through state taxes and benefits. What should be the fundamental principles here? 'The poor', we read, 'will always be with you.' And also, alas, will our range of responses to them.

That saying must have escaped the notice of the rich man at whose gate Lazarus lay in the Gospel parable. The rich man looked after himself rather well. Lazarus missed out even on the scraps. Jesus tells how in death, apparently, the tables are turned (a familiar theme in the stories of many cultures). The lack of neighbourly concern on the part of the rich man is rewarded by torment, whilst Lazarus is given exalted status. Failing to receive the relief he desperately wants, the rich man pleads that his brothers should be given warning of what might befall them, presumably if they don't change their way of life. The suggestion is that Lazarus be sent to them. But would they have recognized him? The plea is dismissed on the grounds that those who will not take seriously what scripture has to say are not going to take seriously some kind of supernatural visitation. Anything can be explained away when accepting its reality would make uncongenial demands.

All this is earthed in the reading from 1 John. Those who do not love the brother or sister they can see (and relate to) cannot possibly love the God they have never seen. Love is not some kind of abstract idea. It is concrete. It is to be expressed. It requires something of us. Love in action is rooted in the God who is love and who lives in those who practise love. Love drives out the fear of punishment that the rich man had in relation to his five brothers. It drives out the complacent or fearful callousness that society can feel and express when called on to offer open-handed generosity to those in need. It militates against judgmentalism and the strength of self-interest. Love comes to perfection as we begin to realize that love is given in the one who first loved us. Love exists to call forth love. Unless it is expressed and shared in our relationships with others, it dies on us.

*Hidden God,*
*you come to us unexpectedly and unbidden,*
*yet you are always with us.*
*Help us to serve you in love*
*as we respond to people's needs.*

# Pentecost 17

## Collect

Lord of all power and might
the author and giver of all good things:
graft in our hearts the love of your name,
increase in us true religion,
nourish in us all goodness,
and of your great mercy keep us in the same;
through Jesus Christ our Lord.

## Psalms 56; 57

## Old Testament *Jeremiah 32.6-15 NEB*

Jeremiah said, The word of the Lord came to me: Hanamel son of your uncle Shallum is coming to see you and will say, 'Buy my field at Anathoth; you have the right of redemption, as next of kin, to buy it.' As the Lord had foretold, my cousin Hanamel came to the court of the guard-house and said, 'Buy my field at Anathoth in Benjamin. You have the right of redemption and possession as next of kin; buy it.' I knew that this was the Lord's message; so I bought the field at Anathoth from my cousin Hanamel and weighed out the price, seventeen shekels of silver. I signed and sealed the deed and had it witnessed; then I weighed out the money on the scales. I took my copies of the deed of purchase, both the sealed and the unsealed, and gave them to Baruch son of Neriah, son of Mahseiah, in the presence of Hanamel my cousin, of the witnesses whose names were on the deed of purchase, and of the Judaeans sitting in the court of the guard-house. In the presence of them all I gave my instructions to Baruch: These are the words of the Lord of Hosts the God of Israel: Take these copies of the deed of purchase, the sealed and the unsealed, and deposit them in an earthenware jar so that they may be preserved for a long time. For these are the words of the Lord of Hosts the God of Israel: The time will come when houses, fields, and vineyards will again be bought and sold in this land.

## New Testament *Galatians 2.15—3.9 RSV*

We ourselves, who are Jews by birth and not Gentile sinners, yet who know that a man is not justified by works of the law but through faith in Jesus Christ, even we have believed in Christ Jesus, in order to be justified by faith in Christ, and not by works of the law, because by works of the law shall no one be justified. But if, in our endeavour to be justified in Christ, we ourselves were found to be sinners, is Christ then an agent of sin? Certainly not! But if I build up again those things which I tore down, then I prove myself a transgressor. For I through the law died to the law, that I might live to God. I have been crucified with Christ; it is no longer I who live, but Christ who lives in me; and the life I now live in the flesh I live by faith in the Son of God, who loved me and gave himself for me. I do not nullify the grace of God; for if justification were through the law, then Christ died to no purpose.

O foolish Galatians! Who has bewitched you, before whose eyes Jesus Christ was publicly portrayed as crucified? Let me ask you only this: Did you receive the Spirit by works of the law, or by hearing with faith? Are you so foolish? Having begun with the Spirit, are you now ending with the flesh? Did you experience so many things in vain?—if it really is in vain. Does he who supplies the Spirit to you and works miracles among you do so by works of the law, or by hearing with faith?

Thus Abraham 'believed God, and it was reckoned to him as righteousness.' So you see that it is men of faith who are the sons of Abraham. And the scripture, foreseeing that God would justify the Gentiles by faith, preached the gospel beforehand to Abraham, saying, 'In thee shall all the nations be blessed.' So then, those who are men of faith are blessed with Abraham who had faith.

## Gospel *Luke 7.1-10 JB*

When Jesus had come to the end of all he wanted the people to hear, he went into Capernaum. A centurion there had a servant, a favourite of his, who was sick and near death. Having heard about Jesus he sent some Jewish elders to him to ask him to come and heal his servant. When they came to Jesus they pleaded earnestly with him. 'He deserves this of you', they said, 'because he is friendly towards our people; in fact, he is the one who built the synagogue.' So Jesus went with them, and was not very far from the house when the centurion sent word to him by some friends: 'Sir,' he said, 'do not put yourself to trouble; because I am not worthy to have you under my roof; and for this same reason I did not presume to come to you myself; but give the word and let my servant be cured. For I am under authority myself, and have soldiers under me; and I say to one man: Go, and he goes; to another: Come here, and he comes; to my servant: Do this, and he does it.' When Jesus heard these words he was astonished at him and, turning round, said to the crowd following him, 'I tell you, not even in Israel have I found faith like this.' And when the messengers got back to the house they found the servant in perfect health.

# The foolhardiness of faithfulness

*I will call to God Most High,*
*to the God who will fulfil his purpose for me. (Ps 57.3)*

Exercising faith can make you look like a fool. Jeremiah was prepared to take this risk. He'd taken plenty of risks in his time as a prophet with a word that people did not want to hear. Now he follows God's prompting in paying good money for a completely unusable and unsaleable field at Anathoth, a village presently cut off from Jerusalem by enemy forces. Jeremiah was in prison. The enemy was at the gates of Jerusalem. For the people of the city, life as they knew it was about to come to an end. What possible point was there in engaging in buying land that, as like as not, would soon be devastated? What point was there in expecting any normal kind of life in the future?

Yet Jeremiah goes through the legal process in the presence of witnesses. He has the evidence stored for the future as a sign that, whatever is to happen in the short term, in the longer term property in the Jewish kingdom would once again be traded by God's people. Jeremiah's wrestling with God had severely tested his faith. Even in prison, it had not broken it.

A different kind of faith is exercised by the centurion from Capernaum. Its depth and assurance seem to have startled even Jesus. As one who had built the synagogue, the centurion was surely a God-fearer. As a Gentile, he does not presume to approach Jesus, whom he would regard as a noted Jewish prophet and healer. Instead he takes the precaution of sending Jewish elders on his behalf, to plead with Jesus to come and heal a favourite servant. On his way there, Jesus is stopped by a group of friends sent by the centurion. His sense of unworthiness combines with a sense of the authority Jesus must have—for, as the friends explain, the centurion knows about exercising authority. 'Give the word', is his message, 'and let my servant be cured'.

There is a double faith here: faith in Jesus, certainly; but also faith in the two sets of messengers the centurion has sent to Jesus. We are often challenged as to the depth of our faith in God. Perhaps we also need to be challenged as to the extent of our faith in our friends and others we ask to act for us—or who would, if we dared to trust them.

The centurion is a striking exemplar of faith from one outside the people of God. In Galatians, Paul instances Abraham as the paradigm of faith—the one who believed and who through that belief received the promise of God's blessing for all the world. It is not the keepers of the Jewish law who are Abraham's heirs in faith. It is those who, whether Jew or Gentile, live in faith relationship with Christ.

*Faithful God,*
*help us to catch the faith*
*shown by Abraham and the prophets,*
*that in our quest to trust you more*
*we may begin to trust others.*

# Pentecost 18

## Collect

Almighty God,
you have made us for yourself,
and our hearts are restless
till they find their rest in you.
Teach us to offer ourselves to your service,
that here we may have your peace,
and in the world to come may see you face to face;
through Jesus Christ our Lord.

### Psalms 145.14-end; 90.13-end

## Old Testament *Nehemiah 6.1-16 NEB*

When the news came to Sanballat, Tobiah, Geshem the Arab, and the rest of our enemies, that I had rebuilt the wall and that not a single breach remained in it, although I had not yet set up the doors in the gates, Sanballat and Geshem sent me an invitation to come and confer with them at Hakkephirim in the plain of Ono; this was a ruse on their part to do me harm. So I sent messengers to them with this reply: 'I have important work on my hands at the moment; I cannot come down. Why should the work be brought to a standstill while I leave it and come down to you?' They sent me a similar invitation four times, and each time I gave them the same answer. On a fifth occasion Sanballat made a similar approach, but this time his messenger came with an open letter. It ran as follows: 'It is reported among the nations—and Gashmu confirms it—that you and the Jews are plotting rebellion, and it is for this reason that you are rebuilding the wall, and—so the report goes—that you yourself want to be king. You are also said to have put up prophets to proclaim in Jerusalem that Judah has a king, meaning yourself. The king will certainly hear of this. So come at once and let us talk the matter over.' Here is the reply I sent: 'No such thing as you allege has taken place; you have made up the whole story.' They were all trying to intimidate us, in the hope that we should then relax our efforts and that the work would never be finished. So I applied myself to it with greater energy.

One day I went to the house of Shemaiah son of Delaiah, son of Mehetabel, for he was confined to his house. He said, 'Let us meet in the house of God, within the sanctuary, and let us shut the doors, for they are coming to kill you—they are coming to kill you by night.' But I said, 'Should a man like me run away? And can a man like me go into the sanctuary and survive? I will not go in.' The it dawned on me: God had not sent him. His prophecy aimed at harming me, and Tobiah and Sanballat had bribed him to utter it. He had been bribed to frighten me into compliance and into committing sin; then they could give me a bad name and discredit me. Remember Tobiah and Sanballat, O God, for what they have done, and also the prophetess Noadiah and all the other prophets who have tried to intimidate me.

On the twenty-fifth day of the month Elul the wall was finished; it had taken fifty-two days. When our enemies heard of it, and all the surrounding nations saw it, they thought it a very wonderful achievement, and they recognized that this work had been accomplished by the help of our God.

## New Testament *1 Peter 4.7-11 NEB*

The end of all things is upon us, so you must lead an ordered and sober life, given to prayer. Above all, keep your love for one another at full strength, because love cancels innumerable sins. Be hospitable to one another without complaining. Whatever gift each of you may have received, use it in service to one another, like good stewards dispensing the grace of God in its varied forms. Are you a speaker? Speak as if you uttered oracles of God. Do you give service? Give it as in the strength which God supplies. In all things so act that the glory may be God's through Jesus Christ; to him belong glory and power for ever and ever. Amen.

## Gospel *Matthew 25.14-30 JB*

Jesus said, 'The kingdom of Heaven is like a man on his way abroad who summoned his servants and entrusted his property to them. To one he gave five talents, to another two, to a third one; each in proportion to his ability. Then he set out. The man who had received the five talents promptly went and traded with them and made five more. The man who had received two made two more in the same way. But the man who had received one went off and dug a hole in the ground and hid his master's money. Now a long time after, the master of those servants came back and went through his accounts with them. The man who had received the five talents came forward bringing five more. "Sir," he said, "you entrusted me with five talents; here are five more that I have made." His master said to him, "Well done, good and faithful servant; you have shown you can be faithful in small things, I will trust you with greater; come and join in your master's happiness." Next the man with the two talents came forward. "Sir," he said, "you entrusted me with two talents; here are two more that I have made." His master said to him, "Well done, good and faithful servant; you have shown you can be faithful in small things, I will trust you with greater; come and join in your master's happiness." Last came forward the man who had the one talent. "Sir," said he, "I had heard you were a hard man, reaping where you have not sown and gathering where you have not scattered; so I was afraid, and I went off and hid your talent in the ground. Here it is; it was yours, you have it back." But his master answered him, "You wicked and lazy servant! So you knew that I reap where I have not sown and gather where I have not scattered? Well then, you should have deposited my money with the bankers, and on my return I would have recovered my capital and interest. So now, take the talent from him and give it to the man who has the five talents. For to everyone who has will be given more, and he will have more than enough; but from the man who has not, even what he has will be taken away. As for this good-for-nothing servant, throw him out into the dark, where there will be weeping and grinding of teeth."'

## *Building on trust*

*May the gracious favour of the Lord our God be upon us,*
*prosper the work of our hands,*
*O prosper the work of our hands. (Ps 90. 17)*

The Letter of 1 Peter seems to have been written in the context of persecution. Yet imminent crisis is no reason for people to depart from what they have learned of Christian principles. It should rather be an incentive to put them into practice. The extract set for Sunday echoes other New Testament writings in calling its readers to maintain their community as well as their faith. They are to keep up their worship, mutual love and hospitality. Whatever gifts individuals have received are to be shared in mutual service. Service itself is to reflect the ways of God and the strength of God. The recipients cannot know how things will turn out for them. But they are to live to God's glory, so that whatever they do may be seen to be of God, the one who is served in giving.

That God's giving to us is somehow related to our ability to respond seems to be implied in the parable taken from Matthew's Gospel. The master in the parable shares out talents (representing his possessions) between his servants and according to their ability. The master seems to expect little from the third servant, otherwise he would have been given more in the first place. So it comes as something of a shock when the master berates the third servant, who had at least carefully looked after the talent, even if his ability to increase its value had not matched that of the other two servants. The point is that he had not even tried. He should at least have made sure that interest had been earned on it.

Merely preserving things as they are does not represent good stewardship. What is given needs working with and developing. Those who have nothing to show for the trust God has placed in them must answer for their fearful caution—or is it sloth?

How does this fit with what we learn from the extract from Nehemiah? Nehemiah's 'mission' was basically restoration, rather than enhancement. But it certainly involved a break with the status quo. And it certainly involved taking risks in getting to work on things as they were. His efforts to rebuild the walls of Jerusalem suffered continual harassment. He was misrepresented. He was threatened. He was tempted to run away. Yet he sees his achievement in completing the walls and gates as a God-given task, something that could not have been completed without the support and help of the God he served. His active endurance for God's sake and in God's strength brings not only the reward of a job well done. It carries with it the bonus of witnessing to 'all the surrounding nations' that Nehemiah's God has been powerfully at work.

*Lavish God,*
*help us work at all that you give us,*
*that your gifts may be used for others*
*and to your glory.*

# Pentecost 19

## Collect

Almighty and everlasting God,
increase in us your gift of faith;
that, forsaking what lies behind
and reaching out to that which is before,
we may run the way of your commandments
and win the crown of everlasting joy;
through Jesus Christ our Lord.

### Psalms 139.1-11; 65.1-7

## Old Testament *Daniel 6.10-23 RSV*

When Daniel knew that the document had been signed, he went to his house
where he had windows in his upper chamber open toward Jerusalem; and he
got down upon his knees three times a day and prayed and gave thanks before
his God, as he had done previously. Then these men came by agreement and
found Daniel making petition and supplication before his God. Then they
came near and said before the king, concerning the interdict, 'O king! Did you
not sign an interdict, that any man who makes petition to any god or man
within thirty days except to you, O king, shall be cast into the den of lions?'
The king answered, 'The thing stands fast, according to the law of the Medes
and Persians, which cannot be revoked.' Then they answered before the king,
'That Daniel, who is one of the exiles from Judah, pays no heed to you, O king,
or the interdict you have signed, but makes his petition three times a day.'

Then the king, when he heard these words, was much distressed, and set
his mind to deliver Daniel; and he laboured till the sun went down to rescue
him. Then these men came by agreement to the king, and said to the king,
'Know, O king, that it is a law of the Medes and Persians that no interdict or
ordinance which the king establishes can be changed.'

Then the king commanded, and Daniel was brought and cast into the den
of lions. The king said to Daniel, 'May your God, whom you serve
continually, deliver you!' And a stone was brought and laid upon the mouth
of the den, and the king sealed it with his own signet and with the signet of
his lords, that nothing might be changed concerning Daniel. Then the king
went to his palace, and spent the night fasting; no diversions were brought to
him, and sleep fled from him.

Then at break of day, the king arose and went in haste to the den of lions.
When he came near to the den where Daniel was, he cried out in a tone of
anguish and said to Daniel, 'O Daniel, servant of the living God, has your

God, whom you serve continually, been able to deliver you from the lions?' Then Daniel said to the king, 'O king, live for ever! My God sent his angel and shut the lions' mouths, and they have not hurt me, because I was found blameless before him; and also before you, O king, I have done no wrong.' Then the king was exceedingly glad, and commanded that Daniel be taken up out of the den. So Daniel was taken up out of the den, and no kind of hurt was found upon him, because he had trusted in his God.

## New Testament *Romans 5.1-11 RSV*

Since we are justified by faith, we have peace with God through our Lord Jesus Christ. Through him we have obtained access to this grace in which we stand, and we rejoice in our hope of sharing the glory of God. More than that, we rejoice in our sufferings, knowing that suffering produces endurance, and endurance produces character, and character produces hope, and hope does not disappoint us, because God's love has been poured into our hearts through the Holy Spirit which has been given to us.

While we were yet helpless, at the right time Christ died for the ungodly. Why, one will hardly die for a righteous man—though perhaps for a good man one will dare even to die. But God shows his love for us in that while we were yet sinners Christ died for us. Since, therefore, we are now justified by his blood, much more shall we be saved by him from the wrath of God. For if while we were enemies we were reconciled to God by the death of his Son, much more, now that we are reconciled, shall we be saved by his life. Not only so, but we also rejoice in God through our Lord Jesus Christ, through whom we have now received our reconciliation.

## Gospel *Luke 19.1-10 NEB*

Entering Jericho Jesus made his way through the city. There was a man there named Zacchaeus; he was superintendent of taxes and very rich. He was eager to see what Jesus looked like; but, being a little man, he could not see him for the crowd. So he ran on ahead and climbed a sycomore-tree in order to see him, for he was to pass that way. When Jesus came to the place, he looked up and said, 'Zacchaeus, be quick and come down; I must come and stay with you today.' He climbed down as fast as he could and welcomed him gladly. At this there was a general murmur of disapproval. 'He has gone in', they said, 'to be the guest of a sinner.' But Zacchaeus stood there and said to the Lord, 'Here and now, sir, I give half my possessions to charity; and if I have cheated anyone, I am ready to repay him four times over.' Jesus said to him, 'Salvation has come to this house today!—for this man too is a son of Abraham, and the Son of Man has come to seek and save what is lost.'

# Faithful unto death

*You are to be praised, O God, in Zion,*
*to you shall vows be paid, you that answer prayer. (Ps 65.1)*

'Dare to be a Daniel', urges the old children's chorus. Stand out faithfully for God and God will honour your faith. Daniel is an astute example to take, for his adventures of faith invariably had a happy ending (for him, at least, if not for his detractors, cf Daniel 6.24). After a night in the lion's den 'no kind of hurt was found upon him, because he had trusted in his God'. But, as many over the centuries have found to their cost, trusting God does not always lead to such miraculous deliverance. The book of Daniel was probably put together during the oppressive times of Antiochus Epiphanes (167–164 BC), when the purity and practice of Jewish religion were being radically threatened by an alien culture and a hostile regime. Some elements of the Daniel story set for Sunday would speak into the heart of the situation, not least the jealous conspiring of power-hungry officials. Here also was a ruler driven by delusions of deity, and therefore susceptible to skilful manipulation. Here too was the consequent condemnation of the innocent. What is absent is the actuality of brutal martyrdom for those seeking to stay true to their God. There were those who, like Daniel, trusted in God—and who, unlike Daniel, died because of it.

Courageous faith does not guarantee a pain-free life. It does open us up to the vulnerable, yet saving, love of God. So Paul proclaims to the Christians at Rome, some of whom a few years' later might well have come to test his teaching during the fierce persecution occasioned by yet another tyrant (Nero). Paul himself had had considerable firsthand experience of suffering and its effects on faith. He is not preaching a message he has not already made his own. The fruit of faith is enjoyment of what the sacrificial love of God has brought about. Whatever our outward circumstances, we have peace with God, ready access to the grace of God, and sure and certain hope of sharing the glory of God. And we have the love of God poured into our hearts through the gift of the Holy Spirit. These realities do not depend on our feelings, nor on a congenial situation. Because of who God is and what God has done, they hold true at all times and in all places. In this context, times of trial can strengthen staying-power and deepen hope. Though allegiance to Christ might not make life easy, it is the making of us.

For it is not only Paul who practises what he preaches. God does so too. In every sense, *God's* love is faithful unto death. It is also living and active in the most unpromising of situations. It extends as far as a despised 'superintendent of taxes' working both for himself and for the occupying power. For some reason, Zacchaeus was curious about Jesus. As far as 'the

Lord' is concerned, Zacchaeus is certainly worth a visit, whether other people approve or not. God's love is not limited by human expectations.

For Zacchaeus, the encounter with Jesus turned his life around, releasing well-springs of generosity. Faith for him was responding joyfully to one who valued him enough to search him out and come to where he was. So God values us all.

*Trusting God,*
*you come to us as we are.*
*Help us respond with generous trust,*
*even when times are hard*
*and the future seems bleak.*

# Pentecost 20

## Collect

Almighty God,
your Son has opened for us
a new and living way into your presence.
Give us pure hearts and steadfast wills
to worship you in spirit and in truth;
through the same Jesus Christ our Lord.

### Psalms 37.35-end; 121

## Old Testament *Genesis 32.22-30 RSV*

Jacob arose and took his two wives, his two maids, and his eleven children, and crossed the ford of the Jabbok. He took them and sent them across the stream, and likewise everything that he had. And Jacob was left alone; and a man wrestled with him until the breaking of the day. When the man saw that he did not prevail against Jacob, he touched the hollow of his thigh; and Jacob's thigh was put out of joint as he wrestled with him. Then he said, 'Let me go, for the day is breaking.' But Jacob said, 'I will not let you go, unless you bless me.' And he said to him, 'What is your name?' And he said, 'Jacob.' Then he said, 'Your name shall no more be called Jacob, but Israel, for you have striven with God and with men, and have prevailed.' Then Jacob asked him, 'Tell me, I pray, your name.' But he said, 'Why is it that you ask my name?' And there he blessed him. So Jacob called the name of the place Peniel, saying, 'For I have seen God face to face, and yet my life is preserved.'

## New Testament *1 Corinthians 9.19-end TEV*

I am a free man, nobody's slave; but I make myself everybody's slave in order to win as many people as possible. While working with the Jews, I live like a Jew in order to win them; and even though I myself am not subject to the law of Moses, I live as though I were when working with those who are, in order to win them. In the same way, when working with Gentiles, I live like a Gentile, outside the Jewish Law, in order to win Gentiles. This does not mean that I don't obey God's law; I am really under Christ's law. Among the weak in faith I become weak like one of them, in order to win them. So I become all things to all men, that I may save some of them by whatever means are possible.

All this I do for the gospel's sake, in order to share in its blessings. Surely you know that many runners take part in a race, but only one of them wins the prize. Run, then, in such a way as to win the prize. Every athlete in training submits to strict discipline, in order to be crowned with a wreath that will not last; but we do it for one that will last for ever. That is why I run straight for the finishing- line; that is why I am like a boxer who does not waste his punches. I harden my body with blows and bring it under complete control, to keep myself from being disqualified after having called others to the contest.

### Gospel *Matthew 7.13-27 NEB*

Jesus said, 'Enter by the narrow gate. The gate is wide that leads to perdition, there is plenty of room on the road, and many go that way; but the gate that leads to life is small and the road is narrow, and those who find it are few. 'Beware of false prophets, men who come to you dressed up as sheep while underneath they are savage wolves. You will recognize them by the fruits they bear. Can grapes be picked from briars, or figs from thistles? In the same way, a good tree always yields good fruit, and a poor tree bad fruit. A good tree cannot bear bad fruit, or a poor tree good fruit. And when a tree does not yield good fruit it is cut down and burnt. That is why I say you will recognize them by their fruits.

'Not everyone who calls me "Lord, Lord" will enter the kingdom of Heaven, but only those who do the will of my heavenly Father. When that day comes, many will say to me, "Lord, Lord, did we not prophesy in your name, cast out devils in your name, and in your name perform many miracles?" Then I will tell them to their face, "I never knew you; out of my sight, you and your wicked ways!"

'What then of the man who hears these words of mine and acts upon them? He is like a man who had the sense to build his house on rock. The rain came down, the floods rose, the wind blew, and beat upon that house; but it did not fall, because its foundations were on rock. But what of the man who hears these words of mine and does not act upon them? He is like a man who was foolish enough to build his house on sand. The rain came down, the floods rose, the wind blew, and beat upon that house; down it fell with a great crash.'

# Struggling with God

*The Lord himself is your keeper,*
*the Lord is your defence upon your right hand. (Ps 121.5)*

Being committed to God can sometimes be a hard struggle. Not only is it likely to provoke hostility and/or ridicule from those not so persuaded; it also involves the believer in an engagement with God which is both demanding and wounding. In the life of faith, 'endurance' (Sunday's theme) is certainly very much needed.

Jacob is a fascinating example of this syndrome. He is not the most attractive of patriarchs. Power hungry, given to deception, trickery and favouritism, he creates around him all kinds of unhappy circumstances. Though according to the Genesis narrative, God consistently and ultimately makes them good, the pain they cause remains a reality. At the point when Sunday's extract begins, Jacob is bracing himself to face again the brother he cheated out of his birthright. It is at this critical moment that he wrestles through the night with a mysterious stranger. Whatever we make of this encounter, it seems to bring the fighter out of Jacob, the determination to stay with the struggle and to prevail. He is rewarded with a new name and a blessing. The name, 'Israel' ('he who contends with God'), replaces the rather less heroic connotations of 'Jacob' ('he who supplants'). And it becomes, of course, a synonym for the whole people of God. God's people are those called to struggle with God. That rings true. Like Jacob, they are not granted to know the 'name' of their assailant—for despite all their pretensions and motives and longings, they cannot have God under their control. But they can receive God's blessing. They can know God more profoundly, even in wounding encounter. Somehow the struggle is worth it.

Paul undoubtedly found it so. His conversion to Christ brought him a great deal of suffering and heartache. As he reminded the Corinthians, it involved him (and should involve them) in rigorous spiritual discipline. But, as he says to another group of Christians, these travails are as nothing compared with the surpassing worth of knowing Christ Jesus his Lord (Philippians 3.8). He is also convinced that at the heart of the engagement with God is 'gospel'—good news saturated with blessings. His life's vocation is to share that reality by identifying with people where and as they are. Struggling with God becomes sharing God's struggle to release good news in the world.

That good news, though full of the joy of God, is no easy option. The teaching of Jesus which Matthew collects together in the 'Sermon on the Mount' makes this very clear. Sunday's extract stresses the need to be firmly grounded in the truth of God as expressed in Jesus, for the storms that threaten it will be severe. In another vivid picture, believers are warned that the way in to God's life is difficult both to find and to negotiate; for the attractions of the other way are obvious and very inviting. They include the temptation to perform high-profile wonders in the Lord's name, without entering into that searching relationship with the living God which changes lives for good. The condemnation of such 'false prophets' is spine-chilling. Better to struggle painfully with God than to be driven out of God's sight.

*Struggling God,*
*you seek to bring forth blessing.*
*Strengthen us to hold to you*
*through thick and thin,*
*even as we struggle with you.*

# Last Sunday
# after Pentecost

## Collect

Merciful God,
you have prepared for those who love you
such good things as pass man's understanding.
Pour into our hearts such love towards you
that we, loving you above all things,
may obtain your promises,
which exceed all that we can desire;
through Jesus Christ our Lord.

## Psalms 15; 146

## Old Testament *Isaiah 33.17-22 RSV*

Your eyes will see the king in his beauty;
they will behold a land that stretches afar.
Your mind will muse on the terror:
'Where is he who counted,
where is he who weighed the tribute?
Where is he who counted the towers?'
You will see no more the insolent people,
the people of an obscure speech
which you cannot comprehend,
stammering in a tongue which you cannot understand.
Look upon Zion, the city of our appointed feasts!
You eyes will see Jerusalem,
a quiet habitation, an immoveable tent,
whose stakes will never be plucked up,
nor will any of its cords be broken.
But there the Lord in majesty will be for us
a place of broad rivers and streams,
where no galley with oars can go,
nor stately ship can pass.
For the Lord is our judge, the Lord is our ruler,
the Lord is our king; he will save us.

## New Testament *Revelation 7.2-4, 9-end RSV*

I saw another angel ascend from the rising of the sun, with the seal of the living God, and he called with a loud voice to the four angels who had been given power to harm earth and sea, saying, 'Do not harm the earth or the sea or the trees, till we have sealed the servants of our God upon their foreheads.' And I heard the number of the sealed, a hundred and forty-four thousand sealed, out of every tribe of the sons of Israel.

After this I looked, and behold, a great multitude which no man could number, from every nation, from all tribes and peoples and tongues, standing before the throne and before the Lamb, clothed in white robes, with palm branches in their hands, and crying out with a loud voice, 'Salvation belongs to our God who sits upon the throne, and to the Lamb!' And all the angels stood round the throne and round the elders and the four living creatures, and they fell on their faces before the throne and worshipped God, saying, 'Amen! Blessing and glory and wisdom and thanksgiving and honour and power and might be to our God for ever and ever! Amen.'

Then one of the elders addressed me, saying, 'Who are these, clothed in white robes, and whence have they come?' I said to him, 'Sir, you know.' And he said to me, 'These are they who have come out the great tribulation; they have washed their robes and made them white in the blood of the Lamb.

'Therefore are they before the throne of God,
and serve him day and night within his temple;
and he who sits upon the throne will shelter them with his presence.
They shall hunger no more, neither thirst any more;
the sun shall not strike them, nor any scorching heat.
For the Lamb in the midst of the throne will be their shepherd,
and he will guide them to springs of living water;
and God will wipe away every tear from their eyes.'

## Gospel *Matthew 25.1-13 NEB*

Jesus said, 'When that day comes, the kingdom of Heaven will be like this. There were ten girls, who took their lamps and went out to meet the bridegroom. Five of them were foolish, and five prudent; when the foolish ones took their lamps, they took no oil with them, but the others took flasks of oil with their lamps. As the bridegroom was late in coming they all dozed off to sleep. But at midnight a cry was heard: "Here is the bridegroom! Come out to meet him." With that the girls all got up and trimmed their lamps. The foolish said to the prudent, "Our lamps are going out; give us some of your oil." "No," they said; "there will never be enough for all of us. You had better go to the shop and buy some for yourselves." While they were away the bridegroom arrived; those who were ready went in with him to the wedding; and the door was shut. And then the other five came back. "Sir, sir," they cried, "open the door for us." But he answered, "I declare, I do not know you." Keep awake then; for you never know the day or the hour.'

## Heaven laid open

*Praise the Lord, O my soul,*
*while I live I will praise the Lord;*
*while I have any being*
*I will sing praises to my God. (Ps 146.1-2)*

The scriptures are shot through with stories of the ways in which God delivers his people. There are often graphic accounts of the sufferings and confinements that people have suffered. Often, space is what they cry out for; for space goes along with freedom. Sunday's readings address this quest for space and freedom.

Heaven teeming with people does not sound like a place of comfortable space. Yet the seer of Revelation sets out a vision of the peoples of the world standing gladly before God and the exalted Lamb which was slain. In his comprehensive vision, there is room for all. Heaven is not restricted to those sealed from the tribes of Israel. There are many more, clothed in white robes, those who have come through suffering shared with Jesus. Now they are in a place of shelter. Now they are in a place of safety, with the Lamb as their Shepherd. Now pain and unrequited longing are no more. And the one who loves them more than life itself will wipe away their tears. Here is true freedom. Here is ultimate fulfilment.

It is a different version of the vision Isaiah set before his hearers. He had looked to a Jerusalem that would no more be threatened by invasions and disaster. He had looked, rather more narrowly than the Seer, to a Jerusalem free from foreigners, those whose language was strange and sinister. He had looked to a Jerusalem where there would be no shortage of water—a life-giving commodity that enemies always sought to control. In his vision, Jerusalem would be a place of broad rivers and streams, yet a place unavailable to outsiders with powerful resources. As always, God was invoked as Saviour. In spite of the privations the people were going through at the time, the time would come when they would see God in beauty in a spacious place.

Isaiah was anxious to prepare people to face the coming onslaught, in confidence that their God would save them. He would claim them back for his own. They needed to be ready for that. So did those to whom Jesus ministered. The kingdom of heaven may be spacious, but the way into it can be experienced as very restricted. The perceived restrictions are related to the way people see God and the importance (or otherwise) they attach to being ready for his coming. It is no good assuming that entry into God's kingdom is automatic. People have to be ready for it, prepared and waiting for it. For God comes when he wills. We must be there to welcome him. We must make space for him. In the light of Sunday's parable, 'Watch this space' can take on a whole new meaning.

*All-encompassing God,*
*you give us a vision of spaciousness*
*yet point to a narrow way.*
*Make us so ready for your coming*
*that we may share your unconfined joy.*

# Harvest Thanksgiving

## Collect

Almighty and everlasting God,
we offer you our hearty thanks
for your fatherly goodness and care
in giving us the fruits of the earth in their seasons.
Give us grace to use them rightly, to your glory,
for our own well-being,
and for the relief of those in need;
through Jesus Christ our Lord.

*Psalms 104.21-30; 65 or 67; 145; 147; 148; 150*

## Old Testament *Deuteronomy 26.1-11 TEV*

Moses said to all Israel, 'After you have occupied the land that the Lord your God is giving you and have settled there, each of you must place in a basket the first part of each crop that you harvest and you must take it with you to the one place of worship. Go to the priest in charge at that time and say to him, "I now acknowledge to the Lord my God that I have entered the land that he promised our ancestors to give us."

'The priest will take the basket from you and place it before the altar of the Lord your God. Then, in the Lord's presence you will recite these words: "My ancestor was a wandering Aramaean, a homeless refugee, who took his family to Egypt to live. They were few in number when they went there, but they became a large and powerful nation. The Egyptians treated us harshly and forced us to work as slaves. Then we cried out for help to the Lord, the God of our ancestors. He heard us and saw our suffering, hardship, and misery. By his great power and strength he rescued us from Egypt. He worked miracles and wonders, and caused terrifying things to happen. He brought us here and gave us this rich and fertile land. So now I bring to the Lord the first part of the harvest that he has given me."

'Then set the basket down in the Lord's presence and worship there. Be grateful for the good things that the Lord your God has given you and your family; and let the Levites and the foreigners who live among you join in the celebration.'

## New Testament *2 Corinthians 9.6-end NEB*

Remember: sparse sowing, sparse reaping; sow bountifully, and you will reap bountifully. Each person should give as he has decided for himself; there should be no reluctance, no sense of compulsion; God loves a cheerful giver.

And it is in God's power to provide you richly with every good gift; thus you will have ample means in yourselves to meet each and every situation, with enough and to spare for every good cause. Scripture says of such a man: 'He has lavished his gifts on the needy, his benevolence stands fast for ever.' Now he who provides seed for sowing and bread for food will provide the seed for you to sow; he will multiply it and swell the harvest of your benevolence, and you will always be rich enough to be generous. Through our action such generosity will issue in thanksgiving to God, for as a piece of willing service this is not only a contribution towards the needs of God's people; more than that, it overflows in a flood of thanksgiving to God. For through the proof which this affords, many will give honour to God when they see how humbly you obey him and how faithfully you confess the gospel of Christ; and will thank him for your liberal contribution to their need and to the general good. And as they join in prayer on your behalf, their hearts will go out to you because of the richness of the grace which God has imparted to you. Thanks be to God for his gift beyond words!

## Gospel *John 4.31-38 JB*

The disciples were urging Jesus, 'Rabbi, do have something to eat'; but he said, 'I have food to eat that you do not know about.' So the disciples asked one another, 'Has someone been bringing him food?' But Jesus said,
'My food
is to do the will of the one who sent me,
and to complete his work.
Have you not got a saying:
Four months and then the harvest?
Well, I tell you:
Look around you, look at the fields;
already they are white, ready for harvest!
Already the reaper is being paid his wages,
already he is bringing in the grain for eternal life,
and thus the sower and reaper rejoice together.
For here the proverb holds good:
one sows, another reaps;
I sent you to reap
a harvest you had not worked for.
Others worked for it;
and you have come into the rewards of their trouble.'

# Honouring the generosity of God

*You open wide your hand,*
*and fill all things living with your bounteous gift.*
*(Ps 145.16)*

The scriptures have much to say about sowing and reaping, not always in very comfortable ways. And even when most of us are quite divorced from direct experience of farming, the biblical imagery remains powerful.

Sparse sowing leads to sparse reaping, Paul tells the Corinthian church. The way he puts it is reminiscent of a proverb. Paul uses the words to point to generosity expressed towards others as one of the ways of expressing a basic response to the generosity of God. God is the giver. He provides all that is necessary for life. If this is true of basic necessities, argues Paul, can we not believe that our God will provide for us as we learn to express our thanksgiving to him through our generosity to people in need. Not only will our action show our thanks to God. Our action will also awaken thanksgiving in others. Our acknowledgement of 'God's gift beyond words' will be a way of leading others to recognize that gift in Christ.

The theme of thanksgiving to God permeates the extract from Deuteronomy. The gift that is to be remembered throughout all time is God's gift of liberation from slavery, a gift that led his people to a further gift, occupation of a fertile land. In these verses, sowing and reaping are taken for granted. They are the stuff of life for a people who have settled on the land. But there is always the danger that people will forget the past. There has to be a constant yearly reminder of that liberation and that gift of new life. Here it is epitomized in an offering to God of the first part of the harvest. And to press the point home, the text provides words to be said as a constant reminder of God's generosity and the people's dependence on God, from when they were 'homeless refugees' to their later settled prosperous existence. Moreover, their thanksgiving to God is to spill over to include those who do not belong to the people of Israel. Their feasting is to include outsiders.

Just as these outsiders are enabled to rejoice in the harvest thanksgiving of the people of Israel, so the disciples of Jesus are taught to acknowledge their dependence on all that had gone before. They reap, Jesus tells them, where others have put in all the preparation and prior hard work. The disciples come into the picture long after the main effort had been begun. They are called to bring the work to completion, as far as possible, just as Jesus' task is to 'do the will of the one who sent me and to complete his work.'

Moreover, this work is meat and drink to Jesus. In being sent out to reap a harvest they had not worked for, the disciples are to share that meat and drink. They will find that in ministering faithfully to others, they will receive nourishment in ways they had not dreamed of. God's generosity shows itself in many ways. And it always calls for thanksgiving on the part of those who benefit.

*God of bountiful provision*
*may we find our meat and drink*
*in sharing your gifts with those in need,*
*in ministering in your name,*
*and in helping to bring to fruition*
*your longed-for harvest.*